LIVES AT RISK

COMPARATIVE STUDIES OF
HEALTH SYSTEMS AND MEDICAL CARE

For a complete list of titles in this series, please contact the

Sales Department
University of California Press
2120 Berkeley Way
Berkeley, CA 94720

LIVES AT RISK

Public Health in Nineteenth-Century — Egypt —

▼

LaVerne Kuhnke

University of California Press

Berkeley • Los Angeles • Oxford

University of California Press
Berkeley and Los Angeles, California

University of California Press
Oxford, England

Copyright © 1990 by
The Regents of the University of California

Library of Congress Cataloging-in-Publication Data

Kuhnke, LaVerne.
    Lives at risk: public health in nineteenth-century Egypt /
LaVerne Kuhnke.
        p.   cm.—(Comparative studies of health systems and medical
care; no. 24)
    Includes bibliographical references and index.
    ISBN 0–520–06364–3 (alk. paper)
    1. Public health—Egypt—History.   2. Medical care—Egypt—
History.   3. Epidemics—Egypt—History.   I. Title.   II. Series.
RA549.K83   1990
614.4′0962′09034—dc20   89-33122
                                                                     CIP

Printed in the United States of America

9 8 7 6 5 4 3 2 1

The paper used in this publication meets the minimum requirements of
American National Standard for Information Sciences—Permanence of
Paper for Printed Library Materials, ANSI Z39.48–1984 ∞

To Bob, George, and Elizabeth

Contents

Acknowledgments

This study has undergone a long evolution, and I have accumulated many debts of appreciation for inspiration and support from many people. William R. Polk, Lester S. King, and William H. McNeill encouraged my initial efforts at the University of Chicago. Generous grants from the American Research Center in Egypt and the Center for Middle East Studies at the University of Chicago provided the means to pursue extensive research abroad at the outset, and another liberal award from the National Library of Medicine (LM03172–01) enabled me to complete the work.

Many librarians, archivists, and scholars on three continents extended invaluable assistance for my research. Hoda Banhawi and Jean Catafago at the Egyptian National Geographic Society in Cairo were indefatigable in locating publications needed. Cynthia Nelson and Aida Sourial at the American University in Cairo stimulated and seconded my investigations. At Cairo University, Dr. Ferdos Labib opened new avenues of inquiry and contributed a twentieth-century perspective to my nineteenth-century public health data. Lewis Halim and Muhammad Qadri unfailingly came to the rescue to interpret technical or archaic terms in Arabic documents.

At Northeastern University, colleagues in my department and college demonstrated cooperation in many ways, and the library staff and Gerald Murphy's colleagues cordially facilitated every service possible.

Finally, without John Janzen's guidance, I doubt that this study would have been published. So many colleagues and friends have been generous with support and enthusiasm that this slight work bears a heavy burden of gratitude.

An earlier version of chapter 7, on women health officers, was published in *Clio Medica,* vol. 9, no. 3, September 1974, pp. 193–205; the section on ophthalmological clinics in Cairo in chapter 8 also appeared in an earlier version in *Clio Medica,* vol. 7, no. 3, September 1972, pp. 209–214.

Introduction
Evolving Concepts of Disease and Medicine

Throughout history, one strange, dread disease has periodically become a metaphor for Western man's fear of suffering and death from sickness. Leprosy in the Middle Ages, Black Death in the fourteenth century, and syphilis in the sixteenth century loomed dramatically in Europe's collective traumatic experience and contributed graphic terms—pest, plague, and pox—to denote the ultimately malevolent curse. During the nineteenth century, a succession of cholera pandemics similarly aroused apprehension and fear on a global scale as they swept inexorably overland and overseas, claiming thousands of victims for a sudden, spectacular, "cadaverizing" death.[1] At the same time, men continued to suffer other disabling and mortal ailments—typhus, typhoid, pneumonia, smallpox, tuberculosis—as normal afflictions of daily life to be endured until their outcome brought death or recovery. Pulmonary tuberculosis may have been a greater killer than cholera, in industrializing nations during the nineteenth century, but its insidious and gradual consumption of its victims caused no public outcry; rather, it inspired in popular literature romantic images about its victims' wasting etherealization.[2]

Preoccupation with the alien and exotic has continued to sustain the common notion of disease as an invasive foreign element. The so-called ontological concept of disease, this view holds disease to be an exogenous entity that attacks specific organs or structures of

1

the body. An opposing idea, the physiological concept of disease, understands it to be a generalized phenomenon—an imbalance between the forces of nature within and outside the sick person—or, in more familiar twentieth-century terms, man's adaptation or maladaptation to his environment.[3]

Both of these concepts of disease coexisted in medical thought through the ages, and one or the other predominated at various times. When Morgagni launched the study of pathology at the end of the seventeenth century by shifting attention from the entire body to specific lesions in individual bodily organs as characteristic effects of certain diseases, medical science began moving in the direction of what Alfred North Whitehead called the notion of atomicity: the trend to localize the phenomenon under investigation in ever-smaller structural units. As the use of the microscope in the nineteenth century enabled biologists to pursue a sharpened focus from organ to tissue and finally to the cell, the pace quickened. With the late-nineteenth-century discovery that specific microorganisms may have pathogenic effects in the human body at the cellular level, emphasis on specificity in disease causation, prevention, and cure became a hallmark of cosmopolitan medicine.[4] The ontological concept of disease became dominant in lay and professional attitudes for almost three quarters of a century, exemplified by the "targeted" remedy, the "magic bullet" rather than the shotgun approach of earlier ages panaceas.

This study investigates the clash that occurred in early nineteenth-century Egypt between advocates of contemporary versions of the two ancient, then seemingly opposed etiological theories. The conflict arose when the Egyptian government attempted to avert invasions of plague and cholera by introducing a European maritime quarantine system based on notions of disease communicability or "contagion." Ideas about contagion dominated popular Western consciousness, going back to biblical injunctions against contact with lepers as "unclean" and reinforced by experience with the presumed communicability of plague in the fourteenth century and syphilis in the sixteenth. In 1546, Girolamo Fracastoro elaborated a type of germ theory to explain disease transmission by "contagion" which provided a theoretical justification for quarantine regulations institutionalized in the Mediterranean during struggles with the Black Death.

Earlier, the disciples of Hippocrates had elaborated another hypothesis that attempted to reconcile humoral etiology with the mass phenomena of epidemics by incriminating air as the carrier of the disease. According to this theory, "miasma," the stench arising from swamps and putrefying organic matter, contained a toxic element that could vitiate the atmosphere and cause disease in susceptible individuals who were exposed to the noxious fumes. There were moral implications in this hypothesis—individuals with constitutions debilitated through excessive indulgence were considered particularly vulnerable, for example—which made it congenial to Victorian reformers, and the miasmatic theory provided the rationale for England's sanitary reform movement in the nineteenth century. Its proponents also opposed the quarantine system as a remnant of medieval superstition and an obstacle to progress and became, in effect, "anticontagionists."

In the field of quarantine practice, therefore, the introduction of Western medical technology made Egypt a battleground in a perennial conflict between these two medical ideologies, while the health of the Egyptian people was at risk from recurring epidemic invasions. Egypt was at the center of the disputes because it became the turnstile in trade between Europe and Asia during the nineteenth century. Between the French invasion in 1798 and the British occupation in 1882, the chronological boundaries of this study, the country also became involved in "the Eastern Question": European powers' competition for influence and later dominance in territories of the Ottoman Empire. The sultan's viceroy in Egypt during the first half of the century, Muhammad Ali, was perceived as a threat to European political and economic designs because he attempted to gain military power and wealth by mobilizing the resources of the Nile valley. Although Big Power intervention defeated his political ambitions, the viceroy nevertheless launched a remarkable experiment in economic development during his tenure in Egypt.

A Turkish-speaking soldier of fortune, Muhammad Ali seized the governorship of Egypt in 1805. During the following four decades, while nominally serving as governor of a province of the Ottoman Empire, he undertook to develop the resources of Egypt so as to win autonomy and establish his dynasty. Two of the innovations he introduced, the creation of a conscript army and the promotion of Egyptian exports on the world market, drew attention to the state of public health in Egypt. In addition, calamitous epidemics of cholera in 1831 and plague in 1835 called for measures to prevent repetition of these national disasters.

In response to cholera and plague epidemics, Muhammad Ali

adopted the classic Mediterranean maritime quarantine system and entrusted it to European consular representatives, thus creating the first international body charged with disease control. Ultimately, the consular Quarantine Board's efforts led to the international agreements to contain communicable diseases which are administered by the World Health Organization today.

On the domestic side, when Egyptian recruits' poor health threatened to weaken the armed forces that were to challenge the Ottoman sultan, Muhammad Ali founded a European-style medical school to train Egyptian military physicians. As the need for medical care for other target groups in the country's small manpower pool came to his attention, he extended the number of personnel and agencies, creating a rudimentary public health organization. Its principal accomplishment was to regularize vaccination throughout the country, effectively eliminating smallpox as a major threat to health in Egypt.

The link between the two initiatives was the application of two different preventive medicine technologies, a "halfway" technology in the quarantine practices adopted to block the entry of plague and cholera and a "definitive" technology in Sir William Jenner's vaccination procedure to immunize against smallpox.[5] The effective principles of quarantine—isolation and neutralization of the infective agent—were embedded in an elaborate framework of restrictions and institutions that, by accretion through the centuries, had grown unwieldy, costly, inconsistent, and seemingly irrational.[6] Its advocates pointed out, however, that given the uncertainty about disease transmission, omitting any of the measures might unwittingly annul the single effective procedure.

Ironically, the definitive technique of smallpox vaccination applied the same order of empirical observation as that underlying quarantine. But Jenner had fortuitously found an effective, specific, and economical technique of immunization without having first identified the biological mechanism involved in the infection. Vaccination entailed no administrative costs, inconvenience, or loss of time in international commerce and therefore caused no international disputes. Quarantine procedures, however, sparked violent squabbles among the maritime nations. Almost half a century's efforts to achieve international agreement on standardized practices were futile because there was no sound scientific basis for action in the prebacteriological era and medical opinion on disease transmission was sharply divided.

This study aims to demonstrate two points. First, since etiological theories in the early nineteenth century were in transition from the Greco-Roman humoral system to the European focus on specificity, universal agreement on disease causation and transmission was not possible. As medical historian Erwin Ackerknecht observed, "Intellectually and rationally the two theories [contagionism and anticontagionism] balanced each other too evenly. Under such conditions the accident of personal experience and temperament, and especially economic outlook and political loyalties will determine the decision."[7] Given the uncertainties about disease causation and transmission, prudence suggested adopting the protective measures recommended by both sides. This is what Muhammad Ali did, as a political expedient to win favor with his European trading partners and to gain their support for his bid for autonomy.

Second, at the time Muhammad Ali introduced European medical training in Egypt, there was an alternative to the Western pattern of first concentrating medical care facilities in the cities and only later inducing reluctant personnel to serve the rural population. In a rational and problem-oriented approach to the country's medical needs, it was possible from the outset to provide basic care in the countryside, where the majority of the people lived.

The introduction of European medical theory and practice with the creation of two new institutions—a Western-style medical school and a maritime quarantine service—imported two systems at a time when their underlying rationale, public policy on the delivery of preventive and curative medical care, was evolving. In fact, the etiological division imported with the quarantine system was only one of six paradoxical developments in the Western medical system during the half century following Napoleon's defeat at Waterloo.[8]

One contradiction became evident as theoretical study emphasized specific causation in disease, leaping ahead of therapy, which remained based on the panaceas of the traditional humoral system. Another movement, generalizing the aristocratic prerogative of a personal physician attending an individual patient for a fee as the societal norm, placed medical care beyond the reach of the great majority of the population. In a related development, the state restricted its intervention in medicine to licensing and regulating practice, in effect repudiating earlier views on state responsibility for providing medical care for the people. A fifth anomaly appeared when sanitary reform was hailed exclusively as an engineering triumph, absolving the medical profession of responsibility in the field of public health. Last, with the devaluation of military models after 1815, attention to preventive and environmental medicine gave way almost completely to hospital-based curative medicine, which has remained the norm in the West.

Since these developments were related to political events in France and economic developments in England, the two countries that provided institutional models for Egypt, it will be instructive to describe the circumstances that shaped these characteristics. The gap between theory and practice became most dramatically evident in France where leaders in the medical profession, spurred by the egalitarian and activist élan of Jacobinism, broke away from academic medicine and took the first steps toward localizing the disease process. Endowed with an abundance of old regime hospitals, a brilliant group of clinicians in Paris rediscovered Morgagni's paradigm in pathology: symptoms and signs observed in the patient during diagnostic examination will correlate with lesions revealed in the corpse during autopsy. The "Paris School" embraced Morgagni's focus on individual organs as the locus of pathology, and one of its stars, Xavier Bichat, further pursued structural changes to the level of tissues, while René Laennec's invention of the stethoscope made possible more exact differentiation among specific disorders in the thoracic cavity. Another colleague, Pierre Louis, insisted on enumeration in hospitals' patient returns, introducing a rudimentary statistical method for comparing mortality and recovery rates. These three techniques in clinical medicine—comprehensive physical examinations and case histories of patients, scrupulous necropsies, and regular recording of morbidity and mortality figures—became normative in hospital procedures and in practical training for medical students worldwide. When Dr. Antoine Barthèlme Clot introduced clinical training to the medical school founded in Egypt in 1827, he laid a firm foundation for students to pursue the advances that would follow discoveries in basic biological sciences later in the century.

In the interim, however, while the study of medicine emphasized localized, specific pathological phenomena, the majority of practitioners continued to follow the Greco-Roman humoral system, relying on the time-honored purges, emetics, sudorifics, and above all, bloodletting, of traditional depletion therapy.[9] A number of clinicians in Paris and Vienna, recognizing the discrepancy between training and treatment, abandoned the old remedies and became known as "therapeutic nihilists," but many physicians, particularly in English-speaking countries, adopted the "more is better" attitude of "heroic" treatment, the euphemism for massive overdosing and copious bloodletting. Ackerknecht exaggerated, of course, when he suggested that the saying which became current on the continent, "The English kill their patients; the French let them die."[10]

As members of the ascendant bourgeoisie gained entry to the medical profession, previously the province of aristocratics, they brought about other changes. The professionalization of occupations, a long-term process transforming the organization of work in modern societies, advanced markedly with the Industrial Revolution. Industrialization brought about economic, political, and educational changes that altered the division of labor and increased technicalization in old and new occupations.[11] By requiring hospital-based training in the techniques of clinical medicine, the new class of physicians took a long step toward transforming medicine from an academic pursuit to an autonomous profession.

The dynamics of economic growth guided a remarkably analogous evolution of the medical profession in both England and France in spite of quite different political and social circumstances. In both countries, the rising bourgeoisie that entered the medical field during the post-Napoleonic period was able to challenge the old, aristocratic medical elite by new modes of operation, including political influence. Broad-based professional associations were one innovation that fostered greater solidarity among physicians and promoted legislation in the interests of the profession. Even more important was the medical profession's alliance with hospitals, traditionally institutions for undifferentiated charity, which were transformed into the principal locus for medical treatment, training, and, later, research.[12]

By mid-century the lower-echelon practitioners, apothecaries in England and health officers in France, had gained legal recognition, organized, and secured legislation to prohibit or at least restrict the competition of irregular healers, the despised "quacks." Once established, the medical professions in Great Britain and France pursued characteristically different avenues to success and prosperity: the French took advantage of an already existing bureaucracy by gaining control of private welfare institutions; the British emphasized private enterprise by expanding personal medical care among the growing classes of the well-to-do.

Nevertheless, a great many physicians never advanced beyond extremely modest circumstances, and their rewards went little beyond satisfying the ideal of serving their fellowman that had induced them to enter the profession originally. Even after the rise in prosperity at mid-century, many village physicians in France cultivated a small vegetable farm or vineyard to supplement the marginal income offered by practice among the peasants. And in England, many physicians practicing in poor urban neighborhoods joined fraternal mutual assistance organizations for fear that their families would not be able to bear the burden of burial expenses in the event of their untimely death.[13]

To return to the evolving characteristics of the medical profession, the image of the private physician devoted to personal care of individual patients as the norm and the ideal was reinforced in England by his exclusion from the mid-nineteenth-century sanitary reform movement. Edwin Chadwick, the lawyer who had described urban environmental deterioration in terms sufficiently vivid to arouse public remedial action, saw sanitation problems as essentially public policy issues. By identifying the need for improved water supply and sewerage as engineering problems, he defined public health as a field of technical expertise. The physician had no place in this equation, Chadwick pointed out.[14] Thus, England's success in sanitary reform created the lasting impression in the popular imagination that attention to public health was primarily a matter of providing "good drains." It also absolved the physician and the hospital from any responsibility for environmental or preventive medicine and created a permanent division between personal medical care and public health policy and practice. More important for an agrarian country like Egypt, the English model was a technical solution for an urban problem that was irrelevant to rural sanitation needs.

From the point of view of institution transfer to the non-Western world, however, the most significant characteristic of the medical care delivery systems imported with colonial control was the underlying implicit repudiation of state responsibility to provide care for the general population. Europe's aristocratic university-trained medical profession had embraced the Greek ideal of a near-sacred personal relationship between the practitioner and his patient which was exemplified in the Hippocratic oath. However, Rome's genius for municipal organization emphasized state support for medical care as well, an equally strong tradition adopted by most European towns as they emerged in the Middle Ages. In the Roman Empire and medieval Europe, each town had municipal practitioners who directed public health services, attended the well-to-do for a fee, and were charged to care for the poor free of charge. This public medical service coexisted with private practice, which gradually gained the ascendancy with the rise of the middle classes. Because the industrializing nations became the major imperial powers in the nineteenth century, they exported their commercial, private enterprise, fee-for-service model as the norm, and the old tradition of state medicine was lost to the colonies in the non-Western world. Nevertheless, municipal doctors were common until the end of the eighteenth century in Western Europe and until the middle of the nineteenth century in Germany. In Norway, Sweden, Italy, and other countries, they formed the nucleus of twentieth-century national health care delivery systems.[15]

For a number of reasons, state activism in medicine peaked in the eighteenth century. Mercantilism, the guiding philosophy of absolute monarchies, elaborated a rationale: since power was the first aim of the state and a large healthy population was a vital component of power, the state should promote the health of its people from the cradle to the grave. It was a matter of economic logic as well; to excel in commerce and agriculture, the state required numerous healthy subjects. At the same time, occupational diseases like scurvy among sailors and lung ailments among miners and the work of pioneer social reformers like John Howard, who investigated abuses in prisons and hospitals, also contributed to a growing interest in the state's responsibility for public health in the eighteenth century.[16] The creation of national armies probably added the greatest impetus to state concern for the health of at least the military segment of the population. The French were the pacesetters, as in most matters of military administration. Early in the century, they set up military hospitals, and in the 1770s, they established a modern, professional, military medical corps. The corps' conscious attention to water supply, personal cleanliness, and sewage and the prompt adoption of Jenner's vaccination no doubt contributed significantly to Napoleon's ability to expand the scale of land warfare. The step from protection of soldiers to medical administration for the public at large was logical for some systematically minded bureaucrats in the service of

European princes. The most important was Johann Peter Frank, a government physician in the Austrian Empire whose multivolume work, *A System of Complete Medical Police*, provided guidelines for a national system of public health in Denmark in 1803 and influenced the tsar of Russia to consider public health a matter of state policy.[17]

A comprehensive program of health care also was under consideration in France on the eve of the revolution, and the Assembly reformulated the old regime plan in 1790, but the initiative failed because of disagreement between physicians concerned with regulating medical practice and charitably minded landowners more interested in public assistance for the poor. The question of state-supported medical care arose again in France at mid-nineteenth century when a surplus of practitioners caught the attention of the medical profession. Reorganization seemed called for, not only by overcrowding in the profession but also by an upsurge of interest in socialist solutions to national problems on the eve of the 1848 revolution. However, the Medical Congress of 1845, the first representative assembly of the French medical profession, rejected the idea of state-supported medical care for the nation at large. Among the members' objections, the congress cited their pious conviction—often invoked in the twentieth century—that the poor should have the same freedom of choice as the rich.[18]

In England, there was no move to establish state medicine, apparently because the seventeenth-century civil war destroyed the links of local government with the Crown, and the country thereafter lacked a well-coordinated system of local administration on which a state medical system could be built.[19] As the crown's control relaxed after 1660, local government became a matter of local initiative, specifically, the counties' parishes. Concerned to reduce the burden of maintaining the pauper population, the parishes subordinated the social problems of health to their plans to put the poor to work. This continuing local preoccupation finally resulted in the Poor Law Amendment Act of 1834, which created a national system of workhouses. Private initiative had taken over in the meantime, when wealthy benefactors began founding a broad array of hospitals, clinics, and other philanthropic institutions in the eighteenth century.[20]

The English system of private enterprise in personal and individual medical care was essentially a response to social change guided by the views of the socially and economically dominant classes. Another system that emerged eventually to care for the less fortunate was the fortuitous result of the Poor Law amendment. Workhouse infirmaries and medical officers provided for ailing paupers by that enactment eventually became the organizational framework for England's National Health Service following the Second World War.[21]

As the nations of Europe industrialized, the most familiar route for extending medical care to the less advantaged classes was an expansion of disability and hospitalization insurance systems that evolved from the mutual assistance functions of guilds, fraternal organizations, and, later, trade unions. These plans called for wage earners' regular contributions to a central fund that could be drawn on to meet subscribers' needs, most often the payment of burial costs. Some associations also extended financial aid to members' families following the death or disability of their principal breadwinner. Such systems of disability and hospitalization insurance were nationalized and expanded to cover a majority of the urban working population in Germany under Bismarck and in England under a Liberal government.[22]

Insurance systems were inappropriate, however, for agrarian societies, where some type of state medicine appeared the only feasible avenue to provide medical care on a wide scale. Only Imperial Russia initiated a public health service aimed specifically at the rural population during the nineteenth century. Although the state medical service was an offshoot of the liberation of the serfs in 1861, it was motivated, as was the Poor Law amendment in 1834 in England, by economic pressure to provide a mobile labor force for Russia's budding industries. With the abolition of serfdom, the tsar organized local government around district assemblies called *zemstvos,* which, in spite of numerous deficiencies, provided a framework for public medical services. Zemstvo members built small hospitals and appointed government physicians whose salaries were paid by taxes. They charged the district health centers with sanitation control, recording morbidity and mortality figures, and cost-free treatment for the peasants.

Because the zemstvos were perennially short of funds to pay physicians, they met the demand for practitioners by hiring as auxiliary personnel retired army medics or barber-surgeons called feldshers. Introduced by Peter the Great because of the shortage of trained physicians, feldshers remained the principal medical care personnel in Russia's armies for two hundred years. Following the creation of zemstvo medical centers, they provided the bulk of care for the peasant population.

The zemstvo system thus contributed one possible solution to the problem of medical care for the rural masses by identifying medicine as a public service the community could finance from tax funds. For agrarian societies, it offered an alternative to the insurance schemes evolving in industrializing countries.[23]

On a small scale, Muhammad Ali anticipated the zemstvo system with rural health centers staffed by European or Egyptian physicians assisted by pharmacists, midwives, and barbers. Like Peter and other Eastern European rulers, the viceroy first created a medical school to protect the armed forces that were an instrument of his policies. Like Alexander 200 years later, he also had to turn his attention to medical care for the peasantry that provided manpower for industrialization and agricultural development programs. Unlike the Russian tsars, however, Muhammad Ali faced a public relations problem that threatened the free flow of Egyptian commodities in the international market and the monetary returns required to finance his expansive projects—a long-held myth that Egypt was a disease-ridden country. To market Egyptian commodities abroad, the viceroy had to reassure his European trading partners that the state of health and sanitation in Egypt was good or accept long quarantine periods on Egyptian commodities, resulting in serious economic loss.

Military ambition, political expediency, mercantilist economic principles, and severe vulnerability to public opinion all contributed to Muhammad Ali's eagerness to introduce medical institutions and preventive medicine technology that would safeguard the resources he was attempting to mobilize in the country under his control.

Thus, early nineteenth-century Egypt is a promising focal point for an investigation of medical technology and institution transfer, to determine whether those technologies and institutions were adaptable to local circumstances or whether they were programmed by their underlying value system to evolve in the direction of the urbanized, industrializing societies in which they originated.

The first chapter of this study sketches Muhammad Ali's drive for wealth and power to gain autonomy from the Ottoman Empire. It describes his rigorous manpower mobilization, which aroused the Egyptian people's implacable opposition to government intervention in their lives. It also points out environmental factors that affected the health of Egyptians and their consumption habits concerning water, food, and drugs.

Muhammad Ali's drive for an effective military force, as well as for economic development, required a minimum manpower level that he soon saw threatened by serious chronic and endemic diseases. Alarm over the poor state of the recruits' health caused the viceroy to establish a medical school for Egyptian physicians which later would become the primary resource for civilian medical care after the armed forces' general demobilization. Serendipitously for Egypt, the director of the school introduced the principles and practices of clinical medicine that had become standardized in Paris and would shortly become universalized as one of the first steps toward modern scientific medicine. The vicissitudes suffered by the students and graduates of the Egyptian School of Medicine is the subject of the second chapter.

Chapters 3 and 4 describe the other major stimulus for making public health a concern of Egyptian government policy—the epidemics of cholera and plague that decimated the population in the 1830s. Although it was not recognized at the time, Egypt was threatened by a double convergence of disease carriers: caravans from Mecca could relay cholera carried by Indian pilgrims to the holy city and ships coming by sea from Syria and Anatolia could import plague-bearing rats from Central Asia. Egypt was particularly vulnerable to the newly introduced disease, cholera, as the extension of perennial irrigation during the nineteenth century multiplied the number of canals and therefore also the risk factor of polluted water sources. Plague, however, had played a paradigmatic role in shaping reactions to communicable diseases since the fourteenth-century Black Death, and the fourth chapter proposes that diverging European and Egyptian attitudes toward that disease derived from contrasting historical experiences. The emotional as well as intellectual commitment to strongly opposed views on plague foreshadowed future difficulties in attempting to enforce consistent measures for epidemic control. Since Muhammad Ali's rigorous application of quarantine procedures recommended by his European advisers during the plague epidemic of 1834–1836 had a traumatic effect on the Egyptian people, the chapter concludes with the question "Was quarantine effective?" Given the provisional nature of medical science at the time and the lack of any efficacious treatment, we conclude that the preventive benefits justified the social cost. Once the disease had penetrated population centers, the toll in human life and suffering was inevitably high, and barring entry to infection was vastly more effective than any measures after the fact.

The history of the international Quarantine Board's operations in chapter 5, however, illustrates the contradiction inherent in appointing consular representatives to administer a service that would impose restraints on the commerce their own governments had charged them to promote. Each crisis posed by an impending epidemic triggered an international dispute and delayed agreement on what should have been purely technical or humanitarian measures to stem the spread of disease. In addition to rivalry among the European powers engaged in trade in the Mediterranean, the Egyptian government as well was attempting to gain a share in the increasingly profitable maritime traffic. A remarkable international agreement on control regulations following the cholera pandemic in 1865 was doomed when the Suez Canal opened four years later and ships' captains entered a race to minimize time and maximize profit in trafficking the area's sea-lanes. In the meantime, Egyptians' lives would be at risk from the constantly looming threat of imported epidemic disease.

Meanwhile, the Egyptians' resentment of Muhammad Ali's coercive rule flared in determined opposition to a government campaign to extend smallpox vaccination throughout the country. Chapter 6 describes how the demonstrated efficacy of immunization gradually overcame suspicion of the government's intrusive interventions, fortified by years of resistance to military conscription. Universalizing smallpox vaccination in Egypt was the major accomplishment of a rudimentary public health system created during the second quarter of the nineteenth century.

European powers' intervention in 1841, to remove the Egyptians from Syria and to reduce their armed forces, in effect also abolished the infrastructure of agencies, including schools and home industries, that served the military establishment. For a time, under the Khedive Ismail, educational institutions began to revive and expand. But Ismail's heavy borrowing from foreign lenders forced the country into receivership, and a second European intervention in 1876 brought severer retrenchment than the first. The dual control of Egypt's finances by England and France doomed the budding public health agencies as well as the schools required to support them. Thus, in addition to the threat of imported epidemics, Egyptians' health and lives were at risk from neglected endemic environmental diseases since funds necessary for their control would not be forthcoming. The rise and decline of Egypt's health agencies and personnel are the subject of chapters 7 and 8.

In the conclusion, chapter 9, we return to the question of whether the Western medical technologies and institutions transferred to Egypt were appropriate for the country's health needs and whether they were capable of adapting to the evolution in concepts of disease and medicine that is still continuing today.

1

Muhammad Ali
and the Egyptians

The dynasty that ruled Egypt until the revolution in 1952 came to power in the wake of Napoleon's invasion of the Nile valley during France's postrevolution struggle with Great Britain. Into the resulting power vacuum moved Muhammad Ali,[1] a former Albanian tobacco merchant who had risen rapidly in the sultan's army. Quickly eliminating his rivals, he gained appointment as viceroy of Egypt and embarked on an ambitious program to build up the wealth of the territory under his control and wrest autonomy from the Ottoman sultan. Observing the major powers' intervention on behalf of the Greeks in their struggle for independence from the Ottoman Empire, the viceroy exerted every effort to gain European support for his bid for autonomy. But his plans conflicted with the imperial ambitions of England and France. Egypt's strategic location on the sea routes connecting Europe with the Orient made it unlikely that it could escape domination by one of the powers. Europe's commercial penetration had been growing since the mid-eighteenth century, and it appeared inevitable that Egypt eventually would fall under foreign control. Muhammad Ali's mercantilist policies temporarily interrupted foreign economic inroads by establishing state monopolies in agriculture, industry, and trade and deferred the definitive takeover until the British occupation in 1882.

The viceroy's achievements were substantial. In 1840, thirty-five years after he had been appointed governor, he had increased state revenues nine and one-half times, from about $10 million to $95 million; at the same time, he had created an army of 200,000 men, about 130,000 of whom were Egyptian regulars, and a fleet of some thirty ships manned by 18,000 seamen. In the process, the pasha had transformed the country's agricultural economy, irrevocably linked Egypt's economic future to European trade, and mobilized about 10 percent of the population in the service of the state.

Muhammad Ali exploited the Nile by introducing perennial irrigation and replacing subsistence cultivation with cash crops in demand on the world market. At the same time, he drew thousands of people into state projects in agriculture, trade, public works, industry, and, above all, in the creation of a military establishment. This marshaling of the human resources of the country was particularly remarkable considering that Egypt had only about three and a half million people at the time. Throughout his mobilization drive, Muhammad Ali was concerned about the scanty manpower pool available for the many enterprises he undertook.[2]

Egypt's lack of raw materials also was cause for concern and led the viceroy to invade Syria to claim the area's resources for his development program. By 1838, Muhammad Ali felt secure enough to make a bid for independence, but although the Egyptian army defeated Ottoman forces in Syria, European intervention forced the Egyptians to withdraw in 1841.

The most important consequences of defeat were mandatory reduction of the Egyptian armed forces to 18,000 men and compliance with the Anglo-Ottoman trade convention of 1838, which recognized the right of British merchants to buy commodities directly from producers throughout the Ottoman Empire and eliminated Egypt's government export monopolies. These restrictions were economically disastrous for Egypt. With no central agency to regulate commodities transactions, individual growers were exposed to the fluctuations in world market demand for their produce. At the same time, the country was opened to a flood of European manufactures that hit hard at struggling home industries. In addition, reduction of the armed forces deprived manufactures of the major local market and destroyed the infrastructure of service agencies created for the military bureaucracy.

To deflect the impact of free trade on agriculture, the viceroy awarded huge estates to private owners, creating a class of landed magnates who would be indifferent to industrialization and resistant to land reform in the future. This adoption of agricultural capitalism combined with Egypt's aborted industrialization had two consequences for medical care. First, there would be no sizable urban middle class developing during the nineteenth century to create a demand for personal care from private physicians. Second, it was unlikely there would be cooperative assistance plans sponsored by trade unions or fraternal organizations which might evolve into sickness and disability insurance programs as they had in Europe. It appeared that any medical care for the general population would have to be provided by the government. But the unprecedented invasions by the state into their private lives during Muhammad Ali's mobilization had aroused an enduring opposition among the Egyptians. Implacably suspicious, they would probably resist any further intrusions, even allegedly beneficial public health measures.

The viceroy's etatism cut against the grain of institutions and relationships that had integrated Egyptian life for centuries.[3] When Muhammad Ali came to power, Egyptian society was organized into a mosaic of autonomous but interdependent collectivities—merchants, artisans, and peasant villages. Taxation was the only link between the government and the inhabitants, and this was mediated by the leader, or *shaykh,* of each corporate group.

In urban centers, all occupations were organized into guilds: scavengers, prostitutes, and pickpockets as well as scribes, barbers, artisans, and merchants had trade associations. The city also was divided physically into separate quarters inhabited by families sharing some natural tie of occupation, origin, or religion. Each quarter was self-contained, with its own gates and communal buildings—mosque, church or synagogue, bath, public well, and market—and constituted an administrative unit under its own shaykh, or confessional leader in the case of Jews and Christians. Unless he had business in the law courts, the city dweller probably would meet only two local government officials in his daily life: the market inspector (*muhtasib*), who collected duties on commodities and transactions and enforced retail merchandising standards in the market, and the chief of police (*zabit*).

In the three thousand villages where the majority of the population lived, rural Egyptians enjoyed actual remoteness from the central government. Each village was a self-contained community with a few shopkeepers and potters, a blacksmith, a carpenter, and a barber; the prayer leader (imam) of the local mosque might also teach in the Koranic school, where one existed. The head man in the village, the shaykh al-balad, was the rural community's single link with the country's rulers; as the government's representative, he was responsible for collecting taxes and drafting military recruits or corvée labor for public works. Thus, Egyptians, whether townspeople or peasants, held only local allegiances to religious leaders, the family, the guild, or villages, and they recognized no notion of duty toward state or nation. They had enjoyed anonymity in their communities and had left dealings with the ruling class to their shaykhs, until Muhammad Ali's expansionist government bureaucracy brought them, unwillingly, face to face with the state.

Egypt's burden of taxation, for example, was staggering for a poor country. An English observer estimated that each individual in Egypt paid about two pounds sterling in taxes annually; this was equal to the sum paid by the inhabitants of Great Britain, twice that paid by the French, and four times the amount paid by the Spanish people to their government. Attempted evasion of taxes was widespread, but the peasants' opposition became almost legendary. The peasants paid only as the last resort, coin by coin, it was reported; they hid their money, and they buried their goods and possessions. Every traveler in the countryside remarked on the extraordinary amount of coercion with the lash the peasant would endure to withhold even a pittance from the government.

The villagers displayed even greater tenacity and ferocity in opposing conscription for military service, which was, in fact, impressment of the unwilling peasants. Ordered to produce a certain quota of men, local government officials would enter each village with a soldier escort, seize the number of *fallahin* required to fulfill their quota, and march them off to the recruiting center, bound together in groups of six or eight by ropes around their necks. Many men fled to distant villages, to Syria, or to the desert to escape conscription. Those who were rich or influential might buy immunity from the draft. Those who had no means took drastic steps to disqualify themselves. Mothers allegedly maimed their own children, blinding or crippling them, so they would not be drafted. "The aversion of the Arabs for military service knows no limits," the Russian consul-general reported. "One never sees a boy of eight years who hasn't had one or several teeth pulled out. Many others have destroyed an eye and cut the fingers of their right hand."[4]

Army service was a great economic hardship for the villager. A farmer could leave his land for a short time and ask a kinsman to perform his chores, but to be absent for long periods, he would either have to hire peasant labor to tend his crops or, in the extreme, sell his land. In the customary practice of the day, military service was for life, and the conscripts regarded it as a sentence to perpetual punishment. The navy also had to resort to impressment during its peak period of expansion, and every sailor in the fleet and every worker in the arsenal had an anchor tattooed on the back of his hand to discourage desertion. Reports of absence without leave from the navy appear less frequently than flight from the army, however, probably because seamen and shipyard workers had their families close at hand in Alexandria.

European observers who applauded extending "the privilege of bearing arms" to Egyptians were puzzled by their resistance. An English officer who found it incredible that young men from eighteen to twenty-five should regard leaving home as hardship attributed the Egyptians' invincible attachment to his home village to "limited horizons," the "indolent life" afforded by easily cultivated land, and the ties of early marriage.[5]

Egyptians married young. Girls married from the age of twelve years on, boys usually around sixteen, and all were wed by the age of twenty. Because troop levies removed precisely the able-bodied men who supported them, families followed men impressed into service, and the government found it inexpedient to stop them. Communities of huts sprang up near any government installation where a large number of men were assembled, notably the naval barracks and dockyards in Alexandria. Ibrahim Pasha also permitted the families of conscripts to follow them to Syria, it was said, to raise the draftee's morale. Thus, when Egyptian forces abandoned Syria in 1841, the troops' retreat from Suez took three days, and the retreat of the straggling train of women lasted eleven days. Realizing the difficulties of maneuvering with such an army, Ibrahim Pasha later ordered that new troop levies must separate the men from their families.

Not all government relations with the populace were carried out with coercion, however. Muhammad Ali gradually began to introduce Egyptians into the lower echelons of civil administration, to replace Turks who resented some of his Western innovations, it was said. The process of nationalizing government service accelerated after withdrawal from Syria called for retrenchment. Although the viceroy's primary aim was to reduce administrative costs by replacing relatively highly paid foreign employees with Egyptians, the economy measure eventually led to the formation of an Egyptian bureaucracy.

Another positive step toward rational administration was the founding of an official government organ, the *Egyptian Gazette* (Waqā'ī' Misriya), to inform all levels of officials about political, economic, and administrative developments. The *Gazette* was matched by regular reports from provincial bureaucrats; together, they constituted a communications system between the center and the periphery of government. Under the direction of capable editors who had studied abroad, the *Gazette* became a channel to local government officials for the specialized information and recommendations of the viceroy's technical advisers, such as the Medical Council in Cairo. It explained to provincial functionaries innovations in government activities such as public health measures. Founded about the same time as the Egyptian School of Medicine, the *Gazette* offers an incomplete but revealing record of the school's progress and setbacks, the accomplishments of its graduates, and the evolution of their responsibilities as state physicians. The *Gazette*'s reports on epidemics during the nineteenth century also document a gradual evolution in the Egyptian government's acceptance of state responsibilities for safeguarding the health of the people. As early as 1830, for example, it carried a notice of what may be considered the first sanitary regulation in modern Egypt. The government was concerned to enforce cleaning the streets and markets, the *Gazette* reported, not only to beautify the capital but also "to dispel doubts and misgivings about the incidence of various ills and different diseases."[6]

What were the "various ills and different diseases" common in Egypt during the early nineteenth century? Reports by contemporary observers offer some vivid impressions of the environment and a few hints about the Egyptians' attitudes toward health and sickness at this time.

No discussion of health in Egypt can ignore the ancient symbols of the land's fruitfulness, the Nile River and the sun. Nineteenth-century romantic writers sometimes compared Egypt to a palm tree: a slender line of habitation clinging to the long, undulating trunk of the Nile and spreading out in a profusion of luxuriant branches at the delta. This is an attractive figure for the hard geographic fact that Egypt is a desert country and only 4 percent of the land is naturally cultivable. But deficiency in rainfall was compensated by daily sunshine and by the Nile's rise of about twenty feet every year between

July and November. In the early nineteenth century, basins with earthen banks held the floodwaters for irrigation three or four months after the inundation. Later in the century, large barrages held water all year around, assuring farmers of three or even four crops each year.

Throughout the nineteenth century, the majority of Egypt's people was scattered in some 3,000 villages along the Nile valley and throughout the delta. Since pasturage was restricted to lower Egypt and the riverbanks, stock raising played a smaller role as a supplement to agriculture among Egyptian farmers than in Europe. The peasants' poverty also limited the number of animals they could employ for cultivation. The farmer used oxen or buffalo for field work, and he hired camels from the Bedouin for transporting crops. In country and city, the ubiquitous donkey carried all manner of goods and persons. In addition to restricted pasturage, the fallah had adapted to almost complete lack of timber and fuel. Except for lower Egypt, where occasional rain demanded weather-resistant building material, the most common dwelling south of Cairo was a small house with walls of mud or sun-dried brick, roofed with a thatch of palm leaves and branches. A pigeon roost often crowned the roof of the house, and the fallah usually brought his buffalo, donkey, and perhaps some chickens into the house at night for security.

Almost all visitors from abroad commented on the long days of backbreaking labor the peasant devoted to earning a living. Except for the period when the land was flooded, working the soil required unremitting effort: besides plowing, tilling, and reaping, the farmer was occupied daily maintaining the irrigation canals and, lacking a work animal, operating the water-raising devices by hand. Besides fetching water, spinning yarn, and preparing her family's food, the farmer's wife was responsible for preparing cakes of animal dung mixed with straw and water to serve as fuel. Children began tending the farm animals at the age of five or six, and their small hands, well suited for plucking blossoms, became an economic asset to the farmer after the expansion of cotton cultivation.[7]

The capital, Cairo, had declined from the splendor reported by travelers between the twelfth and sixteenth centuries, according to the savants who accompanied Napoleon's expedition. One of them estimated the city's inhabited area at only three square miles, one-fourth the size of Paris in 1798.[8] The French occupation forces had razed a number of buildings to provide easy access from the central military headquarters to fortifications outside the city, and they had removed gates to most of the quarters to facilitate control of any possible disturbances. Nevertheless, contemporary accounts indicate that the quarters retained their individual character and separatism resulting from their division according to kinship or occupation. The permanent bazaars, or khans, also were laid out according to particular crafts or commodities, and artisans plied their trades outdoors before their shops or homes. The narrow streets were crowded further with donkeys, pedestrians, and peddlers of every variety. Many water vendors plied the streets because the brackish well water was used mainly for baths, laundry, and watering animals and gardens, and most residents preferred to drink water from the Nile. There was an abundance of public drinking fountains—the preferred philanthropic bequest by the wealthy to the city's amenities—and it was the mark of public-spirited merchants and well-to-do homeowners to provide a large, water-filled urn equipped with a dipper near the entrance to their premises for the benefit of passersby, particularly the poor.

Since water supply became crucial during cholera epidemics, it is worth pointing out that a canal fed by the Nile flowed through the city. The canal's banks were considered a choice residential location during the hot summer months when evaporation from the flowing stream added coolness to the atmosphere, and they were lined with the homes of the wealthy. During the four months that Nile floodwaters flowed through the canal, residents on its banks obtained drinking water by lowering pots from their windows to the canal level. Drawing water from the canal was forbidden after the water stopped rising, and houses along the banks were permitted to reopen drains for wastewater and cesspools emptying into the canal. These subterranean drains seem to have been part of the few remaining, more-or-less-functioning sections of an extensive sewage system constructed during the Middle Ages. It seems safe to assume, however, that most dwellings in Cairo relied on the nightsoil collectors mentioned by historian al-Maqrizi in the fifteenth century. The scavengers' corporation, still operating in the same fashion as four hundred years earlier, must have been inadequate for the city's sanitation requirements, but the state of residential privies probably was no worse in Cairo, with a quarter of a million inhabitants, than it was in the greater urban agglomerations of Paris or London.

Refuse disposal also had not advanced from the practices of the

Middle Ages. People abandoned dead animals in ditches or empty lands, and they threw garbage into the street, expecting dogs, cats, and birds of prey to remove the remains. They disposed of every type of refuse in the canal as well when it was no longer fed by the river. Several eighteenth-century travelers wrote pungent descriptions of the variety of debris that floated on the surface of the canal and of the stench that rose as the water level dropped during the dry season.

Canals, ponds, and marshes created ideal breeding places for mosquitoes, and many travelers emphasized the need for mosquito nets to ensure a night's rest. Many more mentioned flies, the bane of all nineteenth century settled communities dependent upon animal transportation. In addition to the omnipresent donkey, many residents kept sheep, goats and fowl within their courtyards, and public barns in every quarter of the city kept cows during the flood season to supply the inhabitants with milk while they were cut off from the inundated countryside.

At least at the outset of the century, Cairo probably was ahead of most European cities in the number of public baths. A French expedition member recorded observing only 100, a mere fraction of the 1,170 referred to in the fifteenth century by al-Maqrizi. However, the fees were very low, and it was said that all those not entirely without means frequented the baths once a week. Besides, there were many private baths among the wealthy, who would not be inclined to take their families to the public facilities.[9]

Egypt's lack of fuel was illustrated in Cairo by the existence of cooks who ingeniously used the public baths' hot cinders to prepare huge earthenware pots of steamed broad beans and chick peas, two staples of the Egyptian diet. Members of the upper class had servants who fetched provisions daily, but many city dwellers apparently ate their meals on the premises of the public cooks and bakers.

All Egyptians seem to have adapted their diet to the country's lack of fuel. Except for the conspicuous consumption of the very wealthy, most had relatively abstemious eating habits, in the judgment of Europeans. The peasants' poverty restricted them to a subsistence diet of sorghum bread supplemented by beans, chick peas, or lentils, and vegetables in season. Melons added sugar to their fare, and if the farmer owned a buffalo or goat, his family might have milk and salted cheese. In the capital as well, however, even people of means appeared content with a light diet of raw vegetables with rice or bread and occasionally fish, chicken, or lamb. On holidays, vendors sold the crowds in the marketplace dishes of beets, cucumbers, onions, or salad greens. A member of the French expedition reported with evident surprise that "an Egyptian can make a meal of romaine lettuce, a cucumber and a watermelon."[10]

A few of the medical men who wrote observations on living conditions in Egypt included the Egyptians' alleged abstemious eating habits among the positive factors contributing to general good health in the country, but many more remarked on the salubrious climate. The physician who contributed most in the introduction of Western medicine to Egypt, A. B. Clot, proposed after ten years of service in the country that Egypt was considerably healthier than Europe because of the felicitous combination of a benign climate, Egyptians' temperance in food and drink, and their habit of frequent hot steam baths. Baron Dominique Larrey, the surgeon general of the French expedition, found the Nile valley's dry, sunny climate very beneficial; wounds healed quickly, and he saw scabies, gout, and other maladies common in France disappear among the troops. General René Desgenettes, the French expeditionary force's chief physician, expressed concern at the high incidence of "dysenteries" among the troops but conceded they were "inherent in armies." In his summing up, Desgenettes observed that in spite of the great toll taken by plague, mainly in Syria, the number of sick in the Egyptian expeditionary force was proportionately less than in any French army in Europe.[11]

There are not as many observations about the health of the Egyptians in the French medical officers' records as one might wish, because they were preoccupied with the communicable diseases that might have threatened their troops—a severe outbreak of smallpox in the winter of 1799–1800 and a catastrophic plague epidemic the following year which overshadowed other illness. Nor were the French curious to investigate whether any practices based on traditional Islamic medicine were still extant. They noted the practical skills of some folk practitioners but dismissed many more as charlatans.

At this time, the indigenous practitioners in Egypt probably drew on three medical traditions—Pharaonic, originally preserved by the Copts but long since assimilated by the entire population; Prophetic medicine (*Tibb-an-Nabi*), which, it has been suggested, was Bedouin folk practice immortalized in the traditions relating to Muhammad

(*Hadith*); and the classic Galenic tradition exemplified in the Avicennian corpus of writings.[12] The professional class of physicians that had flourished during medieval Islam seems to have declined as the great hospitals that had provided an institutional framework for its activities passed out of existence. Only one, the Maristan al-Mansur, remained (in a wretched state of neglect) when the French expedition scholars compiled their survey of Egypt's institutions. Although historian al-Jabarti wrote that shaykhs still wrote on medical subjects and taught students at the Maristan until the last decades of the eighteenth century, we know that his friend, Shaykh Hassan al-Attar, traveled to Istanbul in 1801 to receive an education in medicine that was no longer available in Egypt.[13] Members of Napoleon's expedition and European physicians who traveled in Egypt as late as 1825, however, observed literate practitioners, the *hakims*, who still drew their practice from the works of medieval Arab medicine. Their training consisted in copying the standard works, especially Ibn Sina's *Canon* and Da'ud's *Notebooks*, over and over in order to memorize them; they then sold superfluous copies to the next group of aspiring doctors.[14]

The most common therapeutic measures, variations of bloodletting, were practiced by surgeons who long had been assimilated into the familiar ranks of barbers. Beside their most common function of shaving men's heads, barbers in Egypt performed circumcision, phlebotomy, scarification and cupping, teeth extraction, opening abscesses, and bandaging or applying leeches to wounds and contusions. At the public baths, they were joined by an attendant who specialized in massage. European doctors often commented favorably on the Egyptians' expertise in techniques of manipulation that were also prevalent in Europe at that time. Baron Larrey had remarked that the local practitioners utilized a wide range of "vigorous" measures for treating external ailments, and he suggested that perhaps Europe was neglecting oily and dry massage, moxa, dry and wet cupping, and frequent steam baths.[15]

As a surgeon himself, Clot had few kind words for the barber-surgeons who, he said, had "not a single scientific notion to guide them"; but he and a French colleague affirmed having observed these practitioners remove cataracts and perform lithotomies "with a certain measure of success." Completing the spectrum of local practitioners, which matched that in Europe at the time, were the osteopath and the *daya*, the Egyptian midwife, both of whom visiting European medical men invariably condemned. Dr. Clot dismissed the osteopaths as "clever charlatans," and he carried on a prolonged campaign to replace the daya with a corps of literate, trained midwives.[16]

Like their counterparts in Europe, folk practitioners in Egypt were dependent on other occupations for their livelihood. None appear to have engaged in full-time practice, perhaps because the habit of self-treatment with hot baths and home remedies was widespread among Egyptians. Internal medicine had not died out with the decline of the hakim class but apparently had become the province of pharmacists, in much the same manner that medical lore had passed from physicians to apothecaries in eighteenth-century England. A physician who spent many years in Egypt during the nineteenth century suggested that in fact an empirical familiarity with drug lore was common among the general population. "It is worth remarking about the acquaintance the inhabitants of Egypt have with a great quantity of drugs and with their empirically therapeutic usage," he wrote.[17]

A complete account of Egyptian drug usage at the turn of the century written by a French army pharmacist, Pierre-Charles Rouyer, confirmed the view that urban Egyptians had acquired an effective grasp of fundamental drug lore based on familiarity with the traditional Galenic humoral system. In general, he wrote, Egyptians seemed to prefer to categorize their illnesses in classical humoral terms and to choose their own remedies for the humoral imbalance they perceived as their ailment. An exception to this rule was the wide variety of substances used to treat ophthalmia; primarily powders or solutions of inorganic salts used for dessicating or astringent action, they seemed to have no place in the theoretical system. Rouyer might have classified them as "symptomatic," as he did kohl, which had been used as a cosmetic eyeliner since pharaonic times and was thought to protect the eyes from infection.[18]

According to Rouyer, the Egyptians' Galenic classification recognized only three fundamental humoral imbalances—excesses of bile, cold, and heat—which they matched by three categories of drugs: purges, psychic stimulants and euphoretics, and fattening agents, cosmetics, and aphrodisiacs. Egyptians' preference for the strongest cathartics seemed to demonstrate a commitment to Galenic "depletion" therapy, which was common in Europe at that time as well. The second group, in which Rouyer included cordials, tonics, antidepressants, and stimulants, were not used to treat illness but were consumed in good health. He devoted particular attention to the two drugs that he considered true stimulants, opium and hashish, which he reported the poorer classes used in the same way their counterparts in Europe used fermented liquors. The usual opiates, philonium and theriac, were two relatively weak preparations that contained only a small percentage of the raw opium in laudanum, the most potent and most popular opiate in the Western world at that time. Rouyer reported the wealthier Egyptians resorted to philonium "for restoring strength, for dissipating melancholy, and for gaining confidence and courage." The third group of drugs—again used only by the healthy and chiefly the wealthy—included those ingested to acquire plumpness or embonpoint. Women were the chief consumers of these generally starchy substances, but men also used them after adding stimulants, apparently to arouse the libido. Rouyer's list of eighty-one plant drugs included thirteen that were popularly thought to be aphrodisiacs.[19]

Pharmacist Rouyer did not recognize the parallels between contemporary Egyptian and French drug usage, but recent investigation has established a remarkable correspondence between them and with drug use in the English-speaking world at the time as well. About three-fourths of the drugs recorded by Rouyer were mentioned in several official drug lists in France as well as the Edinburgh New Dispensatory then standard throughout the English-speaking world. Practitioners on both sides of the Mediterranean utilized similar preparations because they chose remedies to correct their patients' humoral imbalances. The spectrum of symptoms and signs observed by both was similar, even if the causes—unknown to physicians of all nations at the time—differed.[20]

Rouyer and some of his colleagues in the French expeditionary force judged the Egyptians' drug usage irrational or superstitious because it did not conform to their European norms. They failed to match their best example, for instance, Egyptians' alleged failure to utilize opium for its antidiarrheal action, against the Egyptians' great demand for cathartics. There is some self-righteousness, too, in Rouyer's disapproval of the Egyptians' preference for a few simple remedies for illness, while resorting to a "prodigious number" of preparations for pleasurable, aphrodisiac, fattening, and cosmetic purposes. Also, the Egyptians' indifference to the impressive therapeutic armamentarium that he and his colleagues were creating in France threatened his conviction that he was a torchbearer of a superior art and science.

Just as they overlooked the parallels in drug usage in Cairo and Paris, the French officers also failed to notice the similarity between Cairo and European cities in prevailing infant diseases, probably because members of the military elite were not likely to be acquainted with the problems of the urban poor. Among their comments on the high mortality among children, Desgenettes's medical officers estimated the mortality rate among infants under three years of age in Cairo at 60 percent and attributed it to their mothers' "constitutional weakness" as a result of too frequent childbearing. Noting the prevalence of marasmus, that is, protein deficiency, among infants and their particular vulnerability to gastrointestinal disorders and smallpox, the French held premature weaning responsible. But since it was not common to wean infants before the age of two in Egypt at that time, the marasmus most likely was associated with general undernourishment of both mother and child. Enteric infections, smallpox, and malnutrition—this was the familiar syndrome of early-nineteenth-century urban poverty and probably matched the picture of child health among the poor of London and Paris at the time.[21]

As for adult afflictions, there was a general consensus among laymen and medical men who traveled in Egypt during the nineteenth century, beginning with Larrey and Desgenettes, that the most prevalent endemic diseases were ophthalmia, dysentery, and plague. In fact, the first Egyptian physician to gain a doctorate in medicine at the University of Paris in 1833 submitted a dissertation on "the three principal endemic illnesses of Egypt—ophthalmia, dysentery and plague."[22] In the 1830s, Clot confirmed these three as the most common diseases; but leprosy still existed, venereal diseases were common among all classes, and smallpox took an alarming toll among children, he wrote. In a later "sketch of the most serious illnesses in Egypt," Clot added "Cachexia aquosa" or "Egyptian chlorosis" to ophthalmia and dysentery as the most prevalent diseases. About one-third of the young men conscripted into the Egyptian army had suffered from chlorosis, which he identified by marked pallor or yellow color, puffiness of the skin, and extreme weakness.[23]

Pierre Hamont, the veterinary surgeon who was Clot's longtime enemy, listed virtually the same common diseases among Egyptians: ophthalmia, dysentery, leprosy, syphilis, plague, and chlorosis. But he rejected Clot's early statement that pulmonary phthisis was rare in Egypt; it was widespread, he claimed, caused by undernutrition, unhealthful living quarters, and forced labor.[24]

Franz Pruner, a Bavarian internist who was a colleague of Clot and Hamont, discovered the cause of Egyptian chlorosis, severe chronic anemia, when he identified ancylostoma among the intestinal worms observed in numerous autopsies, but he made no causal connection between the parasites and the disease in his writings. Pruner found the differences in disease incidence in Europe and Egypt noteworthy: in European hospitals, one encountered most often pneumonia, pulmonary phthisis, typhoid fever, scarlet fever, and cancer; in Egypt, the majority of hospital cases presented intestinal congestions and ulcerations, plague, measles, and leprosy. For centuries, plague, dysentery, hepatitis, and ophthalmia had been considered diseases endemic in Egypt; recently, leprosy and chlorosis had been added to the list. However, he pointed out, plague disappeared for years at a time, neither dysentery nor ophthalmia prevailed continually, and all the diseases named existed almost everywhere on the Mediterranean coasts.[25]

As we shall see later, there was a sharp division of opinion on plague's endemicity in Egypt, but virtually all observers in the nineteenth century referred to ophthalmia and dysentery as endemic and prevalent diseases there.[26] Edward Lane, in fact, included an appendix to his book on Egypt which offered "directions for the treatment of dysentery and ophthalmia," which he recommended to every person visiting the Nile valley.[27]

Muhammad Ali was fortunate that post-Napoleonic reaction in Europe set adrift many physicians and surgeons who found military duty under the governor of Egypt congenial duty. The best-known names were French, but a host of Italians, Britons, Germans, and Spaniards also manned the military medical corps and later staffed the School of Medicine after its founding. As his expanding ambitions called for wider conscription of troops, the viceroy was compelled to give greater attention to the health of recruits who proved unfit for combat or who fell victim to camp diseases before they had finished training. Ailments that undermined the health of a nation year after year and passed unnoticed rose to frightening proportions when men were crowded into limited space. Black troops from the Sudan had perished by the hundreds at the Aswan training camp set up in 1819, and high mortality continued to decimate Egyptian conscriptees assembled near Cairo in the 1820s. Clot, the French surgeon-physician engaged to reorganize and expand the Egyptian army's medical corps, wrote that in 1825, between 1,000 and 1,500 ailing recruits were hospitalized in the training area near the capital. The death toll among the soldiers so alarmed Muhammad Ali that he asked Clot to exert every effort to arrest the disastrous losses. According to Clot, since only fifty European physicians and pharmacists were attached to the 150,000-man army when he arrived in Egypt, the best solution to the problem would be training Egyptian physicians. Against formidable odds, he succeeded in launching Egypt's first Western medical school in 1827.[28]

2

Response: Establishment of the Egyptian School of Medicine

Although contemporary European observers tended to view the Egyptian School of Medicine as a hybrid growth during its early years, the institution conformed to the pattern of hospital-affiliated training centers that had become the norm in France and England by 1830.[1] In aims and administration, however, Egypt's medical school was similar to the eighteenth-century military hospital-allied schools training officers for the armed forces of European monarchs. It resembled most closely the hospital school founded in Moscow in 1707 to serve Peter the Great's army, one of the prime instruments in his Westernizing program.[2]

Dr. Clot had all the requisites to carry out the viceroy's mandate. The son of one of the veterans of Napoleon's army in Italy, he was a self-made man who enriched his background by drawing on several of France's medical traditions: he trained at the Hôtel-Dieu Hospital in Marseille, apprenticed himself to a barber to learn phlebotomy, studied Latin with a local priest to gain admission to the university, and won doctorates in both medicine and surgery at Montpellier, France's oldest school of medicine. Clot had a genius for organization, thorough familiarity with the successful innovations of the French military medical corps, and considerable skill in bureaucratic politicking, military or civilian. He first enlisted the cooperation of court physicians who were close to Muhammad Ali by involving them in an advisory body that would channel his recommendations to the War Ministry with high-level endorsement. Headed by the viceroy's chief private physician, the Medical Council adopted the French model for a military medical corps and approved the establishment of a permanent military hospital near Cairo for the army training camp, another at Alexandria for the navy, and field hospitals for each regiment. The army establishment became a new model facility about 15 miles from Cairo between the villages of Khanka and Abu Zabel. Clot's design included a pharmacy, a botanical garden, and an amphitheater for lectures and demonstrations, for he was determined that the new hospital should be the site as well of the first medical school in Egypt.[3]

Only by training Egyptian physicians could the needs of the armed forces be met, Clot wrote Muhammad Ali. "In order to be lasting, useful institutions should be national and independent of the cooperation of foreigners." He therefore proposed to give a five-year course of medical training at the new military hospital to one hundred Egyptian young men who must be proficient in Arabic and arithmetic.[4]

The requirement that they be well versed in Arabic meant that the first students for the new medical school were almost exclusively drawn from al-Azhar, an Islamic college, and mosque schools (*madrasah*). Because the principal purpose of the Islamic college was the transmission of the Koran, its language, and related religious studies, al-Azhar's curriculum had not changed essentially since the twelfth century. Arabic language, grammar, rhetoric, literature, Koranic exegesis and readings, sacred tradition, canon law, and theology were the primary subjects; studies not related to religion were logic and mathematics.[5] The logical choice of Azharites thus seemed to Dr. Clot to dictate preparatory studies that would provide a transition from classical, tradition-oriented learning in theology and law to the spirit of critical inquiry that was held to animate Western scientific studies. Before undertaking any medical subjects, the entering class received instruction in geometry and natural sciences, emphasizing physics and astronomy to stimulate their interest in observing the natural world. The walls of the study hall were painted with geometric figures and diagrams and sketches of geographic and astronomical phenomena. A collection of natural history specimens supplemented the botanical garden in the school courtyard, and in default of apparatus that did not arrive until the course of studies was under way, instructors improvised experiments to demonstrate basic principles of physics. Finally, to provide a medium for continuing their studies after graduation, the students plunged immediately into learning French.[6]

At the same time, to relate their new studies to the Islamic classics and to lend legitimacy and prestige to the enterprise, the great figures of medieval Arab science were evoked. A well-known picture of the turbaned medical students watching a demonstration in the anatomical amphitheater at Abu Zabel shows the walls inscribed with the names of famous Arab scientists: Abu Musa Jaber, Ibn al-Ainy, Abu al-Qasim, Ibn Zubayr, Ibn al-Faris, Ibn al-Baytar, Abu al-Faraj, and others.[7]

After the introductory first year, the students followed a four-year medical curriculum modeled on the one in force in France at that time. The core studies were anatomy, pathology, and materia medica, progressing to increasingly advanced levels throughout the four-year course. Physiology, surgery, and therapeutics entered the curriculum in the second year. The third and fourth years introduced clinical training in internal medicine and surgery, plus hygiene, toxicology, and forensic medicine.[8]

For teaching staff, Clot was able to draw on numerous Italian physicians and pharmacists who had staffed the Egyptian military medical corps before his arrival, as well as many of his own countrymen.[9] Syrian Christians fluent in French or Italian as well as Arabic served as interpreters and Azharite shaykhs subsequently recast the translations of instructors' lectures in literary Arabic to serve as the first textbooks. When the question of technical terminology arose, professors, interpreters, and shaykhs agreed to adopt from the outset the Greek and Latin nomenclature standard in Europe.

To facilitate comprehension of unfamiliar subject matter, the school adopted the Lancaster method of student monitors, dividing the class into ten groups of ten, each headed by one of the brightest students, who repeated each lesson with every member of his group.[10] Although visitors from abroad applauded this method as a European innovation, it was in fact the time-honored tutorial system of al-Azhar's student hostels (*riwaq*) where good students earned spending money by coaching their colleagues studying the same legal system or compatriots from their home province.[11]

In view of the key role played by pathology in medical studies in Europe at this time, introducing postmortem dissection was as important as breaching the language barrier. Egyptians' repugnance to mutilation of corpses was well known. It was said to be rooted in a Pharaonic belief that the individual continues to experience sensations after death, fortified by the Muslim eschatological expectation, in common with Jews and Christians, of the resurrection of the body for the last judgment. In his memoirs, Clot described dramatically how he resorted to misrepresentations, ruses, and bribes to break down resistance among students and Muslim shaykhs, but the dissections had to be carried on in secret until 1829, when one of the students attacked Clot with a knife. He treated the attack as an inconsequential interruption, he claimed, and necropsies remained unchallenged thereafter in the regular teaching routine.[12]

Clot was equally determined to enforce what he called "unity of doctrine," to spare the students the contradictions in theory he believed plagued the medical profession in Europe. To obviate the confusion that might result from a diversity of medical opinions among the professors, he wrote, "I laid down that instruction should be consistent in theory and practice, based on the principles of the physiological doctrine." He would not tolerate mere "symptomatic" treatment.[13] Clot's dogmatism, which may have been one of the reasons for the rapid turnover in the medical school's European staff in its early years, illustrates the adherence of European practitioners to speculative systems of physiology and pathology in the early nineteenth century.

Two of these systems, Brownism and Broussaisism, apparently were introduced into the Egyptian medical school. John Brown of England held that illness was the result of either excess tension or abnormal laxness of the nervous and vascular systems. Treatment called for remedies that would either increase tone by stimulation or lessen it by relaxing tensions. Gout, for example, was considered a condition of flaccidity requiring stimulation: application of heat, friction, counterirritants, robust diet, and strong drink. In France, François Broussais elaborated a rival system, "physiological medicine," which made him a leader of the Paris school. Broussais's theory was ahead of his colleagues' views in rejecting the idea of specific disease entities as "ontology"; disease was not a foreign element but simply a change in function. Unfortunately, Broussais could not identify the cause of malfunction, and he fell back on an old theory of an "irritation" that spread from one organ to another by way of the sympathetic nervous system and caused generalized inflammation. Most diseases either started or ended as gastroenteritis; therefore, it was the key to pathology. Since disease was hyperirritation characterized by inflammation, therapeutics called for inflammation-reducing, "antiphlogistic" measures, such as the generous application of leeches to the affected area and a diet of soothing liquids.[14]

Because citizens in Paris before sanitary reform drew their drinking water from the Seine and enteric ailments were endemic, Broussais found ample vindication for his theory in the evidence of autopsies he performed in Parisian hospitals, and it seems likely he elaborated his theory on the basis of observations at the dissecting table. Clot also must have found abundant confirmation of Broussais's fixation on gastroenteritis in his autopsies in Egypt's military hospitals. He had abandoned the "old school" Mediterranean doctrines of Montpellier when he became acquainted with the "physiological doctrine," and he remained attached to Broussaisism throughout his medical career.

Although Clot was too diplomatic to make invidious comparisons in his writings, a compatriot who had preceded him in Egypt asserted that the Italian physicians in the medical corps were "tainted with an extreme Brownism." He applauded Clot's success in enforcing physiological medicine as standard treatment in the Egyptian military hospitals.[15] The Italian Brownists were at least partly avenged a generation later when the German pathologist, Wilhelm Griesinger, was appointed director of the medical school in 1850. Griesinger remarked with annoyance that Clot had enforced Broussaisism as a national system of medicine in the interests of "unité de la doctrine." Hence, Egyptian physicians still tended to identify all possible types of acute illness as gastroenteritis; "something like that cannot be uprooted in a couple of years," Griesinger complained.[16]

While Clot was able to maintain a unified approach in teaching Egyptian medical students, their lives and careers were subject to government policies that evolved under the pressure of events and were often erratic and inconsistent. Although the Egyptian medical school acquired new objectives and operated under changed circumstances over a quarter century of evolution, it never lost its character as a service agency for the military establishment during Muhammad Ali's governorship.

Conscripted into a service organization for the armed forces, Egyptian medical students were subject to organizational and operational patterns that remained a permanent legacy for the nineteenth-century medical profession. Like their counterparts at Moscow's military medical academy a century earlier, Egyptian medical students were expected to finish training within a prescribed five-year curriculum. Unlike the Russians, however, who sometimes prolonged their studies to eight or ten years, the Egyptians were washed out rigorously after each annual examination. Those who failed were dismissed from the school, assigned the rank of private in the army, and transferred to orderly duty in the hospitals. The medical school was directly under the jurisdiction of the Ministry of War, and its supervisor was a Turkish army officer. Students wore army uniforms and received food, lodging, and an allowance of 100 piasters a month. They also were subject to military discipline, the Turks' time-honored punishment of bastinado, beating the soles of the feet, sometimes with disabling effect. Clot had attempted to enforce a system of fines levied on students who cut lectures, failed to prepare assignments, flunked quizzes, or were absent without leave from hospital rounds, but as soon as a sizable sum accumulated, he wrote, it was appropriated by the War Ministry.[17] The ministry's subverting of petty funds was symptomatic of the government's serious failure to place the administrative bureaucracy on a sound fiscal basis, which could have regularized salaries and discouraged corruption. All government salaries were chronically a year or more in arrears. Moreover, the medical school and the army medical corps labored under penny-pinching bureaucratic regulation in minutest detail. The school and regimental hospitals had to request authorization from the ministry's executive council to purchase leeches, for example, or candles for the interpreters who worked on students' manuals far into the night.[18]

Among other disadvantages, graduates of the medical school entered the army at a lower rank and salary than Europeans. A European assistant medical officer received 350 piasters a month, while an Egyptian at the same grade received 150 piasters, only 50 piasters more than his student allowance. European physicians headed each regimental medical unit, where ample staffing apparently made their responsibilities relatively light, as one French medical officer with the Egyptian army in Syria wrote: "I have a deputy and four assistants who do all the work, I have to make only one short round of an hour in the morning, and I have the rest of the day free."[19]

Since salaries were perennially in arrears, all government physicians, including Europeans, found it necessary to seek private clientele; but the majority of Egyptians who could afford the services of a private physician were upper-level government functionaries who apparently expected to receive care from state physicians gratis. Even Clot complained that the wealthy considered him obliged to treat them free of charge because he was employed by the viceroy.[20] Well-off Egyptians would be even more inclined to expect free treatment from the neophyte Egyptian government medics.

The greatest disadvantage for Egyptian students attached to the military in wartime was the recurring demand for personnel, which meant they were transferred to active duty before they had completed training. Those eighty students who were assigned to duty as regimental aides during the campaign in Syria, for example, later had to face charges that they were inadequately trained. Eventually, it became necessary to devise a system of continuing education and to require annual examinations for medical officers seeking qualification for promotion.[21]

Some of the medical students in that first class also must have been casualties in the great cholera epidemic of 1831. According to Clot, he withdrew sixty of the advanced students from the medical school, issued instructions in Arabic and a supply of medicines and lancets, and assigned the young men to care for the stricken in different quarters of the city.[22]

Since journals and letters have not come to light yet, one can only speculate on the Egyptian medical student's daily life in that historic first class. The sudden transformation from theological student at al-Azhar to medical trainee at an army hospital in the desert must have been traumatic for many. As an Azharite, the student's schedule had been unstructured and open-ended. He could return to his village as a preacher after a half dozen years of study or he could remain a theological student indefinitely, as long as his family responsibilities could bear the strain of penury. Nothing was more alien to the spirit and practice of the medical school than such a relaxed, laissez-faire attitude. In Clot's view, the task of training Egyptian physicians was a high-priority crash program, with not a moment to be wasted. He abandoned the traditional three-month summer vacation that prevailed in European schools and restricted the Egyptian students to a single month recess during Ramadan, the period of fasting, when they would be unlikely to apply themselves strenuously to studying in any event.

To arouse a spirit of competition among the students, Clot also arranged public examinations to judge their accomplishments at the close of each academic year. Exercising his flair for the dramatic to the fullest, he invited high-ranking military officers, leading shaykhs, European consuls, and any distinguished visitors who happened to be in Egypt at the time. To lend éclat to the event, the study hall was decorated and a band was summoned from the music school. The medical students were called on to answer orally questions they drew by lot from an urn. Whenever a student gained applause from the examiners for his response to a question, the band delivered a triumphant fanfare. The examinations lasted five days and divided students into three groups according to their performance—fail, pass, and superior. Those who distinguished themselves were rewarded by a double raise in allowance. Those who failed were assigned as orderlies in the military hospitals or later joined barbers as vaccinators in the provinces.[23]

Students who successfully completed the five-year program of studies entered the armed forces as medical officers with the rank of second lieutenant. In lieu of a diploma and as a guide to future professional conduct, Clot had translated into Arabic and presented to each graduate a copy of the version of the Hippocratic oath used at his alma mater, the Montpellier Faculty of Medicine.[24]

Clot's efforts aimed at developing the students' esprit de corps, a sense of professionalism, and a competitive drive by psychological incentives—invocation of the great figures of medieval Islamic science, ceremonial recognition of accomplishment at public trials, the inspiring rhetoric of the Hippocratic oath, and monetary rewards for outstanding performance in competitive examinations. As the students transferred into the military medical corps, he also sought to ensure that their salaries, ranks, and prerogatives would match those of their peers in other branches of the military service, and he fought for distinctive insignia on the regulation second lieutenant's uniform.

On one point, however, Clot remained adamant: he refused to permit graduates of the medical school to assume the title "Doctor." The French officiers de santé appeared to Clot to be the appropriate model for Egypt's medical school, and its graduates were designated senior health officers in the government service, with or without an accompanying military rank.[25]

"Egyptianization" of the Medical School

The twelve members of the class of 1832 selected to study for the doctorate in Paris were the object of special recognition; they were expected to become the nucleus of the medical school's future Egyptian teaching staff. It had long been recognized that the weakest aspects of training were transmitting instruction through the medium of interpreters and the lack of texts in the students' own language. Consequently, members of the group sent abroad in 1832 were ordered to acquire the doctor's degree, a sufficiently advanced level of accomplishment in a specialized field to enable them to teach it, and proficiency in French adequate for translating scientific works. In groups of two, the students were assigned to six areas of study that were to become their teaching specializations: natural history, physics and chemistry, pharmacy and materia medica, anatomy and physiology, pathology and internal medicine, and surgery. In Paris, Clot arranged for the students' admission to three leading hospitals and charged a French commission to hold quarterly examinations, to make appropriate modifications in their instruction, and to report their progress to the viceroy.[26]

Five members of the group returned to join the faculty of the medical school in 1836 after receiving the doctorate; the others remained in internships or residencies in Paris hospitals an additional two years. With the addition of Egyptians to the faculty, instruction in Arabic increased, and after 1839, all courses were conducted in Arabic without interpreters serving as intermediaries.[27] Translation and publication of textbooks in Arabic also accelerated after 1836. Between 1833 and 1840, the number of works translated rose from 12 to 24, and when Abbas succeeded Muhammad Ali as viceroy in 1849, the Egyptian staff members and Dr. D. M. Perron, director of the medical school, had translated 55 titles in anatomy, physiology, internal medicine, surgery, obstetrics, gynecology, pediatrics, and dermatology, and undertaken the collective publication of a scientific lexicon.[28]

When the army training camp at Abu Zabel was vacated during the Syrian campaign in 1832, the military hospital's raison d'être vanished and it became necessary to transfer the medical school. Theoretically, the hospital continued to serve the garrison in Cairo, but the distance from the city made transporting seriously ill soldiers impractical. More important, the medical students no longer had access to a large hospital for clinical training.[29] The new military hospital, Qasr al-Ainy, located on the Nile between Bulaq and Old Cairo, was accessible to the Cairo garrison by land and by river. It also replaced Cairo's former garrison hospital, Ezbekiyah, which became the first civil hospital founded in Egypt in 400 years and played an important role in the evolution of a health care system to serve the civilian population.[30]

It is difficult to assess contemporary European observers' judgments of the Egyptian School of Medicine, for they often were colored by an individual's biases or even the perennial Anglo-French rivalry in the Ottoman Empire personalized in a clash between antagonistic French and British nationals. European observers' partisan views of the school most often reflected their reactions to the school's founder, Dr. Clot. Muhammad Ali awarded Dr. Clot the title of "Bey" for his unflagging service during the fearsome cholera epidemic in 1831. He apparently learned to speak Arabic and adopted the exotic garb of an Ottoman higher official. Clot adjusted to Oriental-style living with such ease that he was challenged frequently to refute rumors that he had "turned Turk," that is, converted to Islam.[31] His flamboyant personality and flair for dramatic gesture did nothing to allay the resentment and criticism generated by his autocratic drive to dominate the entire medical establishment, including the Italian-run pharmacy service and the veterinary school headed by a French rival. Even one of his compatriots who applauded his establishment of the medical school cautioned that improvement in the quality of instruction would be necessary if the school were to merit the "somewhat too brilliant" reputation claimed by its founder. Another who visited in the early years of development observed that the school's operations appeared handicapped by "imported" as well as "local jealousies." A visiting English physician was bluntly explicit: "The establishment does credit to Clot-Bey," he said, "however much envious Franks may sneer at his crimson trowsers [sic] and red morocco boots."[32]

The single issue that drew the sharpest criticism from outsiders was nationalization of the school—adopting Arabic as the language of instruction and replacing foreign faculty members with Egyptians. The appearance of Egyptian faculty only ten years after the school's foundation caused some observers to question whether it was possible to create an Egyptian School of Medicine taught by Egyptians. The Russian consul general was unequivocal in his negative judgment.

The medical school left more to be desired than any of the schools established because it was ill-conceived from the outset, he wrote:

> The broad learning which may be rightfully demanded of a good physician is too far above the common intelligence of Arabs to allow any expectation of seeing them succeed in this branch of human knowledge. It might have been better perhaps to send a few distinguished students to study in the European universities [rather] than to create a medical "wash-house" [buanderie] in Egypt, for which the country cannot offer even the basic requirements.[33]

If the diplomat was referring to the chronic lack of preparatory training for medical students, his observation was well taken. The most serious weakness in the enterprise was the failure to create any system of general education in Egypt from which medical school candidates could be drawn.[34]

In Egypt, for more than a generation, until Ismail succeeded to the khediviate in 1863, the only institutions of learning to prepare students for medical training were the Koranic schools (*kuttabs*) and mosque colleges and a growing number of private schools established for Christian communities.[35] But the Russian consul general's comment probably reflected the educated upper-class European's view that only training in the Greek and Latin classics could fit a young man to undertake medical studies. Most European physicians who traveled in Egypt, as well as diplomats, were well-to-do gentlemen with a traditional humanistic education. In Germany, graduates of secondary schools that emphasized instruction in the natural sciences rather than the classics were still denied admission to medical schools as late as 1879. The nineteenth-century Viennese historian of medical education, Theodor Puschmann, declared unequivocally that non-classical gymnasium students were excluded from medical school because the medical profession was concerned to preserve its elevated social position.[36]

It would take time for even his own countrymen to accept the Egyptian "homegrown" physician. And at mid-nineteenth century, the most generous judgment to be expected from an outsider was exemplified by a visitor who found the Egyptian replacements for European faculty "much too hasty"; nevertheless, he conceded that "several of these professors are demonstrating themselves to be not completely beneath their task."[37]

In addition to their medical studies and clinical training, graduates of the Egyptian School of Medicine mastered French, translated technical literature, pursued research in health-related subjects, and assumed teaching and administrative responsibilities after their return to the school. Were they indeed handicapped by their earlier education at al-Azhar, as critics of the school have claimed? It should be remembered that the clinical training that was becoming normative in the formation of physicians was as new a departure in Europe as it was in Egypt. While Bichat was narrowing the focus of pathology studies from organs to tissues, his colleague in Paris, Pinel, was following a more familiar line of investigation, attempting to create a meganosology by classifying all diseases according to symptoms. In this premicroscopic era when natural science studies were still largely taxonomic, students trained at al-Azhar were at no great disadvantage. Nineteenth-century Europeans who declared that Egyptian students lacked the essential background of Western learning to succeed in medical studies were referring to the classical humanities; the association of scientific method with medical training was only emerging in Western education.[38]

Decline, Recovery, and Decline

By focusing on presumed deficiencies in the students' preparation and abilities, European critics of the School of Medicine failed to ask the appropriate and relevant question: had the school succeeded in nationalizing and institutionalizing the study of Western medicine securely enough to survive the neglect that followed the disappearance of Muhammad Ali's patronage? Continuing support was required in three essential areas, lacking which the medical school would inevitably decline: first, expansion of general education to provide a pool of student candidates with adequate preparatory training for medical school; second, consistent and substantial economic and administrative support for the school's operations; and third, regular study missions abroad to keep the medical students in touch with the accelerating pace of discoveries in the basic sciences that had direct application to medicine.

None of these requisites received sufficient attention during the nineteenth century. Under retrenchment in the 1840s and 1850s, reports of miserly payment of students and graduates, familiar during the school's early years under the War Ministry, reappeared, and in 1848, the Ministry of Education acknowledged that the students had received no salaries for six months. The following year, the ministry attempted to rationalize medical officers' substandard salaries by reducing the rank of new appointees to government employment. Henceforth, graduates would be commissioned second lieutenants only after two additional years in aspirant or cadet rank; thus, the government was able to continue paying them only a slight increase over their student allowances for two years after graduation.[39]

Like other minor government agencies, the School of Medicine also became rife with rivalries and intrigues, and politicization undermined its character as an educational and public service institution. However, the conventional view that Abbas Pasha subverted the school's effectiveness by replacing French leadership with German and Italian faculty is debatable. It is not clear what changes the German, Austrian, and Italian faculty members introduced into the medical school curriculum or whether the changes survived repeated reorganization. We do know that they were interested in clinical research. Griesinger, for example, during his tenure as director of the school between 1850 and 1852, rediscovered and definitively identified ancylostomiasis as the cause of the widely prevalent anemia called "Egyptian chlorosis." Theodor Bilharz, a former student who followed him to Cairo and a teaching position at the School of Medicine, became more famous for his discovery of *schistosoma haematobium,* the parasite that had been preying on Egyptians since Pharaonic times, causing the debilitating disease subsequently named for him, bilharziasis.[40]

Evidently neither the German nor Italian administrators who followed Dr. Clot had his skill or taste for exercising political influence, which had enabled him to promote the School of Medicine successfully in spite of indifference or hostility among high-ranking government functionaries. Perhaps more important, at this time their native lands were politically insignificant among international powers. Unlike the French or British who could rely on the prestige and support of their respective empires' ambassadors, Italians and Germans were represented by consular officials of relatively minor states and principalities. Also, top-level support from the viceroy was crucial for the medical school's success or failure. The low point in the school's fortunes occurred when the new viceroy, Saïd, suspended the school's operations in 1855 and dispersed all the students among various army units to serve in the Crimean War.[41]

The following year, Clot was recalled from France to reopen the School of Medicine and to launch a second "French period" in direction. Failing health caused him to retire definitively in 1858; there was a rapid turnover in directors and the school did not regain a healthy operating level until it passed under Egyptian leadership in 1863. A French physician who visited the school in 1862 attributed its evident decline to lack of continuity and stability. The school has been reorganized three times in five years, he observed; it had not yet recovered from its closure six years earlier and had only 25 students. Parents were reluctant to send their sons to the school because medical careers held few advantages for Egyptians. As government medical officers, Egyptian physicians enjoyed no prestige and no assured vacations; nor was it possible for them to earn a living in private practice.[42]

Shifting graduate medical students to schools other than Paris was a constructive change, however, since the French lost ground rapidly after mid-century to universities that emphasized training in the basic sciences. To Abbas's credit, of 41 students assigned to study abroad during his viceroyalty, 31 were sent to study medicine in Munich, Edinburgh, Pisa, Berlin, and Vienna. Under Saïd Pasha, an additional 30 medical graduates went abroad for specialized training, but we are told that many of them were recalled after only one year's study. At least 20 of 172 students who traveled to Europe during Ismail's khediviate were medical graduates, but the study missions have not been investigated yet.[43]

The outlook for the School of Medicine improved considerably during Ismail's viceroyalty. Besides sponsoring graduate study missions abroad, the government provided consistent financial and administrative support, and it promoted general education. Most important was a revitalization of the Koranic village schools, the kuttab system, primarily by private initiative—Egyptian notables and shaykhs who feared the rapid expansion of schools for foreigners, often run by Christian missionaries, threatened Egypt's Islamic culture. In November 1867, the government assumed responsibility for control, reform, and expansion of the kuttab system. At the same time, it required community support, involving a commitment from parents for their children's instruction. In provincial centers, new schools began to offer at least an intermediate level of instruction for those who had completed the elementary curriculum in the kuttabs. Thirty-three such intermediate schools arose between 1868 and 1879, and an institute to train Koranic teachers in secular subjects opened in 1872 to meet the increased demand for instructors.[44]

Ismail followed his grandfather Muhammad Ali's example by expanding the armed forces, establishing military academies to train the officer corps, and providing them with infirmaries. He also increased career opportunities for Egyptian physicians by revitalizing the military medical corps to serve with the armed forces in campaigns to consolidate Egypt's position in Africa. During Ismail's reign, the School of Medicine enjoyed its most illustrious period under Egyptian leadership. The director of the school between 1863 and 1876 was Muhammad Ali al-Baqli, who had been the youngest and brightest member of the first postgraduate study mission sent to Paris in 1832. After his return, al-Baqli first became famous as a surgeon at Qasr al-Ainy hospital, but as director of the medical school, he encouraged research in all areas and launched the first Egyptian medical journal, Ya'sub al-Tibb (the Queen Bee of Medical Science). During his tenure at the school, all but one of twenty instructors were Egyptians who had received specialized training abroad.[45] At this time, the 175 resident students received complete maintenance as well as schooling and in return they were committed to enter military service or some public health agency after graduation. Twenty "volunteers," whose parents paid their living expenses, were free to pursue private practice after graduation if they wished.

Unfortunately, the medical school's most capable director, al-Baqli, died in 1876 while serving with Ismail's military forces in Abyssinia. During the financial crisis in the late 1870s, the system of state support for students was abandoned. Mandatory payment of fees caused enrollments to plummet, and by 1896, there were only 27 students in the School of Medicine. Without high-level support, the school repeatedly became an object of political intrigues and pressures. Politicization of the school's administration became so flagrant and caused such obvious decline that its takeover by British occupation authorities in 1893 was a rescue operation.[46]

During Muhammad Ali's time, however, graduates of the medical school provided the majority of personnel in the military medical corps for about a decade. And following demobilization, the viceroy broadened their mandate to serve the civilian population in urban and rural health centers. For, in addition to the chronic, endemic diseases that crippled the armed forces and aroused Muhammad Ali's concern initially, two devastating epidemics had claimed thousands of victims and heightened his alarm over the loss of people. We shall describe first the murderous cholera pandemic of 1831.

3

Cholera: The Epidemic of 1831 and Later Invasions

Cholera became a constant threat to Egypt during the nineteenth century as expanding and accelerating ocean transport increased the traffic of Muslim pilgrims along the Egyptian coastline and overland across the Nile valley.[1] At least half of the ten epidemics that erupted between 1831 and 1902 have been traced to pilgrims returning from the holy cities in the Hijaz, but this connection was not recognized until 1865.[2] No one inside or outside Egypt early in the nineteenth century was aware of the country's extreme vulnerability to cholera infection because of its dependence on a single source of water. The danger of contaminating the water supply always existed, but we know today that running streams are automatically self-purifying unless grossly polluted. Egypt's nineteenth-century map indicates that urban as well as rural communities drew their drinking water mainly from the Nile or its branches and from groundwater wells.[3] The cholera pandemics threatened Egypt precisely at the time when the country was changing from basin to perennial irrigation, enormously multiplying the number of canals that diverted the Nile into agricultural areas and that became potential health hazards because of the likelihood they might be drawn on for drinking water. Towns like Tanta and Damietta were at great risk because an influx of visitors to a fair in June or July periodically depleted the normal water supply just before the annual Nile flood when all water courses were at their lowest level.

In Egypt as in Europe, many saw an association between cholera and poverty, but nowhere were the reasons for the disease's more rapid spread among the lower classes understood. Since it is necessary to ingest the *vibrio cholerae,* which is exposed through the dejecta of those attacked by the bacillus, the most common mode of transmitting cholera has been through polluted water. But since any contact with materials contaminated by cholera sufferers' feces is dangerous, personal cleanliness also is necessary for protection against the disease. Cleanliness was difficult to achieve and maintain, however, among large groups of people assembled for any period of time in makeshift circumstances—whether they were European barracks or British slums, pilgrimage sites along the Ganges, or the shanty-town huts of workers in Alexandria's Arsenal.

The central fact in the nineteenth-century's collision with cholera was the lack of any effective therapy or even palliative treatment and consequently the overriding importance of preventing invasion by the disease. Dr. Robert Pollitzer, the World Health Organization's first specialist in communicable diseases, identified five initiatives considered necessary today for effective cholera controls: adequate intelligence services, sufficient facilities for isolating patients, a sanitary engineering service to deal with contaminated water supplies, measures to control flies and to ban the sale of potentially dangerous food or drinks, and a large-scale public information program alerting the public to take necessary precautions.[4] Except for the control of flies and sanitary engineering competence, which did not exist anywhere at that time, Muhammad Ali's government eventually took steps toward the controls Pollitzer listed. The viceroy probably sanctioned these initiatives on the advice of Europeans, but he utilized indigenous institutions—some old, like the local police, and some new, like the government *Gazette*—to contain an epidemic in 1848.

Of the ten cholera epidemics Egypt suffered between 1831 and 1903, I describe briefly the outbreaks of 1831, 1848, and 1865. Each posed the problem of disease invasion in different circumstances with varying contributing factors, illustrating the mounting difficulty of maintaining effective defenses as Egypt was drawn more closely into the network of international trade. In 1831, the Egyptian government and Egyptian society were taken unaware by the first cholera pandemic, and the country suffered devastating fatalities. Muhammad Ali's primary concern was to protect the armed forces, poised at that time for a campaign in Syria, and it appears that government measures may have minimized losses among the military to a certain extent. When cholera broke out again in 1848, Egypt's armed forces had been reduced to a nominal level, but the government shifted attention to a wider population and enlisted the medical corps in civilian service. In 1865, cholera entered the country with pilgrims using two new rapid means of transport, the steamship and the railroad. Because this epidemic traveled on to Europe from Egypt, the quarantine establishment in Alexandria became a focus of international attention and efforts that in general seem to have had positive effects in barring the entry of disease. Last, the technology for excluding epidemic outbreaks could not keep pace with population growth, deteriorating environmental sanitation, and the rising volume and speed of maritime traffic following the opening of the Suez Canal. After an absence of almost twenty years, cholera reentered Egypt in 1883 and spread quickly in shockingly unsanitary conditions resulting from neglect by successive Egyptian governments preoccupied with other problems. Because mounting urbanization and population density made environmental sanitation control increasingly difficult, it was imperative to keep cholera out of the country; once the streams became polluted, widespread infection was almost inevitable.

The Cholera Epidemic of 1831

The first visitation of cholera in 1831 was one of the most murderous epidemics in Egypt's history. Within two months, the disease killed about 150,000 of the estimated population of three and a half million; some 36,000 of Cairo's quarter million inhabitants are believed to have perished in only twenty-eight days.[5] The Egyptian government was completely unprepared for this first invasion of cholera. It was a new scourge in the lands of western Asia, first appearing in Muscat with an expeditionary force from India in 1821. The disease also entered Basra and traveled to Baghdad and Mosul; carried by caravan to Anatolia and the north Syrian coast in 1822, it struck Aleppo and Alexandretta and disappeared by the end of 1823. We are told that Arabian chroniclers confronted by the outbreak in Oman had no name for cholera; seeing the healthy struck down suddenly as if by a simoom blast, they thought cholera was carried by a pestilential "yellow wind" (al-rīh al-asfar or al-hawa al-asfar).[6]

During the epidemic in Syria in 1822, Muhammad Ali had sought advice from the French Supreme Council of Health, exchanging correspondence on quarantine procedures for about a year.[7] But his interest waned as the disease failed to reappear in the Levant, and when cholera struck again in 1831, it caught him off guard, coming suddenly from an unexpected quarter in the Hijaz. In spring 1831, an estimated 25,000 to 50,000 pilgrims had converged on Mecca for the communal ceremonies of Qurban Bayram. Early in June, the Egyptian military Medical Council in Cairo received reports from the chief army surgeon in the Hijaz of great ravages of disease among the pilgrims. An epidemic, "analogous to the cholera morbus of India," had broken out in Mecca in March, subsided, and flared again with the arrival of new pilgrims in May. The outbreak had been aggravated by the simoom wind, a severe shortage of potable water, and drenching rain to which thousands were exposed during their overnight encampment on Mount Arafat. It was believed that 30,000 sheep sacrificed the following day also must have added to the "poison" in the atmosphere. Estimates of mortality from the epidemic ranged from 12,000 to 30,000, and among the victims were reported the leaders of the Damascus and Cairo caravans and the governor of Mecca himself.[8]

Although the Egyptian government hoped that the disease would be confined to the Hijaz, a report that 4,000 pilgrims had set out from Mecca for Qusayr and Suez caused a flurry of anxiety and official activity. Well equipped with troops to apply the standard defense measures against epidemic diseases—military cordons and detention stations for travelers from the infected area—the viceroy ordered Suez and Qusayr encircled and all travelers from the Hijaz quarantined. When the physicians dispatched to Suez returned, reporting that pilgrims had broken through the blockades, a battalion of regular troops moved to intercept them. As news arrived that cholera had broken out in Suez and claimed 150 victims in three days, Ibrahim Pasha organized a military sanitary administration in Cairo which promptly established detention stations at Old Cairo and at Birkat al-Hajji for travelers from Qusayr and Suez. The sanitary authorities also ordered a lazaretto set up near Suez for travelers already stricken with cholera and assigned 300 Bedouin to strengthen the military cordon.[9] Before these precautions went into effect, a courier brought news that the great caravan from Mecca had bypassed Suez and was on its way to Cairo. The governor of Cairo immediately dispatched 200 Bedouin to intercept the caravan and order the pilgrims to set up camp in the desert; meanwhile, a cordon of line troops cut all communications between the camp and city.[10]

It appears that these measures were too little or too late. Pushed by fear, several hundred pilgrims had already entered Cairo; several days passed before most were rounded up and interned, and some remained at large in the city. John Barker, the British consul general who had witnessed the cholera epidemic of 1823 in Aleppo, was scornful of what he considered the perfunctory quarantine of a thousand pilgrims who arrived in Alexandria early in August. Although they had left Mecca while cholera was still raging, they were allowed to proceed further after only "a slovenly quarantine of 15 days."[11]

According to Barker, the fact that the disease did not break out during the two-week quarantine period lulled the people and the government of Cairo into a "fatal security." On the sixteenth of August, they were aroused by simultaneous outbreaks of cholera at several sites in the city,[12] and within three days, the disease claimed 335 victims. When two days later the number of dead rose to 450, panic seized the city. There was a mass exodus of Europeans fleeing in terror to the suburbs, to Fayyum, or to the western bank of the Nile bordering the desert. The Nile swarmed with craft of every description filled with refugees from the stricken city. As the disease spread throughout Cairo, the Franks' quarter became a scene of mass rout. In the streets, a continual file of camels carrying the fugitives' effects passed sad bands of peasant laborers returning home to the provinces. Within a few days, funerals for the victims of the epidemic filled the streets with a steady train of mourners. Although religious-minded Muslims believed the scourge was an act of divine vengeance, according to Dr. Clot, fatalistic resignation was not conspicuous among them. Muslims who had never been convinced that plague was contagious fled Cairo or withdrew to their houses, taking precautions they had scorned in the past.[13]

The news that 335 had died in Cairo within three days paralyzed Alexandria with fear; consular and commercial agents' offices closed and business came to a standstill. At this point, Muhammad Ali proposed that the European consular corps organize a board to protect the port city from the epidemic. According to the consuls' reports, the viceroy placed at their disposal 20,000 troops in the area, extended carte blanche for expenditures, and promised to execute any measures they recommended for the common welfare. Seventeen consular representatives assembled and named a five-man committee as the first Quarantine Board in Alexandria: the consuls general of England, France, Austria, Tuscany, and Russia. The board's first move was to order a double cordon around Alexandria and to post European physicians as inspectors at stations on the cordon and in the markets.

The Quarantine Board survived only about a week, for cholera broke out in Alexandria, in spite of the double cordon, with the same explosive force it had exhibited in Cairo. Deaths mounted quickly, and by the end of August the daily mortality in Alexandria exceeded 100.[14] The consular Quarantine Board had resolved to take full advantage of the extraordinary powers the viceroy had granted them, but their efforts were in vain, and within ten days, they admitted defeat at their last session. Since 800 soldiers in the hospital were without medical attention because of the death or desertion of many physicians, the board recalled all physicians stationed on the cordons and designated only a few observation points to be maintained for detaining travelers from Cairo and for fumigating mail. And since both cordons, which were preventing the delivery of provisions to the city's markets, had become infected, the board abolished the blockades. Finally, the members abandoned their commission and dissolved the board itself.

At the time the Quarantine Board prorogued its sessions, the cholera epidemic had peaked and was claiming more than 100 deaths daily in Alexandria and between 500 and 650 in Cairo. During the following two weeks before the disease began to decline, it spread into new quarters at a terrifying rate. There was a rising toll among troops, in the naval barracks, and on shipboard. Cholera penetrated most of the ships of the fleet and eventually broke out on board the viceroy's own frigate, where the staff made every effort to conceal the fact from him. Muhammad Ali returned to Alexandria precipitately and took over the governor's residence. Ibrahim Pasha had already fled Cairo for Upper Egypt when cholera broke out in his harem.[15]

Although Upper Egypt had not been touched by the epidemic, people in the capital feared that pilgrims en route to the Saïd would reignite the disease when they passed through Cairo on river craft;

those who appeared at Bulaq or Old Cairo ports were intimidated and forcibly prevented from disembarking.[16] In Lower Egypt, cholera had spread in all directions, attacking Rosetta, Boulos, Damietta, and almost all the villages of the delta. Fuah, at the entrance to the Mahmudiyah canal where many pilgrims had stopped, was particularly hard hit, and an army regiment garrisoned there was almost wiped out.

Sending conscripted peasant laborers back to their home villages appears to have been the only government-initiated measure for the civilian population during the cholera epidemic. Muhammad Ali had enforced the Quarantine Board's proposals to draft gravediggers for Alexandria and to remove burial grounds outside the city, but he refused to sanction the destruction of cholera victims' corpses by quicklime, which, he said, was forbidden by the precepts of Islam.[17]

The government's primary concern centered on the military forces, stricken with a devastating disease on the eve of their departure for Syria. According to observers' estimates, about 2,000 sailors and 5,000 troops of the 90,000-man army died during the epidemic.[18] It appears that isolating the sick was the principal expedient adopted to contain the disease among the armed forces. As soon as cholera broke out in Cairo, the minister of war ordered cavalry and infantry regiments to the border of the desert to isolate them from the urban population.[19] When regimental infirmaries soon proved inadequate for the growing number of patients, extra tents were set up to separate the stricken from healthy men in their units. In one case where the regiment had no facilities for the sick, the War Ministry approved housing them temporarily in a local caravansary. Government communications invariably emphasized economy, even during an epidemic, but there were some concessions to medical opinion. A regimental commander who requested instructions for disposing of the effects of soldiers who died was directed first to record the amount realized by selling the effects; however, it was then declared preferable to burn the clothing of those who died of cholera. The War Ministry also surprisingly upheld a second lieutenant who appealed his dismissal for failure to follow his regiment while he was recuperating from cholera.

But there was no clemency for medical officers who had deserted their posts during the panic of Egypt's first cholera epidemic. The viceroy ordered all medical personnel who had fled dismissed, because they had failed in their duty when they were needed most.

European physicians' names were stricken from the payroll; they were obliged to return the swords issued to them and to reimburse the treasury for the mount and saddle they had received.[20] The flight of European members of the medical corps had apparently created a serious shortage of trained personnel, for Dr. Clot acknowledged there was mass defection during the epidemic.[21]

By the middle of September, cholera was on the wane and the mortality bills for Cairo and Alexandria had dropped back to pre-epidemic proportions. The official figures forwarded by European consuls reported the number of dead from cholera between August 19 and September 15 as 2,000 in Alexandria and 10,000 in Cairo, including army and navy personnel.[22] The French consul general questioned these figures and suggested as a more accurate toll 4,000 for Alexandria, 30,000 for Cairo, and perhaps 100,000 for all Egypt. Confirming his estimate for Alexandria, he reported the following mortality figures:

Navy men on board ships	678
Arsenal workers	270
Foremen and clerks	50
Navy men and workers in hospitals	200
Penal laborers	60
Four army regiments garrisoned or camped around Alexandria	558
Europeans	92
	1,908
Muslim inhabitants of Alexandria	2,000
Total	3,908

Complaining that reliable statistics were exceedingly difficult to obtain, the French representative offered the following information about the epidemic's toll in different localities. In Cairo, the governor estimated the mortality at 32,000, but European physicians believed the toll was closer to 40,000. Rosetta had lost 4,000 of a population of 15,000, and Damietta reported 5,000 to 6,000 deaths among its 15,000 inhabitants. Suez had lost 300 of 500 inhabitants; Qusayr had practically no survivors; Fuah was virtually depopulated, and Abu Zabel had lost one-half of 2,000 inhabitants. Upper Egypt also suffered losses; according to a French archaeological expedition in Luxor, cholera almost decimated the population of villages around Thebes. Therefore, Mimaut believed that the death toll for all of Egypt must have been between 150,000 and 190,000.[23] Everyone expected that the country would be slow to recover from its first invasion of cholera, but by mid-October, when forty days had passed without a recurrence of the disease, Egypt appeared to have recovered good health. Ibrahim Pasha successfully carried off the expedition to Syria, and the epidemic began to fade in memory. By the end of November, the anticipated long drawn out recovery period had diminished miraculously; prosperity had followed a cotton crop that surpassed all expectations.[24]

Cholera Again in 1848

In the interim between the first cholera pandemic in 1831 and the second pandemic in 1848, several important changes had occurred in Egypt. Most dramatic had been Big Power intervention to thwart Muhammad Ali's challenge to the Ottoman sultan in Syria, forcing him to withdraw his armed forces from the Levant and curtail their number to a nominal level. Reducing the armed forces led to cutbacks in government agencies serving the military establishment and called for replacing relatively highly paid foreign employees with Egyptians who received lower wages than either Turkish officials or European specialists. Retrenchment thus significantly strengthened the trend toward the formation of a professional Egyptian civil bureaucracy.

In the same way, demobilization of the military medical corps permitted their redeployment in an evolving network of civil hospitals and clinics, which will be examined later, as well as in the quarantine service directed by the consular board in Alexandria. Deemphasizing the military establishment also fortified the educational character of the *Egyptian Gazette,* the official organ founded to inform government officials about political, economic, and administrative developments. Abandoning the heavy emphasis of the 1830s on Ibrahim Pasha's military exploits, the *Gazette* became a channel for explaining to local government functionaries innovations in public affairs, such as government activity in new areas like public health. Under the capable direction of editors who had studied abroad, notably

Shaykh Rifa'a Rifai al-Tahtawi, it disseminated among government officials the specialized information and recommendations of the viceroy's technical advisers, including the Medical Council in Cairo. Finally, Muhammad Ali was keenly aware that stripped of his military power, he was completely dependent on international goodwill for the free, uninhibited flow of Egyptian commodities in overseas commerce. Adverse public opinion abroad regarding the allegedly poor state of health and sanitation in Egypt was a major factor in the prolonged periods of quarantine that ships carrying Egyptian produce had to undergo in European ports. Muhammad Ali's concurrence in all the restrictions imposed on traffic by the Quarantine Board in Alexandria therefore aimed not only to protect Egypt from epidemic invasions but also to demonstrate his resolve to uphold the recognized standards in international cooperation for disease control.[25] To gain the confidence of his international trading partners and ensure free-flowing traffic in Egyptian goods, the viceroy was ready to take additional steps to disarm their objections to sanitary conditions in Egypt. As early as 1835, he had commissioned the British consul general to head a committee that would recommend sanitary improvements in Alexandria, but it seems not to have undertaken any concrete projects.[26]

An outbreak of plague in Alexandria in 1841 provided the incentive and the occasion for the viceroy to issue a model sanitary code for the city.[27] The lengthy decree invoked the etiological principles held by Europe's sanitary reformers and laid down comprehensive regulations covering every then-known locus of dirt and possible infection. One set of orders dealt with periodic purification, fumigation, and whitewashing of all residential premises; another series assigned similar duties to those in charge of quarters for the troops, seamen, workmen in the Arsenal, apprentices in government schools, and all hospital employees. Street repair, street cleaning, maintenance of drains, disposal of waste from privies, and ventilation of bazaars and markets were all responsibilities assigned to specific functionaries. Food inspection became one of the new duties for former military medical officers who were to accompany the municipal market inspector (muhtasib),[28] examine all comestibles and the food prepared by public cooks, and deliver any suspect commodities, together with their vendor, to the police. Severe penalties for noncompliance with the regulations were threatened in each chapter of the Sanitary Code. Finally, since cleaning Alexandria alone would not benefit the general welfare of the country, the decree announced the viceroy's intention to extend the regulations for urban sanitary policing to Cairo, Damietta, Rosetta, and other cities in Egypt. It is likely that the presence in Alexandria of merchants and consular representatives of the trading nations whose confidence he wished to win influenced Muhammad Ali's publication of these comprehensive and exemplary regulations. But two points concerning Alexandria's sanitary code are worth noting. First, since the regulations include miasmatist recommendations for ventilation and elimination of noxious exhalations, as well as contagionist stipulations for fumigating effects and filling cracks and holes in walls, it appears that the viceroy had felicitously combined the best practices of two rival schools of thought on prophylactic public hygiene. Second, the comprehensiveness of the regulations probably doomed them to nonenforcement. Only another autocrat concerned, as Muhammad Ali was, to safeguard the health of government employees who were the instruments of his policies as well as to impress Europe favorably by sanitary reform in Egypt would execute such a thoroughgoing program. If, as the viceroy indicated, Alexandria's sanitary code had been extended to Cairo, Damietta, Rosetta, and other cities in Egypt, it might have mitigated some of the tragic losses the country suffered to cholera.

But, above all, at mid-nineteenth century, rigorous vigilance was necessary to prevent the deadly cholera infection from penetrating the country's inhabited areas. In spite of Alexandria's sanitary code and an elaborate quarantine establishment, Egypt did not escape the second cholera pandemic in 1848. The mortality that year was nothing like the frightful toll in 1831, according to official reports: 3,793 deaths from cholera in Alexandria and 6,028 in Cairo during the two months from mid-July to mid-September. Damietta, Rosetta, and Qusayr also reported high losses, many villages in the delta suffered severely, and at the end of the year, the total number of deaths from cholera stood at 30,000 for all Egypt.[29]

The epidemic in 1848 illustrated two factors that aggravated Egypt's vulnerability during the nineteenth-century cholera pandemics. First, because environmental sanitation was so poor, any large assembly of people could overtax the water supply and put the entire area at risk once cholera had entered the country. Second, the evidence of widespread evasion and defiance of quarantine regulations indicated that neither the elite nor the masses were willing to submit to detention, while medical authorities were at odds over the value or futility of preventive measures.

Ironically, the government had been on the alert in 1847, anticipating the infiltration of cholera with pilgrims from the Hijaz, and had issued comprehensive regulations to control their passage through Egypt. Pilgrims arriving by sea either at Suez or Qusayr and those traveling overland via Aqaba were required to undergo five or ten days' quarantine, depending on whether they were well or sick on arrival. Food, drink, tents, and troops to enforce detention were dispatched from Cairo to all three sites. Enforcing the regulations evidently proved difficult, however, because none of the pilgrims showed any signs of cholera and they all resisted detention. So it appears from the *Gazette,* which reported that although 7,000 pilgrims died at Mecca and Medina, nothing occurred among the returnees to Egypt except that the huge crowd fleeing the epidemic swamped one of Ibrahim Pasha's boats at Jiddah. Since the pilgrims arriving in Egypt all seemed to be in good health, the viceroy spared them the well-known vexations of quarantine.

Although the *Gazette* announced in January 1848 that the government had authorized funds to expand the lazaretto in Alexandria,[30] that overtaxed facility failed to screen the pilgrims who carried cholera into Egypt later that year. As Chief Physician Grassi of the Quarantine Service admitted, it was simply inadequate to accommodate large agglomerations of men and goods without hazard to health. At one time during the pilgrimage season, the facility held 1,300 persons "with all their filthy effects," who were crammed into rooms "closer than in a ship." It was no wonder that cholera appeared in the lazaretto, he declared, since "noxious vapors and miasma" undoubtedly emanated from the stagnant air. In June, two deaths occurred at the lazaretto which the chief physician and his colleagues suspected to be caused by cholera; however, they were not permitted to examine the bodies to determine the cause of death because the deceased were Muslim women.[31]

Some of the stricken apparently traveled unhindered from Bulaq port to Tanta, where a semiannual trade fair held on the feast of Sayyid Ahmad al-Badawi was attracting thousands of visitors from all over Egypt and the neighboring countries. Within a few days, a full-scale epidemic was raging, and the panic-stricken visitors stampeded out of the town in all directions, carrying cholera with them. The outbreak in mid-July 1848 occurred under optimum circumstances for the spread of the disease. Ramadan, the month of fasting, was about to begin; hot weather had set in with temperatures ranging between eighty-five and ninety-five degrees; the river was rising, but water was very low in the canals in the delta. Tanta had no resident medical or sanitary officer and was not noted for cleanliness, according to a Russian physician who visited the town shortly before the epidemic broke out. The water supply was patently inadequate for the influx of people and livestock during the fair, and people might be tempted to draw water from a poorly maintained canal encircling the town. This would be extremely hazardous, the visiting physician observed, when the water level was low, as it was when 150,000 to 200,000 visitors to the fair descended on the city of some 17,000 people in July 1848. Instead of continuing for a week as it did in normal times, the fair broke up in confusion and panic on the fourth day.[32]

Although the information available is slim, government communications in 1848 indicate an evolution in official attitudes toward responsibility to the public since the first cholera epidemic in 1831. Then, the only government initiatives had been segregating sick military personnel and returning fallahin laborers to their home villages. In 1848, high-ranking functionaries still retired to seclusion,[33] but government agencies issued directives urging observance of the public and personal hygiene measures detailed in Alexandria's sanitary code of 1842, described earlier.

In Cairo, the chief physician attached to the Police Department was ordered to enforce rigorously regulations for inspecting slaughterhouses and for cleaning streets and public places in the metropolitan area. Above all, he must prohibit the sale and consumption of green, unripe fruit.[34] Schools received special instructions from the Ministry of Public Instruction, which exhorted school supervisors in general terms to safeguard the students' health and specifically urged the following: maintain cleanliness of the school premises and of students' clothing and bedding; assure good ventilation, but do not permit students to sleep uncovered or with windows open at night; forbid the purchase and consumption of all unripe fruit; forbid students to leave and outsiders to enter the premises; forbid games that will tire the students because fatigue and perspiration may predispose them to the disease; if any student is stricken with cholera, place him in isolation and provide medical attention immediately; if cholera spreads to other students, send the healthy home at once.

Although some of these instructions were irrelevant, some were good advice representing empirical hygiene practices of the day. Since no one knew how cholera was transmitted from man to man, the most important ruling was isolating sick students. Quite rightly, the instructions also stressed cleanliness, a sovereign prophylactic against many infections. In keeping with nineteenth-century views, fatigue, perspiration, and sleeping exposed to the night air were all considered predisposing causes of illness and were to be avoided. At this time, Europeans also commonly believed that eating pulpy vegetables and green, unripe fruits would cause dysentery; one observer expressed certainty that in 1848 cholera made the worst inroads among Muslims who "stuffed their stomachs" with watermelons and cucumbers after breaking the Ramadan fast. The prohibition was a step in the right direction for other reasons: pulpy vegetables and fruits like cucumbers and watermelons may harbor several microorganisms responsible for enteric disorders.[35] As for the general public, it appears that the central authorities directed local government officials to utilize the provincial health service created in 1842 and to refer promptly any cases of cholera to district physicians. In Cairo, the government instructed police to urge stricken residents to go to the city's ten health bureaus, where they would receive treatment and medication free of charge.[36]

There were conflicting reports, however, about the availability of medical assistance in Alexandria. The British consul general reported that strict quarantine regulations were enforced only to safeguard "the precious life of Ibrahim Pasha and members of his family," and as soon as he sailed for Rhodes, all suspected cases of cholera were turned out of the lazaretto. The poor of the town were totally neglected, he reported; out of 284 deaths in one day, 214 were listed "found dead," that is, they died without any medical attention. Francesco Grassi, Chief Physician of the Quarantine Service, described the release of detainees in the lazaretto as a considered decision to abandon quarantining and crowding people in cramped quarters after the epidemic was already under way in Alexandria. If many had died without medical aid, he stated, this was due to the speed with which victims succumbed to the disease and to many Muslims' lack of faith in medicine, for the quarantine administration had provided physicians and medicines without charge in every quarter of the city. The French consul also reported that free emergency health stations had been created in Alexandria on the model of those that operated in Paris during the cholera epidemic in 1832. Similar arrangements apparently were available in the provinces.[37]

True to its didactic purpose, the *Gazette* tried to rouse local officials to the danger of failing to notify district physicians immediately when cholera broke out. Cholera appeared in Fariskur, one of the rural rice-growing communities in Sharqiya, it reported, and attacked fifty-five people on the fifteenth of Ramadan. Where the district physician was summoned without delay, he treated them immediately and God cured them all, the *Gazette* asserted. However, it warned, one whose family did not notify the physician promptly departed for the hereafter. During the epidemic, the *Gazette* kept government functionaries informed on the course of the disease with such edifying examples and exhortations. Early in the epidemic it reported that the viceroy had requested scholars at al-Azhar to read Bukhari's *Sahih* publicly, divinity students to read the holy Koran to influential persons, and all the people to pray for deliverance from the scourge that afflicted Egypt. It also reported the epidemic's decline and declared the waning was God's response to the people's humble prayers.[38]

Although the daily routine of life continued normally, government business slowed down with the ministries' adoption of quarantine, and the lack of Muhammad Ali's strong hand was evident, according to observers. The viceroy had retired from government affairs in December 1847, and Ibrahim Pasha had fled Cairo for Alexandria and ultimately Constantinople as soon as cholera appeared in Egypt. The duties of government thus passed to Abbas Pasha, who, being no more ready to risk infection than Ibrahim, boarded ship and sought safety in Upper Egypt. Bagi-Bey, the governor of Cairo, was an early victim of the epidemic, and the capital city was left without a chief executive.[39]

Clot's experience in disciplining the staff of Cairo's civil hospital, Qasr al-Ainy, offers an example of the lack of a central coordinating authority. He claimed that while inspecting the hospital, he found the supervisor, physicians, instructors, and medical students all neglecting cholera patients. He reported his finding to the Ministries of War and Public Instruction and demanded exemplary punishment of the entire staff. The Ministry of War complied, but the Ministry of Public Instruction objected that it was contrary to Islamic law to inflict punishment during Ramadan and therefore ordered the prisoners released.[40]

Clot's experience demonstrated the pitfalls of overlapping bureaucratic spheres of responsibility, but it also illustrated the Egyptian government's good fortune in failing to adopt officially and exclusively his anticontagionist views on communicable diseases. Clot had expressed scorn publicly for the "inhumanity" of physicians who were cautious in attending plague patients, and he held similar views on cholera. His hostility toward quarantine procedures was so well known that the British consul's report that quarantine was "grossly neglected" in Cairo seems plausible; Clot probably was responsible for not detaining the travelers who carried cholera from Bulaq to Tanta.

Observers of the epidemics in 1831 and 1848 remarked that the Egyptians were terrified of cholera; while they scoffed at precautions against plague, they fled or secluded themselves at home in Frank fashion when cholera appeared.[41] Medical staff members at Qasr al-Ainy hospital whom Clot observed neglecting cholera patients were acting on sound, if selfish, instincts, given the dubious hygiene standards of the day. Clot would have preferred that Egypt follow the example of Malta, where the government officially adopted the idea that cholera was a disease transmitted by vitiated air loaded with miasmatic emanations. Citing renowned medical authorities in Paris, a government notice condemned those who upheld "the cruel and unfounded doctrine" of contagiousness and stipulated that such opinions would disqualify medical practitioners who became candidates for government posts. According to the medical historian of Malta, the official stand "fostered an irresponsible familiarity toward the fatal illness" at a time when techniques for handling communicable diseases were wholly inadequate.[42]

In Egypt, however, neither one of the two medical factions prevailed completely at this time. In his observations submitted to the Sanitary Commission of London, Dr. Grassi unequivocally stated his belief that cholera was communicated from man to man. As evidence that cholera was "portable and catching," he pointed to the concentrations of cholera outbreaks at sites along the waterways where travelers stopped. Bulaq port had suffered proportionately far more than Cairo, and two villages that faced each other at the entrance to the Mahmudiya canal, where Muhammad Ali had relocated all the poor people's huts, were struck much harder than Alexandria itself.[43]

The Cholera Epidemic of 1865

The lack of vigilance which had allowed cholera to pass through Egypt in 1848 continued, but two additional contributing factors appeared for the first time in the epidemic in 1865.[44] Most dramatic was the epidemic's easy and rapid progress from the Hijaz to Egypt to Mediterranean Europe, facilitated by new rail and ship transport. Equally disturbing was the discovery that ships' captains were falsifying declarations on the state of health of passengers traveling to and from the Mecca pilgrimage.

Completion of the Alexandria-Cairo-Suez railway line had added the link connecting steamship transport in the Mediterranean with that in the Red Sea in 1858, but pilgrim traffic on that line did not attract attention until 1865. In that year, the feast of Qurban Bayram occurred on a Friday, making the pilgrimage a *"Hajj al-Jum'a,"* a special occasion popularly considered seven times more blessed than the feast on an ordinary weekday. A greater than normal influx of pilgrims converged on the holy cities, and 90,000 reportedly gathered for the principal ceremonies outside Mecca.

At the end of April, the Quarantine Board in Alexandria learned that cholera had appeared in Mecca and Medina. Two Egyptian physicians dispatched to the Hijaz confirmed the outbreak as cholera and described a scene of mass mourning as hundreds of pilgrims died on all sides each day. The Ottoman Commission of the Hijaz estimated the mortality at 15,000, but observers held the death toll must have been twice that number. According to an investigating committee, cholera was imported to the Hijaz at the end of February by two ships from Singapore carrying almost 1,200 Javanese, Malaysian, and Indian pilgrims. During the voyage, 143 persons on board the ships had died of cholera, but the captains declared that the disease had appeared only after they had put in at Mokalla, a port on the southeastern coast of the Arabian peninsula.

Within a period of three weeks, ten steamers, each carrying nine to twelve hundred passengers, arrived at Suez. The ships' official statement declared the passengers' health perfect and indicated that the few deaths that had occurred were due to "ordinary" diseases. A port physician at Suez boarded each of the vessels, reported no evidence of illness, and authorized free entry for the ships. Thereupon, twelve to fifteen thousand hajjis landed and boarded the Suez-to-Alexandria rail line. When cholera broke out among those newly debarked in Suez, it became evident that all the ships' captains had falsified their declarations.

Investigation revealed that each of the ships had cast overboard passengers who died of cholera, and one in fact had lost to cholera more than 100 out of 2,000 passengers. In the meantime, the pilgrims traveling by rail had arrived at Alexandria and camped close to the Mahmudiyah canal. Egyptians in the area who hastened to welcome their coreligionists from the holy cities were the first to be attacked by cholera. The first case occurred on June 2, but through wishful thinking or self-deception, the Quarantine Board authorities failed to acknowledge the nature of the disease until June 11. From that date until July 23, cholera swept over Egypt, causing more than 60,000 deaths, 4,000 in Alexandria alone.[45]

Seized with panic, foreigners in Egypt rushed to any vessel available to carry them away from the epidemic, and an estimated thirty to thirty-five thousand persons scattered from Alexandria to all the chief ports of the Mediterranean—Beirut, Cyprus, Malta, Smyrna, Constantinople, Trieste, Ancona, Marseilles, Valencia—carrying the disease with them. By the time the fourth pandemic ended in 1874, it had circled the globe from the Malayan peninsula back to Java. It had hit European population centers hard, causing an estimated 200,000 deaths on the continent.

Following the European exodus, business came to a virtual standstill in Alexandria and Cairo; all government offices, banks, and commercial establishments extended leaves of absence to employees who requested them and adapted to skeleton staff work. The government suspended all public works projects in Cairo and Alexandria, and the dockyards adopted a reduced work schedule to allow long rest periods for their workers.[46]

As had been the case in Tanta in 1848, communities that drew on sources other than the Nile were at greatest risk from contaminated water supply. In Upper Egypt, villages close to the Nile escaped the epidemic, while those a half-mile or even a quarter of a mile inland suffered seriously. An English resident in Luxor reported that only one death suspected to be caused by cholera occurred in that town, while at Qina, 250 persons allegedly died in one day. "Shaikh Yussuf laid the mortality at Keneh to the canal water, which the poor people drink there," she wrote.[47]

In the poor quarters of urban communities, where the cholera epidemic made the worst inroads, the quarantine service initiated rigorous measures to contain the disease. But the epidemic was out of control before they realized the danger, and their efforts came too late. It is worthwhile describing the quarantine service's procedures, however, to understand the resistance they aroused and the fact that entire villages fled at the mention of a possible quarantine. The community that had become infected was cut off from communication with the rest of the country by a military cordon; no one was allowed to leave or enter, and all provisions, including medicines, were passed through the line of soldiers. The markets, slaughterhouses, and public privies were policed. Fresh fish, vegetables, and fruit were seized; stale fish, hides, and bones were deposited outside the town, and rags and soiled clothing were burned. Drains emptying into the canal were closed and disinfected with quicklime, as were the latrines of mosques, prisons, barracks, schools, and other public places. People were driven out of their houses into tents and sheds; the worst hovels were destroyed, and other houses were cleaned and whitewashed.

In Cairo and Alexandria, government authorities ordered what had become routine measures to clean up the municipality: obstructions were demolished, the streets were swept and sprinkled, and rubbish was deposited outside the city; market supervision was tightened, and the sale of produce considered harmful for any reason was banned. Emergency medical stations were set up at strategic points within the two cities; physicians were assigned to each station on 24-hour call to dispense medication and to move quickly to any place in the city where they might be needed.[48]

Like his predecessors, the Khedive Ismail fled with his retinue and harem, this time to Constantinople. Many considered his sudden departure irresponsible and believed it contributed to panic and to general demoralization. Some Egyptians openly criticized his precipitate flight, the British consul wrote: "They now say it is one more plague which has visited Egypt in two and a half years since his accession."[49] Nevertheless, Ismail's fear of epidemic disease caused him to uphold what some called "needless" quarantines on transport between the Hijaz and Egypt as long as he held the khediviate. Regrettably for Egypt, fear as a motivation in public health policy disappeared, causing relaxation of quarantine controls.

The principal reason for extreme variation in opinions about cholera transmissibility from person to person was the widespread confusion about possible modes of transmission of what was obviously an alien imported disease. The nineteenth century was trying to deal with cholera by measures earlier ages had devised in their struggle with another exotic and fearsome affliction, the Black Death. Egyptians and Europeans differed in their reactions toward cholera because their attitudes had been conditioned by historical encounters with plague. We turn now to that dread disease, which had longtime associations with Egypt.

4

The Plague Epidemic of 1835: Background and Consequences

Since the fourteenth-century Black Death, plague[1] had played a paradigmatic role as the archetypal pestilential scourge that terrified populations into creating elaborate defense systems against its recurring ravages. In the accelerated pace of trade in the nineteenth century, cholera and yellow fever posed greater threats to exposed societies, but earlier experience with plague not only dictated the practices but also defined the principles for disease control. As a century passed without any recurrence of plague in Western Europe, Atlantic seaboard nations began to challenge the elaborate Mediterranean defense system of military cordons, quarantines, and lazarettos that delayed the movement of goods and persons. But there was no demonstrably sound scientific theory to provide a basis for abandoning the system, and there were enormous vested interests in maintaining it. Dispute over the issues thus revealed irreconcilable differences among policymakers, quarantine establishment functionaries, trading interests, and the medical profession.

In Egypt as well, European physicians split into two camps upholding opposing theories and procedures for the control of plague and therefore all epidemic disease. To compound the confusion, attitudes among European and Egyptian laymen apparently arose from differing experiences with plague over the centuries and divergent views on socially acceptable behavior during an epidemic crisis. Each community considered the responses of the other's members irrational or reprehensible.

Europeans had long considered Egypt the cradle of the plague, just as they considered India the home of cholera. The theories elaborated over the years to explain why plague appeared to originate in the Nile valley influenced nineteenth-century European official policy and public opinion vis-à-vis Egypt. Periodic outbreaks of plague in the country, recurring almost as regularly as the annual Nile flooding, early led European observers to make a causal connection between the seasonal inundation and plague epidemics. The Galenic notion of disease causation by noxious miasma from decaying organic matter underwent a nineteenth-century elaboration in Egypt: the "cadaveric virus theory" that held plague was a result of a miasmatic poison emanating from soil in which buried human corpses were decomposing.[2] The most eloquent exponent of the theory was Etienne Pariset, Permanent Secretary to the French Academy of Medicine, who headed a commission to study plague in Syria and Egypt in 1827. Pariset was revolted by the Nile valley graveyards where corpses were annually submerged and surfaced to float on the rising river. He theorized that Egypt must have been free of plague while the ancients practiced embalming and entombing corpses outside the flood area. When Christians substituted burial for embalming, they must have initiated the sixth-century pandemic. The Black Death also must have arisen in Egypt's delta, he said, "because nowhere else in the world does one find . . . extended, flat land which is warm, humid and saturated with animal matter."[3] The cadaveric virus theory underlay the popular nineteenth-century view that graveyards were seed beds of epidemic disease, particularly plague, and should be removed as far from habitation as possible.

Clot rejected Pariset's hypothesis and other theories that ascribed the genesis of plague in Egypt to the *Khamsin,* the hot, sand-laden wind from the Sahara, humidity, or stagnant waters. Plague was endemic in Egypt, according to Clot, because meteorological circumstances peculiar to the country endowed it with a "pestilential constitution."[4] In the meantime, a "localist-miasmatist" hypothesis of disease causation added impetus to the sanitary reform movement in England. Independent of changing medical viewpoints of the time, British sanitary reformers operated on the theory that the stench arising from filth contained noxious particles that were absorbed through the extensive surface of the thin air vesicles of the lungs. Once ingested, these toxic particles caused disease.[5]

In France, concern with sanitary improvement as an aspect of social reform added political corollaries to this theory, and the conviction that the extirpation of plague required radical government reform recurs repeatedly in the writings of continental Europeans who traveled in Egypt during the nineteenth century. One example was Hamont, the veterinarian whose criticisms of the viceroy aimed to counterbalance writings by Dr. Clot, Muhammad Ali's articulate admirer. Hamont asserted that the Egyptians' illnesses had social causes: "the frightful state of slavery in which they live, the abominable despotism which weighs on them, the vexations which they must suffer."[6] The reformist attitude also was evident in a report issued by the French Academy of Medicine in 1846 which declared that investigation in Egypt had demonstrated that plague was not a contagious disease. The academy's commission of inquiry emphasized social causes as primary pathogenic factors in Egypt: accumulations of putrefying animal matter near dwellings, poor and crowded housing, inadequate nutrition, neglect of personal hygiene, and, above all, the governing authorities' lack of initiative to improve the lot of the inhabitants. The academy's report concluded that the progress of civilization was the only preventive against plague and Egypt's greatest need was enlightened, efficient administration.[7]

Pariset's theory that plague was especially associated with waterlogged lands was being disproved while the academy was studying its report; plague was already retreating from its alleged home in lowland Egypt, and it persisted longest in the highlands—in the foothills of the Himalayas, among the mountains of western Arabia, in the Kurdish highlands, and in the Chinese hinterland of Yunnan. The French academy's finding incriminating social and environmental health hazards as pathogenic factors was admirable as a general principle, but it was not an adequate guide for dealing with the specific threat of importing plague with trade in commodities.

Unlike the common people of Europe, who were terrified of plague and were convinced that it was extremely contagious, the majority of Egyptian Muslims at the outset of the nineteenth century apparently had no fear of infection by contact with the disease. They seemed to consider plague simply one among the many trials of living, and they scorned the precautions resident Europeans practiced during plague "season" in Egypt. The usual explanation of that time

for the Egyptians' indifference toward plague—"Muslim fatalism"—
is too facile to be accepted without qualification.

Some of the medieval Arab physicians had recognized the principle of infectivity as well as miasmatic toxicity in disease transmission,[8] and the Egyptian historian, al-Maqrizi, who wrote a generation
after the Black Death, described the plague epidemic's spread in
terms of both contagion and miasma.[9] However, the notion of contagion or infectivity of plague was never generally admitted in Egypt
or other Muslim lands, according to Michael Dols, the historian of
plague in the Middle East. He suggests that there was a consensus
on the plague based on three hadith, or traditions: a Muslim should
not enter or flee from a plague-stricken land; the plague represents
martyrdom and mercy from God for a Muslim and punishment for
an infidel; and there is no transmission of disease. Although the literal
interpretation of these traditions appears to be an exhortation for resignation to inevitable death, Dols points out there was a gap between
prescription and practice in Muslim communities during a plague
epidemic.[10] There were also a great number of magical beliefs and
practices to soften the likelihood of martyrdom and to supplement
unavailing medical remedies. This modified religious-cultural attitude apparently remained one of the shared views of the Islamic
community.[11]

Nevertheless, between the fifteenth and nineteenth centuries,
other factors must have fortified the Egyptians' apparent "indifference" toward plague. One possible explanation may be the fact that
the panic and dread, which Egyptians and Europeans shared during
the trauma of the Black Death, were not institutionalized in pest-
houses in Muslim lands. Isolation in these facilities psychologically
reinforced fear of plague in Europe.[12] There is also the fact that, unlike pneumonic plague, bubonic plague is observably not contagious.[13] After the fifteenth century, pneumonic plague broke out in
Egypt only at infrequent intervals, and Egyptians may have become
accustomed to relatively mild, localized outbreaks of bubonic
plague.[14]

The third pandemic of plague, which erupted in Egypt in 1899
after an absence of fifty-five years, has been studied exhaustively and
has provided data for suggesting a normal season, incidence, and
epidemiological pattern for the disease. Those "normal" conditions
did not necessarily exist in the early nineteenth century, however.
One of the anomalies of plague in the Nile valley is a locus of

pneumonic plague in Upper Egypt around Asyut. According to epidemiologists, only the Egyptian littoral's Mediterranean climate is naturally vulnerable to plague, and Egypt south of Cairo normally is too hot and dry to be susceptible to enzootic plague were it not for the Nile irrigation system. The port cities, Damietta, Rosetta, and Alexandria, had a greater abundance of rats, but the embankments of canals in agricultural areas provided harborage for rats that fled the floodwaters in August and took refuge in the dovecotes on house roofs or in the houses themselves.[15] However, the Khedive Ismail first extended irrigation to Upper Egypt in the 1860s, and the British introduced perennial irrigation with the first Aswan Dam, built between 1898 and 1902. A permanent rat flea population of sufficient density to cause an epidemic in the Saïd was therefore unlikely until the late nineteenth century. Temporary concentrations of rats and fleas at optimum meteorological conditions, however, could and occasionally did trigger an epidemic in Upper Egypt.[16]

European residents in Egypt believed that plague was always imported from Turkey, Asia Minor, Syria, or Crete, but they shared the Egyptians' observation that the plague season had easily defined limits. When plague broke out in Cairo, both Franks and Egyptians assured visitors the scourge would decline by the end of June when hot weather set in. Egyptians looked forward to the plague's disappearance when they celebrated "al-Nuqta," the annual rise of the Nile, which normally occurred in Cairo around the summer solstice.[17] Travelers called the Egyptians fatalist "predestinarians" when they bought and sold in the markets the clothing of those who had died during the last plague season after al-Nuqta. European residents in Egypt, like the Franks in Syria, celebrated "the death of the plague" on St. John's Day, June 26, a festive occasion for friends to visit and congratulate each other on having escaped the last visitation. Some European travelers scorned both traditional observances as Muslim and Christian "superstitution," but a few noted that empirical observation lay behind the local customs: it was "well known that extreme heat checks the plague in the same manner as the cold season."[18]

Except for their common recognition of this phenomenon, Franks and Egyptians held opposed views on the plague. The Italians who settled in Egypt and the Levant evidently brought with them a strong conviction of the communicability of plague, which had raged as late as 1743 in Sicily. They were terrified of the disease and took stringent precautions to avoid exposure to it. Many travelers to the eastern Mediterranean commented on the Franks' rigorous self-imposed quarantine during the plague season; following is a summary of a description by one of the medical officers in the French occupation forces.

When the Franks living in Egypt were certain that plague had broken out in the country, they retired to their homes, closed all the doors, and did not communicate with anyone until the feast of Saint John. One servant not included in isolation was designated *provveditore* (sutler). This man deposited all provisions bought in the market in the home's outer courtyard. The porter washed all the articles of food in urns of water and all money in vinegar and fumigated all papers over a stove, handling them with tongs. Domestic animals were caged, and if they escaped from the premises during the epidemic, they were destroyed. Besides keeping all the doors closed, the Franks sealed all small openings in the walls and shot any stray animals that entered the premises. Some physicians in the Frank community carried their safeguards to extreme lengths. One doctor rode abroad on a saddle covered with wax cloth, with a guard of four servants. Garbed in a protective suit with a mantle of oilcloth, he felt the pulse of patients through a leaf of tobacco with his fingers dipped in oil. This was virtually the same costume worn by physicians during the Marseilles plague in 1720.[19]

Enlightened Europeans of the nineteenth century ridiculed these precautions and pointed out that Muslim Egyptians scorned them as well. While most foreigners ascribed the Egyptians' indifference to fatalism, Clot wrote that their conviction that plague was not contagious was based on long experience. He described their view as follows: "We have cared for our fathers, our children and our brothers, and we have not contracted the disease; if plague is really contagious, why does it carry off Franks who observe quarantine?" According to Clot, "the ignorant" believed that it was a scourge sent from God, while "enlightened" Muslims thought that the infection was present in the air, therefore impossible to escape by isolation.[20]

John Bowring used the Egyptian example to support his case against quarantines and asserted that the Muslim Egyptians never neglected plague patients among friends and relatives, unlike the Christians, among whom instances of inhuman desertion occurred. Such unhesitating self-exposure could not be attributed to fatalism alone, he said, for "I could never discover that the doctrine of fatalism led them to subject themselves unnecessarily to other diseases and dangers."[21]

Bowring and Clot were both special pleaders for the abolition of quarantines. But the views of al-Jabarti, the historian who recorded the antiplague measures adopted during the French occupation and the early years of Muhammad Ali's rule, may be representative of educated Egyptian opinion. Al-Jabarti gives the impression that he saw plague as a natural phenomenon, an endemic, periodically recurring disease caused by miasmas, as well as one of the human trials permitted by God. During the plague epidemic of 1798–99, the French issued many orders to control the spread of the disease. Early preventive measures seemed to be based on miasmatic principles, but as soldiers returned from the plague-stricken expedition to Syria, rigorous quarantine procedures were instituted and public health in Cairo came under strict surveillance.[22] Al-Jabarti accepted the early measures but disapproved of the later restrictive regulations. When the authorities prohibited burials in cemeteries in inhabited areas, he agreed with the theory underlying this order. "It was said that miasmas accumulated in cavities in the earth; that these cavities were cooled in the winter by the water of the Nile, by rain and humidity; and that [afterward] the miasmas expanded into the air and brought the plague." The French also ordered all clothing, furniture, and other effects of deceased persons aired on the roofs of houses for two weeks, he pointed out, "dissipate the bad odors which could have engendered plague." Al-Jabarti observed that the measure was opposed by the masses, who, "in their ignorance, saw in it only a means to learn what each one possessed. However, they [the authorities] had no other objective but to destroy miasmas and to prevent an epidemic."[23]

Al-Jabarti had no sympathetic comments, however, for an order commanding immediate notification of any suspected cases of plague and threatening severe penalties for noncompliance: shaykhs in the quarters who had information about the disease and did not inform the commandant would receive 100 lashes as penalty for negligence; leaders of the religious confessions who did not report death resulting from bubonic plague in their communities would be punished with death; men or women who washed the dead, who recognized or suspected that a dead person was stricken with buboes, and who did not report this within 24 hours would also be punished with death.[24] From all accounts, the plague of 1798–99 struck Alexandria severely but spared Cairo, and there was no necessity to enforce these Draconian regulations.

When plague broke out again in February 1801, however, the French immediately established quarantines and cordons, according to al-Jabarti.

They [the French] exercised the greatest severity in the application of sanitary measures [which] harass the people and frighten them. When someone fell ill, the doctor visited him, and if he was recognized as stricken with plague, he was immediately transferred to quarantine without any of his family being able to see him afterwards. . . . If he recovered, he returned home; otherwise they had him buried, fully clothed. . . . His house remained closed for four days, and all his clothes were burned, . . . if any passerby was imprudent enough to touch the door of the house or to overstep the boundary drawn around it, he was immediately arrested by the guards and sent to quarantine. . . . Those individuals who undertook to wash the dead, to carry them or bury them, . . . left their quarantine only to perform their functions. These measures . . . induced many inhabitants to leave Cairo to settle in the villages.[25]

The plague of 1801 took a high toll among the inhabitants of Cairo as well as the French forces; according to the army's chief physician, the mortality among the people averaged 100 a day during April, and a total of 2,937 died of plague during that month alone.[26] Even greater ravages occurred in Upper Egypt, no doubt from pneumonic plague. Al-Jabarti chronicled this phenomenon and included a letter from his friend, Shaykh Hasan al-Attar, dated May 1801.

Plague raged in all Upper Egypt, but especially in the city of Asyut, where more than 600 persons died every day. Such a scourge has never been seen in the memory of man. I think the country lost two-thirds of its population. The streets are deserted; friends or relatives only learn of the death of those near to them long after the event for everyone is absorbed in his own family's misfortunes. Corpses remain in the houses for days on end, for only after a great deal of trouble can one find biers, washers and porters. The scourge's attacks showed preferences for men and especially young men; it spared neither the virtuous nor the shaykhs, thus the celebration of religious ceremonies has been suspended as a result of the deaths of imams and muezzins. Artisans are also wanting; for a whole month I have not been able to find a barber to shave my head. . . . The most eminent and distinguished person [notable] has no more than ten people to conduct him to his final resting place, and those ten are paid for the service. The entire city is plunged in mourning; wherever one passes one finds only corpses and biers, only moaning and weeping are to be heard. The crops are still standing; there is no one to harvest them, and soon the wind will have dispersed them.[27]

Al-Jabarti does not mention plague again until December 1812, when news of an outbreak in Constantinople caused Muhammad Ali to establish a quarantine in Alexandria. The latter part of his chronicle describes plague epidemics in 1813 and 1815 and mentions rumored outbreaks in 1814, 1819, and 1821. From these accounts we learn that, as in Europe during the sixteenth and seventeenth centuries, a pattern of official activity developed during the plague "season."

In January, when plague usually broke out in one of the port cities, quarantine was established at Alexandria and Damietta, and Muhammad Ali sent his sons and household retainers to join Ibrahim Pasha, then governor of Upper Egypt. During the early years, the pasha secluded himself in Giza; later he went into isolation in his own palace at Shubrah. As a Muslim head of state, Muhammad Ali ordered the reading of Bukhari's *Sahih* in the mosque at al-Azhar and public recitations of the Koran every evening. Sometimes he had alms distributed to the poor and to orphans in Cairo's schools, enjoining them to pray to God to avert the pestilence.[28]

When plague appeared in Cairo in 1813, the police ordered all the inhabitants to air their clothing outdoors; they were to sweep and sprinkle the streets and keep them clean thereafter. Al-Jabarti noted that Ibrahim was as terrified of plague as his father. When he was recalled from Asyut in 1813 to receive the title of governor of Upper Egypt from the Ottoman sultan's special envoy, Ibrahim traveled by boat to Giza, bypassing Cairo. On arrival, he ordered all the people who had accompanied him to bathe and wash their clothing in the Nile before landing, whereupon the boat was sunk. "All this because of fear of plague and of death," observed al-Jabarti.[29]

These comments on fear of death probably exemplified the believing Muslim's attitude of detachment, which Europeans identified as fatalism. "It was believed that quarantine prevented plague; . . . and the Pasha and persons in his entourage also had become convinced of it, for they were very attached to life in this world." His descriptions of the rigorous quarantine imposed on Giza repeated disapprovingly, "all this because of fear of plague and death." They went so far in Giza, he wrote, as to prevent boats from crossing the Nile. Only official communications to the viceroy were transferred across the river, on two boats held in readiness opposite each other at Old Cairo and at Giza.

> If his lieutenant . . . sent him a paper, this paper, after being disinfected with resin and sulphur (fumes), was passed to the boatman on the Cairo side by means of a long [cleft] stick; he in turn approached the other boat and passed the paper, also by means of a long stick. The second boatman again used a similar stick to pass the letter to someone on the riverbank. The latter dipped the letter in vinegar, fumigated it, and delivered it to the Pasha.

The ruthless treatment of the people in Giza particularly aroused al-Jabarti's indignation. For three consecutive years, they were ordered out of the city during the plague season if they did not have sufficient provisions to tide them over sixty days' detention while the pasha remained in quarantine. In 1814, he wrote, many of the inhabitants had to spend the night in the open country, with their children and belongings, because they had been given only three days' notice to evacuate and to reach another city. Moreover, many soldiers who did not want to be locked in the city also left, and they robbed the evacuees of their belongings and their draft animals. "The inhabitants of Giza suffered a great deal . . . all because of pure fear."[30]

In 1816, al-Jabarti recorded the death of the viceroy's son, Haj Ahmad Tusun Pasha, presumably from plague. And when plague broke out in 1819, Muhammad Ali ordered all high-ranking functionaries in the government to observe quarantine. They secluded themselves like the Christians and did not admit anything into their homes from outside. "These precautions frightened the population," al-Jabarti claimed.[31] An epidemic in 1824 lingered on the following year, according to a visiting physician, and by this time, in Alexandria there was a pesthouse for Europeans "of the lower orders" which was dismal in the extreme.[32]

The Epidemic of 1834–1836

During the interval between the plague epidemics of 1824 and 1834, far-reaching changes had heightened the Egyptian government's concern about the threat to Egypt's manpower from epidemic disease. Muhammad Ali had transformed the country's agricultural economy by introducing perennial irrigation and replacing subsistence cultivation with cash crops in demand on the world market; state monopolies of exports, especially cotton, augmented revenues increased by more extensive cultivation and taxation. Alexandria revived as the principal port of the eastern Mediterranean, and rehabilitation of the old canal linking Alexandria with the Nile—renamed the Mahmudiya—provided passage for Egyptian commodities to the Mediterranean and the European market. Launching a military campaign to win Syria's raw materials for his industrialization program in Egypt, the viceroy built up a military force that effectively challenged Ottoman control of the Levant. Large numbers of men were mobilized to work in the dockyards and Arsenal in Alexandria and in numerous factories producing material for the military establishment. Technical schools were training specialists for the government and military bureaucracies, and state primary schools were reaching out to the younger generation.

The rising traffic in Egyptian ports, the rehabilitation of Alexandria and the Mahmudiya Canal, and increased production of cotton also attracted many foreign commercial agents; from sixteen in 1822, their number approached seventy by 1834. No longer restricted to segregated caravansaries, the foreign merchants built European-style villas in the new port area of Alexandria or along the banks of the Mahmudiya Canal. After Muhammad Ali gained control of Syria, many European governments transferred their consuls general from the Levant ports to Alexandria, and twenty-five consular agents soon joined the business representatives there.[33]

The first cholera epidemic in 1831 had invaded the country when the Egyptian army was poised for its first campaign in Syria and had killed 150,000 people, including 7,000 men in military service, during a scant two-month siege. It had a traumatic effect on the pasha; clearly, the day had passed when he could retire to Shubra Palace during the plague season and ignore the epidemic preying on the country. When plague broke out in Alexandria in November 1834, therefore, the government was prepared to uphold any measures recommended by the consular Quarantine Board and to institute its own controls as well.

Within that month, the Egyptian government representative on the Quarantine Board, who was also the chief of police of Alexandria,

had to exercise his enforcement power as the board members zeal-
ously hurried to issue regulations that provoked fierce opposition
among the city's Muslims. In December the corps of ulama in
Alexandria addressed a petition to the viceroy protesting outrageous
measures: investigators were examining the nude corpses of deceased
Muslims, which was "not in harmony with the law." Moreover, they
were transporting families of persons who allegedly died of plague
outside the city, placing them in quarantine, a tyrannical measure
that removed the poor from their work and deprived them of their
daily bread. The families of the deceased and their household effects
were being carried off in carts at night by torchlight, and the noise
of these sinister processions was shattering peace of mind and arous-
ing terror among the people. Some were throwing their dead into
the streets so that no one could identify them; others were fleeing
and abandoning the corpses in their houses. It was evident, the petition pointed out, that quarantine would never be successful among
Muslims for they were not afraid of plague. However, now if someone were afflicted, he would not mention it for fear of being removed
from his home.[34]

Muhammad Ali immediately ordered the police chief to instruct
the Quarantine Board members to avoid any measures that might conflict with Islamic law or offend Muslims. They should not require
examination of bodies, or the destruction of corpses of Muslims by
quicklime, or the removel of families of the deceased outside their
homes. It would be sufficient to designate a cemetery in an isolated
location outside Alexandria, where graves could be dug to the proper
depth. "Compromised" families could be quarantined in their own
homes, under surveillance, for the prescribed period, and the government would provide daily rations for the needy among them. The
board members also should solicit the advice of two shaykhs who
had signed the petition in future discussions of control measures.[35]

At the same time, to ensure that work at the dockyards would continue uninterrupted, the viceroy approved the board's proposal to
place the entire Arsenal under quarantine. He opposed sending the
workers' families back to their home villages as a potential threat to
the rural communities' health and proposed instead housing the
families temporarily in army tents, while the workers' huts were
leveled and replaced with new barracks.

As the number of deaths from plague rose to more than 100 during
December, the Quarantine Board ordered a *cordon sanitaire* around

Alexandria to contain the epidemic. This time opposition came from the European merchants in Alexandria, who claimed they would suffer from the suspension of trade. "Do not listen to such excuses," the viceroy ordered his secretary. "Quarantine aims to protect the entire population, therefore it is a lesser evil adopted to avoid a greater one.[36] In January, additional Quarantine Board measures for Alexandria included airing and exposing to sunlight the household effects of all inhabitants; whitewashing the interior of all dwellings; daily removal of rubbish from courtyards and passageways; disinfecting and whitewashing all workshops in the Arsenal; and mandatory bathing and an issue of new clothing for all workers in the Arsenal.[37]

The Egyptians apparently continued to evade isolating the sick. Fear of being transported to the lazaretto caused people to hide the stricken, and illness was rarely reported to the Quarantine Board until it had ended in death. To avoid discovery of plague, families buried their dead in the courtyards or under the floor of the house or secretly deposited their corpses in the streets at night.[38] As the number of cases multiplied, the city notables and ulama again protested to the board that dividing families was contrary to custom and tradition. According to the French consul, Muhammad Ali had the shaykhs quarantined in their own homes, in Frank fashion, and threatened them with seven months' penal labor if they did not set a good example to the public.[39]

Resistance to the isolation of those stricken with plague apparently mounted as the epidemic spread and claimed more victims. Early in February, Muhammad Ali ordered his secretary to take action, invoking religion in the following terms:

> The aversion of the inhabitants of Alexandria to health measures rises from their ignorance. . . . the adoption of appropriate measures to ward off the evil is authorized by the precepts of religion, and aims only at the general welfare. Since the plague . . . is a scourge emanating from His divine will, fleeing the wrath of God to take refuge in His mercy is not contrary to the sacred law. . . . One cannot deny that the reigning disease is contagious; and what God has said by . . . His Prophet: "Flee my vengeance, as you would flee the presence of the lion," does this not apply to contagion? . . . Do not the fleet, the hospitals, and the Arsenal, which have been protected from the prevailing scourge by observing sanitary regulations, thanks be to God, provide adequate evidence?
>
> Consequently, the health measures in force will not be relaxed in

the slightest. . . . You will therefore assemble the notables of the city, the chief of police, the directors of hospitals . . . in order to adopt the most effective measures for the welfare of the city.[40]

As the epidemic grew more intense and the number of deaths rose from day to day, it proved impossible to enforce the regulations. The quarantine of infected homes was lifted early in March, and, since plague was already raging outside Alexandria, the cordon sanitaire was abandoned.[41]

There was alarm in Cairo as soon as the epidemic was declared in Alexandria, and the viceroy immediately ordered the people to maintain cleanliness of their persons and their premises to avert the disease.[42] In January, all high-ranking government functionaries and the European community hastened into seclusion. According to Clot, the Egyptians and Turks were amused by the Franks' panic and took few precautions; they feared the government's isolation more than the plague.[43] In April, when the number of new plague cases was approaching a thousand a day, the military Medical Council proposed evacuating the entire city population, but the viceroy disagreed, suggesting that assembling a large number of people would be more likely to propagate the disease than segregating some among them.[44]

If enforcing restrictive measures on the entire population of Alexandria or Cairo proved infeasible, the government nevertheless did not relax quarantine regulations for hospitals, schools, military garrisons, the fleet, and all government installations, including factories, as well as the ruling family's palaces and harems. In Cairo and Alexandria, cordons had been ordered around all hospitals early in December: only those physicians who felt obliged to continue their service outside the institution were exempted from detention. The military Medical Council instructed physicians in all hospitals and government installations to isolate immediately any suspected cases of plague in tents remote from the establishment, to bury the dead in graves six feet deep, and to report the number of deaths daily to the health authorities.[45]

Supervisors at the installation under quarantine were enjoined to observe traditional Frank precautions against admitting any objects "susceptible" to contagion: papers and letters should be immersed in vinegar and fumigated with chlorine fumes; wood and other fuel were to be exposed to the air for twenty-four hours before entry to the premises. Finally, government physicians were to remain at their posts but to avoid contact with the plague-stricken in order to continue attending other patients. "Whatever your opinion, you are to consider plague a contagious disease and to act accordingly," Dr. Clot ordered.[46]

Ezbekiyah, the military hospital for the Cairo garrison, was reserved exclusively for plague patients and, according to Clot, accommodated more than 3,000 during the epidemic. Government personnel suffering from other illnesses were sent to a hospital outside Cairo. All the special training schools in the Cairo area—the cavalry school in Giza, the artillery school in Tura, the music school at Khanka, and the Polytechnic school at Bulaq—maintained strict quarantine over their students. At the polytechnic, where 150 students were confined in the main building ringed by a military cordon, we are told that the school director, Hekekyan-Bey, enforced detention by standing guard at his window with a loaded rifle, threatening to shoot the first person who attempted to break the quarantine.[47]

In Alexandria, all barracks were quarantined and surrounded by a double ring of barriers and sentinels. Rigorous quarantine was maintained among the 6,000 workers at the Arsenal; when a case of plague appeared, the individual was removed immediately to a lazaretto near the Mahmudiyah Naval General Hospital. All workers who had been in contact with a plague patient had to undergo temporary detention, a bath, and a change of clothing.[48] Similar regulations applied to the fleet; if plague broke out among naval personnel, the individual was evacuated immediately to the Mahmudiyah lazaretto, and the vessel was placed under quarantine for eleven days. Toward the end of March, when the epidemic reached its peak in Alexandria, claiming 180 to 200 deaths a day, the fleet at anchor in the harbor set out for Crete.[49]

The plague epidemic of 1835 was notable for extending into areas rarely touched by the disease—Upper Egypt as far as Thebes and west into Fayyum province. As the plague made fresh inroads in all directions, public baths were ordered closed for the duration of the epidemic,[50] and many regiments garrisoned in cities or villages were evacuated to the desert.[51] Recruitment for the armed forces was suspended, and the war minister was reprimanded for having permitted conscription to continue when some recruits died en route from their villages.[52] As the epidemic expanded throughout the Nile valley, Muhammad Ali fled to his palace in Shubrah, where he maintained rigorous quarantine: all avenues to the palace were surrounded by a double barrier guarded by 400 men.[53] By mid-April, plague had begun to wane in Alexandria and mortality figures dropped below 100 a day; in Cairo, however, the epidemic was reaching its peak, carrying off 600 to 1,000 victims daily.[54]

One of the few foreign visitors in Cairo during the plague year of 1835 vividly described the psychological terror that gripped even the most self-assured traveler in the empty, echoing streets of the city, which had become a charnel house. Arthur Kinglake must have stayed in Cairo at the very peak of the epidemic for he observed that during the nineteen days he spent in the city, the mortality rose from 400 to 1,200 a day. During that time, almost everyone he had contact with perished: the Levantine banker who accepted his letters of credit with iron tongs and purified them with the smoke of burning aromatics, his landlord, his donkey boys, a magician whose performances he had watched, and the Bolognese doctor he had consulted when feeling unwell. Kinglake noted a preoccupation with cleanliness during the epidemic. "It is said that when a Mussulman finds himself attacked by the plague he goes and takes a bath," but he apparently did not learn that it was motivated by the Muslim's concern to die in a state of ritual purity.[55] One of the features of the epidemic that he found most disquieting was the steady procession of funerals every day from dawn until noon; the passing of howling mourners was so incessant that Kinglake believed one-half of the inhabitants of Cairo must have perished.

As the epidemic raged through May and into June, Cairo and Alexandria took on the appearance of ghost towns; virtually the entire surviving population had withdrawn into isolation and all normal activity came to a halt. Europeans began to count off the days to the onset of the Nile flood and took heart in the old-timers' observation that plague never extended beyond the feast of Saint John. If summer had not been late this year, we might be rid of this "eternal epidemic," one of the consuls wrote.[56]

Apparently relying on the reliability of this seasonal phenomenon, Muhammad Ali abandoned isolation on June 21. Public officials were notified that quarantine restrictions were lifted and they were to resume normal activity on that date. European consuls left the viceroy's palace for Cairo and Alexandria, making way for provincial governors summoned to Shubrah to take up long-neglected administrative matters. Early in July, quarantine was lifted from military units and schools.[57]

No one in Egypt needed the evidence of official mortality figures to convince him that the plague epidemic that tapered off at the end of June 1835 had been one of the worst in Egypt's recent history. "Only now, when the mind is no longer excessively absorbed by the fear of contagion, have we begun to realize the enormity of the evil," the Russian consul wrote. "Those who have lived longest in Egypt do not remember a plague as terrible as this last." Many villages had lost half of their inhabitants, especially men twenty to forty years old, agriculture had suffered an irreparable loss of labor, and wide areas formerly cultivated were now wasteland. In Giza almost three-fourths of the village's 2,400 inhabitants had perished. Rosetta had lost two-fifths of the survivors of the cholera epidemic and in two months had dwindled to a village of 4,000 souls.[58]

Compilations of the official mortality figures gave the total number of deaths from plague in Alexandria as 7,800 for the period January through mid-June, and in Cairo, the mortality was reported to be around 34,600 from mid-March until mid-June. All the consuls declared these figures gross underestimates. Functionaries charged with burial rights confirmed that the daily number of deaths in Cairo had been at least 1,000 for the last twenty-two days of April, and on some days, mortality had exceeded 2,000. It was believed that 20,000 of the 80,000 Copts in Cairo had perished and that members of other confessions had succumbed in proportionate numbers. The government reportedly had sequestered 1,200 homes left vacant by the death of all members of the family. Whether the discrepancy arose from the Egyptians' refusal to report deaths in the family or whether it was the government's policy to release only partial statistics, a consensus held that the official figure indicated only one-half of the total mortality and that at least 75,000 had died in Cairo, perhaps 200,000 in all Egypt.[59] Although all the figures are open to question, table 1 gives a rough indication of the distribution of the disease as it appeared to observers at the time.

Relief was general when the epidemic waned at the end of June, but sporadic individual outbreaks suddenly increased in September.[60] Again, the government appears to have been unsuccessful in separating the sick and the well in Alexandria. On the viceroy's orders, officials attempted to convince the leading notables and ulama of the city that it was their duty to isolate those stricken with plague and to place their families under observation. They were assured that the well-off could take with them in detention anything they wished and

Table 1   Deaths from Plague in Alexandria, 1835 [a]

	Population	Reported Mortality	Estimated Mortality	% of Group
Muslim Egyptians	20,000	5,468	10,936	54.6
Soldiers	3,000	235	470	15.6
Negroes and Berbers	4,000	764	1,528	85.0 [*sic*]
Turks	6,000	339	678	11.3
Copts, Armenians, and Jews	4,000	241	482	12.0
Greeks	1,800	257	257	14.2
Maltese	600	367	367	61.0
Europeans	2,600	170	170	6.0
Total	42,000	7,841	14,888	35.4

[a] Sticker, I, 312. Sticker does not identify the source for this information but presumably drew the figures from the Alexandria Quarantine Board records, to which he referred earlier in his history. All the figures cited in the table vary widely from the consuls' dispatches, notably the total population of Alexandria, which they reported as approximately 60,000. Also, De Lesseps, who was a member of the board, wrote on May 20 that 450 Europeans had died in Cairo and Alexandria, not including the Maltese, who mourned 750 dead in Alexandria alone.

the poor would have all their needs provided at government expense; moreover, heads of families who failed to report outbreaks of plague in their households would be executed. Neither promises nor threats availed to stop evasion of the regulations, for another khedivial message later bade the ulama to forbid Muslims to bury the dead in their courtyards, "because that is one of the things which brings about diseases."[61]

Officially and technically, the great plague epidemic ended October 30, 1837, when Consul General Patrick Campbell, president of the Quarantine Board for that month, notified the viceroy's government that no cases of plague had appeared in Egypt during the preceding forty days. In reporting to his own government, the British consul general pointed out that Egypt had been officially in an epidemic state for forty months, from July 1834 to November 1837.[62]

Since European governments based their commercial policies vis-à-vis Egypt on their conclusions drawn from observations during the plague epidemic, it is worthwhile to note again the divergent attitudes toward control measures in Egypt. The viceroy and upper-level government officials were convinced that plague was contagious and had adopted rigorous Mediterranean quarantine practices. The majority of the Egyptian people, however, either did not believe plague was contagious or believed it was morally reprehensible to try to escape inevitable death; perhaps many held both views. Certainly, they abhorred the isolation and detention procedures of quarantine as outrageous invasions that disrupted the solidarity of family life, to be resisted as long as possible.

European physicians in Egypt at the time were similarly divided. In Alexandria, the majority Italian staff of the quarantine service was committed to rigorous contagionist theories and procedures. In Cairo, the military Medical Council was headed by Dr. Clot, a leading opponent of both the principle and practice of quarantine. Many of his like-minded colleagues served in the Egyptian fleet, in military units, in government installations, and in schools and hospitals.

At the onset of the epidemic, Clot created the official Egyptian Plague Commission to settle the dispute of whether or not plague was communicable. Members of the commission examined many cases of plague and conducted one hundred postmortems without special precautions. They carried out several experiments exposing human subjects to plague sufferers' effects or inoculating them with the victims' pus or blood. Clot inoculated himself three times with the blood of a plague patient with no effect. The results convinced him and many of his colleagues that plague was not communicable.[63]

While the views of Clot and his anticontagionist colleagues decisively influenced official policies in France, England, and Austria,[64] they did not undermine the Egyptian government's stand. Clot wrote that when he announced to the viceroy that he and other European physicians would form a commission to investigate the disease and that they would treat plague like other ailments, Muhammad Ali accused the doctors of foolhardiness, called their decision a "piece of madness," and advised them to observe quarantine.[65]

Although he considered them useless, Dr. Clot did not oppose quarantines at government installations; they were reassuring precautions good for mental hygiene, he wrote; besides, they were ordered by Muhammad Ali.

> In spite of our ideas on the uselessness of . . . all the isolation measures . . . we had to submit to the law, to respect prejudices and pub-

lic opinion; as chief of the service we were required to draft instruction for . . . quarantines which we made mandatory.[66]

Other European physicians in Egyptian government service were not as scrupulous in observing Clot's directive, "Whatever your opinion, you are to consider plague a contagious disease and to act accordingly." As early as January 1835, the War Ministry dismissed the European chief physician, Louis Aubert-Roche, and the Turkish supervisor at the marines' hospital in Alexandria for failing to enforce quarantine.[67]

Noncompliance with quarantine regulations appears to have been common among members of the navy medical corps, who were able to function independently of the authorities in Cairo and Alexandria. Perhaps typical of the European attitude were statements made by Dr. Abbott, naval surgeon aboard the *Abu Qir*, a line vessel with a crew of more than 1,000 men. Abbott declared that he never observed "any kind of quarantine or fumigations" because he felt these precautions were useless. Consequently, when the fleet was ordered to Crete at the peak of the epidemic in Alexandria, he dispensed with "the usual ceremony of fumigation" of supplies, including tarbooshes, blankets, and woolen clothing; nor did he prevent the wives and relatives of the sailors from bringing additional blankets and clothing on board ship the day before sailing.[68]

Similar views were expressed by Dr. Koch, head of the navy medical corps and chief surgeon for the Egyptian fleet and a known noncontagionist. In a letter to Clot, Koch described the circumstances that convinced him that plague was not contagious.

> One day I received from the Admiral the command to order all sailors on board their respective ships and to prevent all communication between them and people in the infected quarters of the city. All the dwellings through which the disease had passed were to be cleaned, fumigated and whitewashed, and effects used by plague patients were to be burned. . . . Many sailors . . . brought from their homes blankets and clothing which had served the sick as well as the healthy. And not a case of plague appeared in the squadron. . . . However, during the voyage to Crete and at Crete itself, in rigorous quarantine, several cases of plague broke out on board different ships.[69]

It was inevitable that evasion of the regulations would come to the attention of the pasha and arouse his wrath. Orders to have seamen stricken with plague removed to the Mahmudiya lazaretto and to impose an eleven-day quarantine on the ship and crew were not being followed, the viceroy observed in a directive to the admiral of the fleet; navy physicians were neglecting surveillance of personnel stricken with the pestilence. The body of one who had died had been discovered in the Mahmudiya Canal with an 88-pound iron weight around his neck. Since the signs of the disease on his body had been lanced, this could have been performed only by those physicians who were failing to transfer the stricken men to isolation. The admiral was ordered to punish the offenders severely and to warn all medical personnel that His Highness would treat them harshly if they failed to carry out their responsibilities.[70]

Apparently Koch was one of many European physicians discharged from government service for failure to comply with official regulations. Clot was bitter in blaming the quarantine service medical staff in Alexandria. "Ardent partisans of contagion," they were hostile toward colleagues who held different opinions and expressed their resentment in official reports that caused many physicians to be dismissed, he claimed.[71]

Was Quarantine Effective Protection Against Plague?

Opposed to Dr. Clot and his noncontagionist colleagues' evidence of their failure to transmit plague by exposure, contact, and inoculation, the contagionists could only point to the (admittedly relative) immunity of those who went into seclusion during the epidemic. The issue was: were the quarantine procedures enforced by the Egyptian government effective at all or were they, as the Egyptians no doubt saw them, simply additional hardships inflicted on an already suffering populace? On this point, Clot and his miasmatist colleagues were weak, for positive evidence outweighed the negative, and the establishments that escaped plague during the epidemic were those isolated from the community. The Music School at Khanka, ordered into quarantine in an old army depot, had no plague cases among its students, and the Polytechnic School, where Hekekyan-Bey personally stood guard, was spared throughout the epidemic. Both the Arsenal, where 6,000 workers were effectively detained by a military cordon, and the viceroy's palace at Shubra, where elaborate restrictions were enforced, were struck only after quarantine regulations were lifted.[72]

The partisans of noncontagion neglected to mention in their writings what the European consuls reported in 1836: plague broke out primarily among those who had been quarantined the year before—workers in the Arsenal, navy personnel, and students in schools. Clot wrote that in spite of rigorous quarantine maintained over 300 inmates at Shubrah Palace, three servants died of plague; but he failed to specify that the deaths occurred in 1836, after quarantine had been lifted.[73] The miasmatists also allowed no margin for human error or neglect in the preventive measures and declared that a single case of plague in an establishment under quarantine invalidated the principle of isolation. Clot's colleague, Aubert-Roche, emphatically denied the efficacy of protective barriers and asserted, "It is wrong to say the Mahmudiya hospital did not suffer from plague; after six months of quarantine, one of the orderlies was attacked."[74]

Although neither side to the dispute recognized it at the time, the cumbersome, hit-or-miss quarantine procedures traditionally excluded and destroyed stray animals, which must have kept infected rats and fleas from the segregated premises. The government regulations also eliminated fleas by burning clothing and bedding used by the plague striken. For populations at risk, like the 6,000 workers at the Arsenal, government measures extended to leveling their huts and building new barracks, or at least cleaning, fumigating, and whitewashing the dwellings.

Although it had proved infeasible to enforce controls over all the citizens of Alexandria or Cairo at the peak of the epidemic, as we have seen, the viceroy allowed no relaxation in restrictions on government service personnel. The British consul general, Patrick Campbell, reported that "the Pasha gives every support, as well by his example, as by his orders, to the efforts of the Quarantine Board." During his presidency of the board, Campbell had quarantined the entire Twenty-second Regiment garrisoned in Alexandria for eleven days when a single case of plague broke out in the unit. He also ordered the admiral of the fleet quarantined, and we know that the order was enforced, for government records include an official reprimand to the admiral for protesting the restriction. Two ship commanders were sentenced to seven years penal labor for breaking quarantine before the end of the prescribed detention period. And when one of Ibrahim Pasha's officers in Syria reportedly violated quarantine, he inquired what penalty European regulations prescribed; informed the usual punishment was death, he had the officer summarily tried and executed.[75]

As for the pasha's daughter-in-law who was quarantined, Muhammad Ali ruled his own family with an iron hand and there was no question of noncompliance with regulations. When Saïd accompanied the fleet to Crete, provincial officials decided to waive quarantine restrictions for the young prince, but his first question on arrival was how many days of detention he had to undergo.[76]

In November 1835, the Quarantine Board issued new regulations "to avoid misunderstanding" in future outbreaks of plague. All houses where plague appeared would be placed in thirty days quarantine and fumigated. Stricken individuals with means could be attended by their own physicians, while those in need would be removed to the lazaretto and attended by the Quarantine Board's medical officers.[77]

It appears that Europeans resident in Egypt later followed the Egyptians' example of hiding the sick or the dead during an outbreak of plague,[78] but at this time, it was common for them to resist quarantine by force. These incidents often became armed confrontations between Quarantine Board officials and police, on one side, and a crowd of supporters for the family threatened with detention, on the other. We are told that the viceroy, "tired of these scenes," instructed the police that in cases where Europeans resisted enforcement of regulations, they should call on them three times to comply and fire if they continued to resist after the third summons.[79]

The enforcement of domestic quarantine for plague ceased to be a major problem when the disease mysteriously declined in the 1840s. But the main point of contention between miasmatists and contagionists—the necessity for maintaining traditional maritime quarantines—remained a bitterly disputed issue, seriously impeding efforts to control outbreaks of cholera, which, unlike plague, continued to ravage the civilized world throughout the nineteenth century.

The history of the international Quarantine Board that Muhammad Ali commissioned in 1831 reveals that in the dispute over quarantines, economic and political factors shaped the board's policies, rather than technical or humanitarian. We shall survey that history next.

5

The International Quarantine Board

In retrospect, the Quarantine Board in Alexandria was a premature experiment in international cooperation doomed to failure in the hypernationalistic climate of the nineteenth century. The principle of cooperation could not survive the intense economic and political rivalry exemplified in the drive for colonial empires at that time. It was too much to expect that European consuls, specifically commissioned to promote their countries' commercial interests, would disadvantage those interests to collaborate in initiatives of dubious value to control communicable disease. Apart from their responsibility to maximize their countrymen's trade opportunities, European consular representatives shared a keen sensitivity to the notion of national sovereignty and to the necessity of asserting their own personal prerogatives and their nations' rights, honor, and prestige.

The consuls also were ill-prepared to deal with the technicalities of containing epidemic disease. An Italian physician resident in Egypt when Muhammad Ali established the first international Quarantine Board[1] expressed approval of the viceroy's initiative but pointed out the consular representatives' lack of professional expertise.

> The representatives of civilized nations were thought to possess an abundant store of knowledge for the utility of so important an institution; but it would have been a wiser plan to seek such knowledge . . . in persons of the trade; . . . with one or two exceptions, the others had not the slightest idea of the topics they undertook to discuss.[2]

The history of the consular Quarantine Board's activities in Alexandria reveals that each of the delegates was preoccupied with his own government's policies; they also sought and gave preferential treatment for their own nationals' ships. In fairness to the European consuls, however, it should be pointed out that the traditional practices of the Mediterranean maritime quarantine system, elaborated during the age of sail to contain plague, became increasingly cumbersome and costly to international traders as the pace of sea traffic accelerated during the nineteenth century. The regulations almost encouraged circumvention, evasion, and eventually defiance.

The Maritime Quarantine System

The maritime quarantine system consisted of three instruments: the bills of health issued to ships on departure from port; the periods of detention, called quarantines, imposed on ships, passengers, and cargo originating in ports judged infected with disease; and the facilities for detention and isolation called the lazaretto. The issuance of bills of health designating the ascertainable state of health in a ship's port of origin was the principal measure for preventing exportation of plague, an "international intelligence network" to alert authorities in the port of debarkation to the possible danger of infection abroad. All major trading nations maintained sanitary authorities at their chief ports in communication with the Mediterranean: Marseilles and Toulon in France, Trieste in Austria, Odessa in Russia, and the principal ports of the Italian states. After 1815, England required vessels from the eastern Mediterranean to undergo quarantine at Malta before proceeding to the British Isles.

According to Italian ports' usage, vessels were issued passes in four denominations: "unclean" or "foul," designating a port where plague existed at that time; "suspect," indicating a recent incidence of plague at the locale or on board ship; "clean," if the port of origin had no incidence of plague for forty days; and "free," if the ship came from a land where there was not even a suspicion of plague. The latitude for error, disagreement, and deception in such a system is obvious. And there were frequent complaints that quarantine officials could be induced to falsify information or to waive regulations for sufficient compensation.[3]

The Venetian system of quarantine, which became the model for most other sea powers, was based on the experience of some seventy plague epidemics in 700 years and rested squarely on the conviction that infection was carried in shipments of goods. Venetian regulations provided for the isolation of plague-stricken passengers, fumigation of their personal effects, and purification of the cargo carried aboard ship. Paralleling the designation of clean, suspect, and foul bills of health, goods were classified as materials not susceptible, doubtful, or susceptible to absorb infection. The quarantine period of forty days apparently was based on the belief that it took this length of time to dissipate the infection absorbed in merchandise by exposing it to sunshine and fresh air. Rules for purification varied according to the commodities' supposed degree of susceptibility, but in the course of time, the classification of goods had been elaborated to the point of absurdity.[4]

Nevertheless, it was the only system extant for attempting to mitigate the threat of pandemic killer disease. The twentieth century would acknowledge the value of early international disease control efforts, unaware that the viceroy of Egypt had commissioned the first international Quarantine Board in Alexandria in 1831. It was a common assumption, according to one international health official, "that the board is a body originally imposed on the government of Egypt by the European powers."[5] In fact, Muhammad Ali had adopted the principle of quarantine before any European consular representatives arrived in Egypt. Maritime quarantine was an old, familiar idea throughout the Mediterranean, and as early as 1812, his Italian physicians had persuaded Muhammad Ali to restrict the entry of ships from Turkey when plague broke out in Constantinople.

Alarms about the threat of plague from Syria and Asia Minor recurred and stimulated the establishment of quarantine stations in Alexandria in 1828, in Damietta in 1829, and in Rosetta in 1831.[6] But Egypt lacked a lazaretto, which Mediterranean Europe considered an essential defense against plague. The lack of a lazaretto became a serious handicap for the viceroy after his campaign in the Levant because it was impossible to import commodities from Syria and Asia Minor without such a facility. Persons and goods had to remain on board ship for forty days; if the vessel was not carrying sufficient provisions for that length of time, the ship's captain often returned to his port of debarkation or made for another harbor where quarantine was not enforced.[7] Since plague appeared almost every year in Syria or Asia Minor, this meant inordinate delays and losses in delivering materials from the viceroy's Syrian dependency.

When the consular Quarantine Board reconvened after the cholera epidemic in 1831, therefore, Muhammad Ali specifically charged the members to create a European-style lazaretto as the core facility of an effective quarantine system. The board accordingly drafted a comprehensive program that stipulated that the lazaretto would be modeled on the best European facilities, that all its principal employees would be European, and that ships' and passengers' fees would be calculated to cover the cost and maintenance of the establishment. An outbreak of plague in Damietta spurred lagging construction, and the new lazaretto was in operation by January 1833.[8]

In view of the role the pilgrimage was to play in carrying cholera from South Asia to the Mediterranean via the Arabian peninsula, it is important to note that Muslim pilgrims' movements constituted the bulk of traffic through Alexandria's lazaretto from the outset. In January 1833, 2,000 pilgrims were quartered in the lazaretto, Muslims from all parts of the Ottoman Empire and a large number of Russian Tartars from the Black Sea area. All pilgrims transiting Egypt thereafter routinely stayed in the lazaretto before setting out on the caravan to Mecca, and the Egyptian government provided sustenance for the poorest among them. The British consul general, who visited the lazaretto at that time, found the travelers' quarters "clean and convenient" and ample enough to accommodate 2,500 persons.

The lazaretto compound also included warehouses for quarantined goods and a small garrison of soldiers to guard the merchandise and to prevent communication between the lazaretto and the city. Duties were levied on ships according to tonnage, on cargo according to "susceptibility" to contamination, and on passengers according to the number of persons in a group requiring accommodations. These duties amounted to considerable revenue; in 1833, it was estimated that ships in quarantine paid an average of $14,000 to $15,000 annually in quarantine fees, which were applied toward the lazaretto's operating expenses. Salaries for personnel was the largest single expenditure; the lazaretto and its subsidiary bureaus employed 19 Europeans, 47 Egyptians, and 80 Egyptian guards.[9] In spite of seemingly sufficient staff and operating funds, this was the establishment that, fifteen years later, proved inadequate to handle the great influx of pilgrims who brought cholera into Egypt and sparked the epidemic of 1848.

One obstacle to efficiency in the quarantine service operations was the difficulty of gaining agreement among Quarantine Board members for consistent policy enforcement. The situation became clear in 1838 when the board's first elected president found his attempts to enforce regulations blocked by his colleagues' defensiveness in protecting their national prerogatives. One source of friction developed in the relations between the quarantine services in Alexandria and Syria. Following the Alexandria board's recommendations, Ibrahim Pasha had established quarantine stations in Syrian ports, and his commander in the Levant, Sulayman Pasha, apparently enforced the regulations with a military rigor resented by local consuls and merchants alike.[10] When the board's president proposed that, since intelligence from Syria indicated that plague had appeared on the coast, all ships from the Levant should be placed under observation on arrival in Alexandria, his colleagues disagreed. Their consuls in Syrian ports were issuing clean bills of health, which they felt should permit their ships free entry. Instead, they called for discussion of travelers' complaints and merchants' reports of discrimination in the lazaretto's operations. The Quarantine Board members also refused to uphold the president in firing quarantine service employees, who apparently were consular protégés, for malversation of funds. Finally, the president resigned when Board members passed a resolution that their ad hoc rulings could waive any of the board's statutory regulations.[11]

Histories of the quarantine service claim that at this point, angered by the European powers' rejection of his bid for independence from the Ottoman sultan, Muhammad Ali decided to withdraw the prerogatives he had granted the consuls in 1831.[12] No doubt the pasha was aware of the board's proceedings. An opportune moment to intervene arose at the end of 1839 when a Turkish ship from Smyrna that arrived in Alexandria with a clean bill of health was placed in quarantine, while an Austrian steamship that arrived from the same port on the same day was granted free entry. Muhammad Ali promptly notified the board that the quarantine service had been regularized sufficiently so that henceforth it could be administered by the Egyptian government.[13] Muhammad Ali's move to nationalize the Quarantine Board was to prove short-lived, in view of his impending defeat in Syria, but it temporarily and partially Egyptianized the agency. In 1840, the Egyptian liaison officer, Tahir Effendi, was named permanent president. And in August 1841, the board was declared responsible directly to the viceroy. Two months later, Muhammad Ali had to reaffirm the sovereignty of the Ottoman sultan, and the Egyptian board technically became subordinate to the sanitary administration in Constantinople.[14]

In the meantime, European consular agents had refused to recognize the board's authority or the validity of bills of health issued by the Egyptian police. Their ambassadors in Constantinople secured an order from the sultan demanding the viceroy's adoption of the Ottoman board model, which included official European representation.[15] With his customary pretext of lacking directives from the Sultan exploded, Muhammad Ali had to concede European consul's participation in the agency. A new decree in November 1843 invited the consuls general of Austria, France, Great Britain, Greece, Prussia, Russia, and Sardinia to name delegates to a reorganized board. Egyptian government appointments included the minister of war, Khurshid Bey, and Shaykh Khalil Ghazali, counsel for canonical law and popular religious beliefs. The viceroy's chief secretary pointed out that there was no hope of moderating the rigorous quarantine measures imposed on Egyptian commodities in European ports, which severely handicapped the country's commerce, as long as foreign nations withheld their confidence in Egypt's sanitary administration.[16]

In the 1840s, the rising volume and speed of international trade caused by the expansion of steam transport provoked a strong challenge to the time-honored practice of detaining ships from localities where plague prevailed. Commercial interests in France felt particularly disadvantaged, for England and Holland had long virtually ignored quarantines and Austria followed suit early in the nineteenth century, apparently relying on land controls along the border with Turkey to exclude plague. Following the first invasion of cholera in 1831, the stringent quarantine measures elaborated after the Marseilles plague of 1720 had been renewed at precisely the moment when England took a long step to outstrip France in the trade race by launching the Peninsular and Oriental Steam Navigation Company. Increasing pressure by shipping interests then caused the French government to commission the Academy of Medicine in 1844 to examine, and if possible to revise, the Marseilles code. The academy attached great weight to the evidence of experts with experience in Egypt, as we have seen, and it accepted the investigating commission's conclusion that plague was not transmissible from person to person. The commission further asserted that there was no convincing evidence that plague could be transported in merchandise. Persons stricken could vitiate the air of ships, creating a localized "pestilential constitution," but imported plague could not cause a serious outbreak unless favorable climate and sanitary conditions existed.

Health authorities in Great Britain also upheld a noncontagionist view that an "epidemic atmosphere" might extend over thousands of square miles and yet affect only particular localities—those in an unsanitary state. On this hypothesis, quarantine was no safeguard for the public health but was an obstruction to commerce. England therefore officially abandoned quarantines and exclusively relied on local sanitary improvements.[17] In both countries, the opinion gained ground that quarantines were not only useless but were, in effect, institutionalized instruments of extortion. Bowring's judgment that "ignorance instead of safety, evil instead of good pervade the whole field of sanitary legislation" epitomized the progressive's reaction to the inconsistencies and excesses of antiquated quarantine practices.[18]

Countries in the western Mediterranean, unconvinced by the evidence advanced and holding enormous vested interests in quarantine establishments, refused to follow the lead of the Atlantic seaboard nations in abolishing maritime quarantine. Specifically, in regard to Egypt, reports that the annual plague outbreaks had waned to the vanishing point after 1842, a trump card in the arguments for eliminating quarantines, aroused strong skepticism. During the 1840s, several European govenments sent special envoys to observe actual health conditions in Egypt and to assess the effectiveness of the quarantine service operations.[19] It was difficult to reconcile the idea of plague's disappearance with the notion held for so many years that Egypt was the cradle of plague.

Muhammad Ali therefore attempted to respond to two opposed viewpoints, both of which incriminated health conditions in Egypt in disease causation, so as to gain the "confidence" required for uninhibited commerce. On the one hand, he upheld a maritime quarantine system that was extremely disadvantageous for Egyptian trade. During the decade from 1834 and 1844, when Egypt was rarely completely free from plague, vessels carrying Egyptian commodities routinely were denied clean bills of health and were subject to long periods of detention in European ports. On the other hand, trading nations unconcerned about contagion were wary of the "pestilential" or "epidemic constitution" that they believed arose from unsanitary conditions in Egypt. The sanitary reform introduced in Alexandria in 1842 and theoretically projected for future implementation in other major cities seems to have been the viceroy's attempt to disarm those objections.

Profit Challenges Principle in the Age of Steam

Muhammad Ali's concern to promote Egypt's cash crops in international trade remained basic policy for his successors, who were among the great landowners profiting from the system of agricultural capitalism. Following the introduction of steam power, the khedives, particularly Ismail, also entered the field of maritime passenger transport, an area of sharp competition among the European powers. Rivalry intensified after the opening of the Suez Canal in 1869. By 1870, most major trading nations—England, France, Austria, Italy, Germany, and Russia—had established regular service between their home ports and Alexandria. The Khedive Ismail had taken over the Nile Navigation Company founded earlier by Saïd, expanded it, renamed it the Khediviyah, and with it captured a busy trade plying westward from Alexandria to Piraeus and eastward to Constantinople and the Syrian coast. Apparently, there was ample custom for all in the Mediterranean, but as early as 1865, the Khediviyah clashed in the Red Sea with a fleet of steamers sent from Bombay by the Indian Steam Navigation Company to carry pilgrims between Jiddah and Suez. The English steamers were superior, the British consul general reported, and they were realizing substantial profits that, he predicted, would pose "wholesome" competition for the Egytian company and force it "to act more for the benefit of the public."[20] During the next ten years, the Khediviyah continued to expand and soon matched the number of British vessels in the Red Sea traffic. Consuls' reports listing the various nations' ships carrying pilgrims from Jiddah to Suez showed that Egyptian and British flag ships were far ahead of other countries and were abreast of each other in the race.[21] For passenger volume, however, the British surpassed any combination of other nations' transport. Consular reports for the pilgrimage season in 1880 show that the number of pilgrims from South and Southeast Asia represented almost one-half of the entire world traffic, close to 29,000 of the total 59,650. Although the largest group of pilgrims came from the Dutch East Indies, there was only one Dutch ship involved in transport, compared with sixty-one English vessels.[22]

Egypt was in dangerous competition with England, particularly after Ismail sold his majority of shares in the Suez Canal Company to the British government in 1875 for an immediate cash payment that forestalled bankruptcy for only a year. In 1876, the Debt Control Commission was established, and by 1877, more than 60 percent of all Egyptian revenue went to the servicing of the national debt. The financial crisis during the period 1875 to 1877 undermined the khedive's authority and offered an opportunity to nationalist army officers and some ambitious Assembly delegates to gain a greater share in government at the expense of the ruling house. In the meantime, Egyptian journalists started attacking foreign control of the country's financial affairs, and the press began to lead political agitation by the country's intelligentsia. One of the issues the intellectuals adopted to attack the European presence in Egypt was alleged obstruction of the pilgrimage by unnecessary or prolonged detention of the hajjis in quarantine. It is worthwhile to look at how Muslim pilgrim traffic[23] became an object of international attention following the cholera epidemic in 1865.

Egypt had been a transit area for Muslim pilgrims from Africa, Asia, and Europe since the Middle Ages. Until the end of the nineteenth century, the Maghribi caravan and smaller groups of pilgrims from West Africa, the Caucasus, and Asia Minor joined the Egyptian caravan outside the gates of Cairo for the overland journey to Mecca. Traveling via Suez, Aqaba, and the eastern shore of the Red Sea, the caravan took about 35 days to reach Mecca. Including the pilgrims' stops in Mecca and Medina, the entire journey lasted at least 110 days. An alternate sea route took pilgrims from Egypt up the Nile to Qina and across the desert to Qusayr, where they took ship for Jiddah. With the introduction of steam transport at mid-nineteenth century, Suez gained a virtual monopoly over the sea traffic.[24]

Although the pilgrims' primary aim was the religious reward for participation in this large-scale demonstration of faith, some pursued private business as well. Earlier, the last three days of the pilgrimage had been the occasion of a great trade fair at Mecca, and some pilgrims continued to carry on a surprising volume of trade even after the majority began traveling by steamship. One writer noted that on pilgrim ships coming from Singapore during the 1860s, passage was reckoned according to the number of parcels of merchandise the pilgrim carried.[25] An English physician described at the end of the century the difficulties of disinfecting the effects of pilgrims:

> The ordinary pilgrim coming from Egypt and the north is in many instances a trader, who combines religion with business and brings back with him a large amount of goods to be sold in his own country. Ten or twelve boxes may form the luggage of such a man and I have seen one pilgrim with no less than 80 boxes of luggage.[26]

Besides the encumbrance of baggage that would be difficult to disinfect, other circumstances of the pilgrimage posed health problems. Many pilgrims were old, having deferred the journey as the climax of their lives, and a long desert trek or a rough sea voyage in accommodations similar to those of slave ships could tax the endurance even of younger travelers. Many pilgrims literally observed the Prophet's admonition that piety was the best provision for the journey to the holy cities and relied on the benevolence of coreligionists along the way to supply food and shelter, if needed, and above all water.[27] The majority of pilgrims were poor; numerous accounts refer to "penniless" and "destitute" pilgrims unable to pay for passage home.[28] Destitution was so closely associated with disease in the mind of the nineteenth-century educated European that he naturally assumed the pilgrim to be a disease carrier. The hajji's willingness to endure unbearably crowded conditions on board ship and at the pilgrimage sites was seen as a sign of excessive religious zeal that made him indifferent to discomfort and sickness. From the sanitarians point of view, intuitively linking human congestion with infection, it was obvious that the pilgrimage must be a starting point for epidemic disease. British functionaries with experience in India no doubt could imagine vividly the daunting problem of attempting to maintain cleanliness in areas where thousands of pilgrims congregated or of providing adequate drinking water for the assemblage.[29]

"The Cholera Conference:" and the Constantinople Agreements of 1866

The cholera pandemic of 1865 aroused maritime nations to the fact that cholera had invaded Mecca in 1831 and had since reappeared almost annually at the time of the Muslim pilgrimage. The unmistakable implication of vulnerability for every European country with a Muslim colonial population or in communication with Muslim lands lent urgency to the call for an international sanitary conference in 1866 to institute controls over the annual pilgrimage traffic. The maritime nations' delegates to the meeting in Constantinople disagreed on whether the Hijaz was the breeding ground or the relay station for cholera, but they were unanimously concerned to check its expansion westward to Europe.[30]

Key recommendations adopted at the conference made Egypt the linchpin in the defense system by establishing an international sanitary commission at Suez, the Red Sea Sanitary Service, to supervise the operations of quarantine stations at El Tor and Al-Wajh and of five sanitary posts on both sides of the Red Sea. Soliciting cooperation from the nations represented, three agreements called for suspending embarkation of pilgrims at their home ports whenever cholera was epidemic in India; restricting the number of indigent pilgrims who would need assistance by requiring a "proof of means" certificate affirming the pilgrim's possession of adequate funds to complete the voyage and to maintain his family during his absence; and, last, applying to all pilgrim vessels the minimum standards of accommodation and hygiene required for British ships by the Native Passenger Act.[31] For the first time in history, an international group had organized a rational collective defense against the threat of epidemic disease.

Even more noteworthy than the adoption of resolutions for future action was the delegates' unusual concurrence on some fundamental principles discussed at the Cholera Conference. Perhaps because fear aroused by the pandemic had equalized some of their differences, the delegates agreed that Asiatic cholera originates in India where it is endemic in the Ganges valley, that man is the principal agent in disseminating cholera, and that the transmissibility of cholera was "an incontestable truth." These conclusions were based on epidemiological considerations, and it was remarkable that an intergovernmental conference should have been able to agree on them unanimously at a time when they were anathema to an influential body of medical opinion.

It appears that the countries involved in the Mecca pilgrimage attempted to observe the Constantinople agreements for several years. There was a general desire for cooperation, we are told, among the governments of India, Turkey, and Egypt. British authorities in India renewed efforts to enforce the Native Passenger Act and to control the number of pilgrims at departure by applying a "minimum means" requirement. In 1872 and later when cholera broke out in the Hijaz, the Red Sea Sanitary Service at Suez prevented the epidemic from entering Egypt by rigorous measures: they closed the Suez Canal to all ships touching the Hijaz and imposed ten days' detention on all pilgrims wishing to transit Egypt. The *London Times* observed that Egypt's reported freedom from cholera might have been due to the government's enforcement of the Constantinople agreements and conceded that "so much of the scheme as affected Egypt had a certain practicability about it."[32]

Opening the Suez Canal facilitated vastly expanded and accelerated dissemination of communicable diseases, however, while a strong drive to maximize profits in rapid and large-scale transport of persons and goods through the canal soon outstripped the move to contain disease transmission. As early as 1873, consular representatives on the Quarantine Board in Alexandria began reporting exploitation of Muslim pilgrims by unscrupulous ships' captains who crammed passengers on their vessels without even providing adequate drinking water. One notorious case involved three ships' captains who sold part of their coal supplies at Jiddah and struck an agreement to take turns towing each other to Suez. Unfortunately, the plan was not feasible, and one of the ships drifted in distress in the Red Sea without water for the passengers. Another was able to reach El Tor, but the captain, fearing reprisals from the passengers, put off for land with his officers and abandoned the ship in the harbor.[33]

Overcrowding the ships carrying pilgrims was the most common violation of the Constantinople agreements. Captains who herded passengers on their vessels at Jiddah and Yanbu went unchecked by authorities, and rarely did a transport arrive at Suez carrying only the number indicated on its passenger list. The British Native Passengers Act of 1858, which all national shipping companies were enjoined to observe, prohibited taking on more than two passengers per ton of the ship's weight. By 1878, when an epidemic in the Hijaz refocused attention on pilgrims' transportation, it was discovered that none of the shipping companies, not even the English, was observing the restrictions. "Competition almost always caused the regulated number to be exceeded," one observer pointed out.[34]

Another abuse developed following the cholera epidemic in 1878, when the Quarantine Board had ruled that pilgrims could not travel overland through Egypt directly after leaving the Hijaz but must spend fifteen days under observation at the quarantine station. Ships' captains then seized the opportunity to debark one boatload of passengers at El Tor and return immediately to Jiddah to embark another boatload. Unable to travel overland, the pilgrims were stranded without onward passage after completing their detention period. The Quarantine Board tried to require a written guarantee from the shipping companies that they would transport pilgrims to the ultimate destination indicated on their passage ticket, not simply to the quarantine station. Shipping companies then took the stand, which the British consul upheld, that vessels could not be required to wait for passengers who were quarantined; if the Egyptian government wished to detain pilgrims at El Tor, it was the Egyptian government's responsibility to repatriate them. In mid-February 1878, there was a backlog of 3,000 pilgrims awaiting passage to destinations in North Africa. Because the captains insisted they had discharged their obligations by transporting their passengers to the quarantine site, the Suez Canal Company had to intervene and contract transport for the pilgrims at company expense.[35]

In addition to the importunings of stranded pilgrims, consular members of the Quarantine Board had to deal with shipping companies' complaints that the board was really a tool of the Egyptian government. In 1878, a number of British companies charged that prohibiting pilgrims from landing anywhere on the coast except at quarantine stations aimed "to discourage foreign navigation and insure a monopoly of pilgrim transport to the government firm, the Khediviyah."[36]

In an effort to deflect future criticisms of their rulings, in 1879, the Quarantine Board drew up a code for ships transporting pilgrims. To the members' chagrin, the most frequent and flagrant violator of their code was the Khediviyah. From all accounts, the Khediviyah Line overcrowded pilgrim ships beyond belief, deposited passengers at Suez with no provision for onward transportation, and put in arbitrarily at Mediterranean ports while loaded with pilgrims from the Hijaz. Consular members of the board threatened to withdraw their support for all the board's rulings if they were not applied impartially to all companies transporting pilgrims in the Red Sea.[37] In 1881, however, a serious outbreak of cholera severely overtaxed the board's logistic capacities, at precisely the time when it came under Egyptian administration, precipitating a crisis that led the British to take control of the board's operations.

The British Takeover

Between 1865 and 1882, the cause and prevention of cholera became partisan issues politicized by several factions. Most important, Egyptian nationalists were competing with the British Foreign Office to discredit and gain control of the Quarantine Board. Europeans resident in Egypt, the Egyptian government, the nationalists' military clique, international shipping companies, and the annual surge of Muslim pilgrims to Mecca all played a role in a political crisis precipitated by epidemic disease control. These actors' roles are worth examining, especially that of the European consular Quarantine Board.

By the 1870s, European opinions had evolved since the plague and cholera epidemics forty years earlier, but two major professional points of view were opposed: the Mediterranean, exemplified by Italy, and the Atlantic, championed especially by Great Britain. Educated lay opinion, as well as the medical profession in the Italian states, supported the contagionist view of disease transmission for several reasons. For one, experimental science had always been strong in medical training at Italian universities, and Pacini's[38] discovery of the cholera vibrio, although unacknowledged, came out of a long tradition of empiricism. The Italian states also had the longest history of devastating experiences with plague and had created the most elaborate array of institutions to exclude the disease. Finally, the Latin nations in the western Mediterranean, particularly Italy, had acquired great vested interests in quarantine organizations; controls over the movement of persons and goods provided employment to many of their countrymen, who also furnished personnel for the Egyptian and Ottoman sanitary establishments. It was unlikely that Spaniards or Italians would repudiate the rationale for their own maritime restrictions by sanctioning less stringent controls in the eastern Mediterranean or Red Sea.

On the opposite side of the quarantine issue were Austria, Holland, and, above all, Great Britain. As the French delegate to one of the sanitary conferences pointed out, it was natural for England, an island country distant from the locus of any of the dread killer diseases and possessing, the French physician conceded, far superior hygienic conditions than the continent, to feel less threatened by possible disease invasion than the Mediterranean countries. Also, it was an article of faith in Victorian England that the only safeguard against epidemic diseases lay in abundance of fresh air, pure drinking water, sanitary disposal of organic wastes, avoidance of overcrowding, and temperate personal habits. The well-known English sanitarians were confirmed anticontagionists; they expressed their opposition to the idea of a specific contagion with the conviction of unimpeachable sincerity. Under their leadership, England had provided an admirable example in sanitary reform to the industrializing world. However, sanitary reform was only a partial solution to the problem of communicable disease and could not be carried out in classic English fashion—an energetic campaign by voluntary organizations of public-minded citizens, like the Health of Towns Associations—in all countries.[39] Unfortunately for the cause of international cooperation, England's success in sanitary reform caused her spokesmen to express impatience with quarantine systems they considered obstructive. A leading physician in 1862 expressed a typical judgment:

> It is certainly a noteworthy coincidence, that the stringency and severity of the quarantine regulations in a country have been of late years, very much in inverse ratio to the progress there of exact medical observation as to the circumstances which favour the rise and spread of epidemic disease, and also the advance of enlightenment on social and political science among the people generally.[40]

France, with an Atlantic and a Mediterranean seaboard, shared both points of view. There was no national consensus on disease transmission or on appropriate prophylaxis, and public opinion was divided by the opposing interests affected by preventive measures. Conflict between Atlantic shipping interests and Mediterranean advocates of quarantine had induced the French government first to appoint sanitary physicians to key cities in the eastern Mediterranean in 1847. The widely varying quarantine regulations among commercial nations then inspired the French government to promote a series of international sanitary conferences, beginning in 1851 in Paris, to seek trading nations' agreement on the principles underlying quarantine practices.[41]

The khedivial government, particularly during Ismail's frantic search for new sources of revenue, seems to have been oblivious to the effect of its actions on the health or welfare of its subjects. We have already seen that the Egytian government-owned steamship line was the worst offender in jeopardizing pilgrims' health and safety by overcrowding its ships. Historians also have noted the ill-considered taxation of every possible commodity and service in Egypt; one example nullified the Quarantine Board's efforts to eliminate a health hazard. Alarmed by the common practice of disposing of dead animals in canals and streams, causing wholesale pollution of the country's water supplies, the board in 1878 secured an enactment requiring owners of dead animals to bury them. The khedivial government promptly imposed a tax on animal burials, virtually ensuring that the ordinance would not be observed.[42]

In the meantime, the quarantine service in Egypt became a target of resentment in the rising nationalist movement which ultimately provoked the British occupation in 1882. The conspicuous presence in Alexandria of European functionaries in the Egyptian government was a constant irritant to nationalists supporting "the Colonels," the military faction calling for "Egypt for the Egyptians." Political activists among army officers and the intelligentsia began to rally the religious establishment to the cause of Muslim pilgrims allegedly obstructed or mistreated by foreigners in the quarantine establishment. Muslim pilgrims were the most important actors in the conflict over quarantine regulations; they were "the masses" crammed into ships to ensure maximum profit for shipowners and herded into detention camps to undergo all the disputed practices of quarantine.

When cholera broke out in the Hijaz in 1881, the Quarantine Board in Alexandria ordered strict measures to protect Egypt, including 28 days detention for pilgrims at three quarantine stations. Within days, the camps were swamped beyond capacity and lack of water contributed to unhealthy crowding to allow a cholera outbreak to develop into an epidemic in the camp itself. To contain the epidemic, the Quarantine Board ill-advisedly extended the pilgrims' detention. When rations and water ran out, some of the pilgrims who had been detained as long as 40 or 50 days became enraged; three caravans burned the lazaretto and fled the camp.[43] The pilgrims' outraged reaction to their treatment became the cause of an investigation promoted by Egyptian nationalists to discredit foreign functionaries of the Quarantine Board and arouse antiforeign feelings. The nationalists apparently aimed first to discredit the board in Alexandria, then to abolish it and transfer its responsibilities to the Board of Health in Cairo which was under Egyptian direction.[44]

For lack of government support, the investigation of pilgrims' grievances eventually ground to a halt; meanwhile, protests from steamship companies outraged by the paralysis of shipping through the Suez Canal during the epidemic had mounted. In September 1881, the Quarantine Board had restricted movement through the canal, and by the end of the year, the British Foreign Office as well as the Suez Canal Company were deluged with complaints from shippers, accompanied by bills for compensation for delays, extraordinary expenses, and losses from detention.

It was the British companies' threats to abandon the Suez Canal and return to the Cape route that drew Ferdinand de Lesseps, president of the Suez Canal Company, into the etiological debate on cholera. Addressing the French Academy of Sciences in April 1882, he declared the board's measures futile and inconsistent with current enlightened opinion, which held emanations from local miasma responsible for infectious disease transmission.[45] There is no indication whether his fellow academician, Louis Pasteur, had any comments on de Lesseps's etiological views, but they were challenged by Dr. A. M. Fauvel who, as an official delegate to the Constantinople conference in 1866, had approved the rationale for the practices de Lesseps condemned as "barbaric." Fauvel conceded that the procedures in force were far from ideal, and he foresaw a time when quarantines would disappear as progress in science discovered new types of preventive measures, but in the meantime, they were justified for lack of anything better.[46]

The epidemic crisis of 1881 might have passed into oblivion, but the Quarantine Board in Alexandria never forgot that cholera had been introduced into the Hijaz from Aden. The Board routinely quarantined all vessels calling at that port, the main coaling station for British shipping from East Asia and South Asia. The Foreign Office repeatedly relayed to Alexandria complaints that all passenger and mail ships from India which stopped in Aden were detained at Suez and delayed for long periods. Eventually, the Foreign Office and British directors of the Suez Canal Company as well as British shipping companies became convinced that the Quarantine Board in Alexandria was deliberately obstructionist. Earlier, the board's measures had been concerned primarily with pilgrim ships, which appeared reasonable to them since the assembly of pilgrims at the Holy

Places in Arabia every year "under circumstances likely to engender cholera and to communicate it to other countries" required quarantine measures. Since 1881, however, restrictions imposed on passengers, mail, and cargo from India had become extremely obstructive. In fact, Suez Canal Company directors found it "monstrous" to reject the clean bills of health carried by ships from Indian ports.[47]

As the Quarantine Board continued to restrict shipping from Aden and ports in India moving through the Suez Canal, the Foreign Office grew increasingly impatient. Impatience escalated to exasperation during the troubled months after June, when attacks against foreigners in Alexandria had raised the possibility of European intervention. In late July, a ship from Bombay carrying 500 pilgrims and crew members provided an occasion to stand on principle. Although four pilgrims had died during the voyage "from accidents and chronic diseases," the ship had a clean bill of health from Bombay. The British consul therefore was instructed that the ship should not be detained in quarantine and that he should inform the Egyptian government that Her Majesty's Government expected all Egyptian board members to support British representations.

The handwriting was on the wall. At the next Quarantine Board meeting, the British delegate challenged a ruling renewing quarantine on ships from Bombay and Aden and put it to a vote. In favor of the ruling were France, Germany, Austria-Hungary, Italy, Spain, and Portugal; opposed were England, Greece, and three Egyptian government functionaries. No doubt under instructions from the Egyptian government, the president of the board cast the deciding vote and the motion was defeated. Ships from India henceforth would be able to travel freely through the canal. Within six weeks, Italy had imposed a quarantine on all shipping originating in the Indian Ocean or the Red Sea and traveling via the canal; the age of sanitary reprisals had begun.[48]

The British government's suspicion that quarantine restrictions on British shipping were a form of harassment motivated by Mediterranean jealousy and Egyptian government obstructionism provided justification for first dominating and later controlling the board. At the same time, there was a hardening of British medical opinion on the theoretical basis for preventive practices. Few of the British delegates to the international sanitary conferences, either medical or diplomatic, had ever subscribed to the efficacy of quarantines. British India, particularly, had been traditionally anticontagionist and had suffered, never supported, observance of quarantines. After 1878, the views of medical men in India became more widespread, and the profession in general moved away from the agreement of 1866 on the origin and propagation of cholera. British personnel from India who arrived in Egypt suggested that the prevalence of cholera in India was highly exaggerated, a false impression created by native officers recording deaths who invariably assigned the cause to cholera when in doubt. Paradoxically, the British position retreated from the consensus of 1866 and hardened into a denial of the existence of a specific causative agent for cholera on the eve of Koch's identification of the cholera vibrio.[49]

Of course, the British sanitarians were right to insist that an exclusive and obsessive concentration on exotic imported disease must give way to more enlightened attention to environmental health hazards and chronic, endemic sickness. One disease that aroused no dispute was smallpox; everyone agreed it was contagious and devastating. But universalizing smallpox immunization among the Egyptian population was not a simple matter, for here Muhammad Ali's government encountered strong resistance among the peasants. We turn next to the introduction of vaccination in Egypt.

6

The Conquest of Smallpox: Variolation and Vaccination

The successful campaign for wide-scale smallpox immunization in Egypt, as elsewhere in the nineteenth century, was a triumph for public health for two reasons. First, immunization demonstrated that prevention was simpler and less costly than attempted cures and spared both community and individual the ghastly ravages of the unchecked disease; second, official vaccination programs more than anything else accustomed people to the notion of government intervention in matters of health by providing a service of demonstrable, manifest benefit.[1]

Smallpox had been a recognized scourge in the Middle East since the sixth-century epidemic struck Ethiopian invaders threatening Mecca, which the Koran interpreted as a sign of divine protection for the Prophet's birthplace. The tenth-century Islamic scholar-physician, al-Razi, wrote the classic clinical description of the disease, definitively distinguishing between smallpox and measles. Al-Razi's treatise implied that smallpox was a very common disease in the tenth century and was endemic to the entire Islamic world from Spain to Persia.[2] The terror of plague outbreaks overshadowed smallpox in the Mediterranean for several centuries, but it remained widespread and continued periodically to claim great numbers of victims until the early nineteenth century.

At that time, we are told, 60,000 died of smallpox each year in Egypt. In 1813, John Burckhardt wrote that in the small village of Isna alone, there were 250 deaths from smallpox. Clot claimed that smallpox was the chief cause of child mortality when he arrived in the country in 1825. Another French physician who served in Egypt in the 1840s declared that one-third of the children died of smallpox each year.[3] This estimate appears exaggerated in view of the reported prevalence of other diseases, but smallpox undoubtedly was a major factor in child mortality in Egypt, as it was in Europe before the introduction of vaccination. At the time Jenner wrote his inquiry on the cowpox vaccine, smallpox accounted for one-tenth of the deaths of all children in Sweden and was said to claim one-half of the children who died in London.[4]

Variolation in Egypt

Although Clot recorded the introduction of smallpox immunization in 1827 as his own personal accomplishment,[5] there is evidence that both variolation and vaccination were practiced earlier in Egypt. The loose use of the term "vaccination" generically for all types of immunization has obscured the fact that it was variolation—the transfer of smallpox matter, variola, from one person to another—that stimulated the study of this preventive procedure and launched the science of immunology.[6]

Variolation was an ancient folk medicine practice common in Asia, Africa, and Europe; historians have identified it in China as early as the sixth century of the Christian era and have postulated that it existed in India perhaps even earlier. From China, nomad merchants passed on the practice to Circassians in Georgia, who transmitted it into Anatolia, Armenia, Persia, the Levant, Arabia, Egypt, and the Balkans. The Chinese method, called "sowing the pox," consisted in inserting a scab from a smallpox pustule into the nose. Circassians caused an irritation on the skin and applied a thread soaked with variolic pus to the affected area. A third method, making a wound in the skin with a needle, knife, or lancet dipped into purulent matter from a smallpox sufferer, was widespread. Seventeenth- and eighteenth-century travelers reported the custom of "buying the pox" by such procedures in rural communities in nearly every country of Europe, in the Caucasus, in the Balkans, and among the nomads

of the Arabian and Saharan deserts. The Turkish method of variolation by small incisions or punctures on the upper arm was the procedure imported into England early in the eighteenth century. Italian
physicians had adopted it somewhat earlier, and from those two
countries the practice spread throughout Europe.[7] From such wide
distribution, it appears that variolation arose spontaneously, out of
empiric observation, wherever the need for it occurred.

At the time of the French expedition in Egypt, Napoleon's sur-
geon-general, Dominique Larrey, reported that inoculation with
smallpox was known and practiced up to the sources of the Nile. He
described the procedure, which was called "finishing with smallpox"
("tikhlyseh el-gidry," i.e., *takhilis al-jadari*), as follows. "Midwives
take a small band of cotton, apply it to suppurating smallpox pustules, then place it on the arm of the child they wish to inoculate."
Larrey admitted that the practice usually succeeded but expressed
fear that smallpox so transmitted might become dangerous in adverse
environmental conditions.[8]

Another French observer, who served as medical officer in Upper
Egypt in the 1840s, reported that the nomads of the deserts and
oases vaccinated themselves with cowpox. Acquaintance with this
folk custom might have accounted for their ready response to the government's vaccination campaign; they accepted it with enthusiasm,
he wrote, unlike the fallahin who feared that their children were being
marked for conscription into service. Visitors also mentioned that the
fallahin resisted vaccination, whereas the Bedouin had no objection
to it and even came to town to ask for the vaccine.[9]

Vaccination in Egypt

Muhammad Ali apparently became convinced of the benefits of vaccination as early as 1819, for in that year he ordered his
deputy to introduce vaccination among children in different sectors
of society, to set an example for people who were rejecting vaccination of their children as "contrary to their customs."[10] The next reference to vaccination occurs in connection with the alarming mortality
among Sudanese conscripts for the army. In 1821, the pasha authorized a disbursement for Dr. Dussap, a survivor of Bonaparte's
expedition to Egypt, who had been charged with inoculating the
troops assembled in Upper Egypt against smallpox.[11] Unfortunately,

the Sudanese in Aswan continued to perish of nostalgia, and the people of Upper Egypt forever after associated vaccination with "marking" recruits for military service.[12]

In 1824, Muhammad Ali commissioned several French physicians to travel in the countryside vaccinating children and instructing village barbers in the procedure. The government directed the district supervisor, shaykhs, and "responsible people" of Mansura to facilitate their mission. We know that this tour took place, for six months later, a local official forwarded a complaint that many children vaccinated by the team had broken out with smallpox, and some had died; in response, the government ordered an investigation into the numbers of children vaccinated and those who died. In 1826, it directed the governor of Fayyum to facilitate another French doctor's mission to vaccinate children and to instruct local barbers in the technique. His counterpart in Asyut was requested to forward information on the number of children who had been vaccinated and the number of barbers familiar with the practice.[13]

The creation of a medical corps for the Egyptian armed forces provided a framework for regularizing and extending vaccination among widening circles of the population, Clot wrote. First, all students selected for the new medical school were vaccinated when they appeared for training at Abu Zabel. Next, all men under arms and wives and children living in army camps were vaccinated. Then vaccination was made compulsory on all vessels in the Egyptian fleet, in arsenals, factories, schools, and groups of laborers collected for government work projects.[14]

From the outset, it was acknowledged that village barber-surgeons were the logical personnel to extend smallpox immunization to the countryside. All medical officers sent to the provinces were charged to train the most capable local barbers to continue vaccinating on a regular basis. Later, groups of barbers were called in from the provinces for training at the medical school as well.[15] As an incentive for the correct and conscientious performance of his responsibility, every barber received one piaster for each vaccination that showed a positive reaction after the eight-day incubation period.[16]

Incentive awards might prove effective with village barbers, but winning the cooperation of the villagers themselves posed serious problems. The greatest obstacle was the peasants' fear that vaccination was a subterfuge to "mark" children for future conscription. Another objection noted by one of the provincial medical officers was the repugnance of the fallahin to what they considered indiscriminate mixing of blood drawn from Muslim and Christian arms. Clot also mentioned, among the objections he encountered to vaccination in 1827, the opinion of some religious leaders that immunization flouted the submission to the will of God required of all Muslims.

To break down opposition to vaccination at the outset, Clot prepared a detailed instruction that was sent to the ulama, to provincial governors and village shaykhs, and to all barbers selected as vaccinators. The directive included an explanation of the analogy between cowpox and human smallpox, a description of the signs distinguishing "successful" from "unsuccessful" vaccination, and specific instructions on the preferred technique of vaccinating. Perhaps most important for ensuring continuity in immunizations were detailed directions for collecting and preserving the vaccine.[17]

Following a smallpox epidemic in Shibn al-Kum in May 1836,[18] the Egyptian government undertook to coordinate immunization efforts by creating a central administration to enforce the following regulations: (1) The Medical Council would maintain contacts with medical councils in Europe for the supply and preservation of vaccine;[19] (2) physicians traveling through the country to administer immunizations would teach the technique to surgeons at provincial schools and to barbers designated by officials in towns and villages; (3) surgeons attached to provincial schools and physicians and pharmacists in hospitals and military units should vaccinate all military personnel, cadets, and children in the area who have not had smallpox; (4) vaccinators should keep records of all individuals immunized, and the completed lists should be sealed by the village shaykh, the district supervisor, and the provincial governor and forwarded promptly to the Ministry of Education; (5) surgeons and barber vaccinators would receive one piaster for each successful immunization confirmed as positive, and payment would be made every three months after verification of the records; and (6) all vaccinators were forbidden to receive any compensation from the families of those they immunized.[20]

The wide-scale immunization program envisaged in the directive of 1836 apparently gained momentum only after the establishment of a provincial health service in 1842. In the capital, a permanent vaccination station was established in 1837 at Ezbekiyah Hospital, where women health officers formed the nucleus of a municipal vaccination service. According to Clot, a depot created at the hospital maintained a supply of vaccine sufficient to immunize 15,000 children each year. Twice a week, the hospital held a public clinic where lower-class women brought their children to be vaccinated and women health officer trainees visited private homes to introduce vaccination among the city's upper classes.[21] In 1856, another immunization center for children in Old Cairo opened at the medical school in Qasr al-Ainy, and police advised people to have their children vaccinated only at these two authorized stations.[22]

The first figures on vaccinations reported in the *Gazette* in 1840 do not indicate what share of the total was administered in Cairo. The announcement stated simply that some 61,000 children had been immunized against smallpox between April 1837 and July 1840. In 1848, however, the *Gazette* began to publish monthly reports on the number of children vaccinated at Ezbekiyah Hospital. During a six-month period, the hospital immunized 3,673 children, averaging more than 600 each month.[23]

Resistance to Vaccination in the Provinces

The Egyptian government's immunization program encountered strong opposition from the villagers in the provinces. While the religious scruples mentioned earlier may have fortified an attitude of passive resistance, it was the fear that children were being branded with permanent scars to be dragooned into the army that aroused violent opposition. The Egyptians' opposition to conscription was unappeasable by any possible appeals to self-interest, and vaccination appeared patently linked to the detested troop levies by its resemblance to tattooing; among the common folk, in fact, it was called "tattooing smallpox." Had not the pasha ordered smallpox tattooed on all the conscripts from the Sudan when they were herded into the training camp at Aswan? And did not all the men drafted into the navy have an anchor tattooed on their hand to prevent their escape?[24]

This fear caused the villagers to flee from the doctors, to hide their children, to resist the vaccinators, and sometimes to mistreat them. Charles Cuny, a health officer in Middle Egypt, reported that he had to appeal to the viceroy for protection for barber-vaccinators who were being beaten by the villagers and imprisoned or burdened with corvée duty by authorities.[25] Officials in the provinces who, fearing punishment from above, tried to force the fallahin to bring their children to them for vaccination were bribed to leave the children unmarked. Poor women living on alms would sell their only possessions for a handful of coins to persuade the shaykh to skip over one or two of their children, it was said.[26]

Cuny's experience confirmed that fear of losing their children to government service motivated the villagers' resistance to immunization. While they might be bribed, threatened, or cajoled into allowing vaccination, they would refuse to produce the children for examination the following week. On two occasions, Cuny wrote, he had to flee for his life when angry fallahin, aroused by the rumor that he was going to carry away the children he came to inspect, attacked him, the district physician, and their soldier escort. The village of Dai'rut al-Sharif, which had held out stubbornly against vaccination for three years, finally permitted twelve children to be vaccinated, but when Cuny and the district medical officer returned to check the immunizations, they were surrounded by 200 armed fallahin within minutes after their arrival; only the fortuitous appearance of the governor of the canton with his troops snuffed out the rebellion and allowed the doctors to escape.[27]

The habit of opposition to the government's measures persisted long after the limitation imposed on Muhammad Ali's armed forces removed the threat of mass conscription. Resistance died out gradually as people observed the results of vaccination; when their "marked" children escaped, while the "unmarked" perished in a local wave of smallpox, the mothers' suspicion and fear finally gave way to acceptance. By 1843, one government official could write that women were going spontaneously to village doctors or to city hospitals to have their children immunized, and the Bedouin and Nubians were seeking out traveling vaccinators in their areas.[28]

Years of resistance, however, combined with lack of personnel and supervision, continued to thwart universal immunization, ordered in repeated government directives, well into the 1840s. When Cuny went to Minya as a medical inspector in 1844, he found only two or three barber-vaccinators—of a corps trained earlier by the government vaccinator in Bani-Suayf—remaining to serve the entire province. Even these had ceased vaccinating because the death of their former chief deprived them of a channel for payment from the government as well as their protection from the villagers' hostility.

Cuny's task, which was typical for provincial medical inspectors at that time, called for recruiting and training a sufficient number of barbers as vaccinators for the population and assuring them payment of the premiums provided in government regulations. The viceroy's order (which Cuny claimed he solicited) identifying barbers as sanitary functionaries entitled to the protection of government officials immediately raised the number of volunteers for immunization training. Cuny selected 150 barbers and had them instructed and subsequently tested in vaccination procedures. Each candidate who passed the examination successfully received a certificate of competence, a lancet, and printed instructions to serve as a reminder of the preferred method of vaccinating. When he was transferred to Qina in 1848, Cuny found the people less hostile to government measures, and he was able to revive an active vaccination service by training 214 barbers in a year and a half.

At his next post in Asyut, Cuny claimed that he ran into vested interests. Some of the district physicians used their position to extort favors from village shaykhs and recruited only friends or relatives as vaccinators to serve as buffers against the fallahin. Wishing to maintain the status quo, these individuals combined to oppose him. However, by "corporal punishment visited upon the most recalcitrant vaccinators . . . and by withholding wages from the most mutinous effendis for several days, they were soon brought to reason." Overriding their opposition, Cuny trained 362 barbers who helped to vaccinate more than 30,000 children in less than two years.

Table 2 is a summary of Cuny's record in smallpox immunizations during his six years, from 1844 to 1850, as a medical inspector in Upper and Middle Egypt.[29]

Meanwhile, in 1846, the *Egyptian Gazette* announced that government training for barbers as vaccinators was continuing in other regions of the country. In the coastal provinces, forty-nine barbers were sent to the governorate headquarters for instruction in the theory and practice of vaccination. After completing training, they received a lancet and an admonition to practice their art faithfully in their village when they returned home.[30]

The Russian physician who toured Lower Egypt in 1848 observed that by that time, the immunization campaign was well under way in the delta provinces. According to the chief physicians in the governorates, almost 20,000 children had been vaccinated in three regions during 1847: 2,230 in Qalyubiya, 6,654 in Dakhaliya, 10,674 in Gharbiya—a total of 19,558.[31]

Table 2   Smallpox Immunization under Cuny, 1844–1850

Department	Barbers Trained	Children Vaccinated
Minya	149	11,222
Qina	214	10,953
Asyut	362	31,591
Total	725	53,776

No doubt it took a long time to narrow the gap between the government's announced intention and actual realization of universal smallpox immunization. But the government had a vigilant eye while Muhammad Ali was viceroy. When smallpox broke out in Cairo, he ordered a quarantine on the palaces and schools in and around the city and commanded his deputy to investigate and report back immediately whether the fathers of the ten children who died because of their failure to vaccinate them had been punished or not.[32] According to Clot-Bey, the Egyptian government's smallpox eradication program extended into the countryside between 1827 and 1850 mobilized more than 2,500 barber-vaccinators who were able finally to vaccinate 80,000 children each year.[33]

One Hundred Years of Vaccination and Variolation

In describing the smallpox immunization program he helped to introduce in Egypt, Clot-Bey pointed to the rise in population as evidence of its success. The increase in Egypt's inhabitants from some three million in 1825 to five million in 1850 was directly attributable to reducing child mortality by eliminating smallpox, he claimed.[34] It is difficult to evaluate Dr. Clot's contention because consistent population figures are not available for the first half of the nineteenth century. It appears that he extrapolated from the accepted estimate of two and one-half million people in 1821 and the government census of almost four and a half million in 1846 to arrive at his figures for 1825 and 1850. So many other reports are at variance with those figures, however, that one can only conclude that the population increased between 1825 and 1850. The magnitude and rate of increase for that period are debatable, as is the extent to which the control of smallpox accounted for the rise.[35]

It seems clear, however, that smallpox declined as a principal cause in national mortality bewteen 1825 and 1850, following the extension of vaccination throughout Egypt. In 1861, one of the doctors attached to the quarantine service in Alexandria wrote that vaccination was practiced in all provinces and districts, and he believed that the common people had grasped its importance as a prophylactic measure.[36] At the turn of the century, the physician to the British embassy in Constantinople observed that "Egypt has been comparatively free from smallpox since the introduction of vaccination in 1827."[37]

In spite of apparent administrative neglect in the latter half of the nineteenth century, the system inaugurated in 1827 survived into the twentieth century. When Dr. Sandwith, the first British administrator of the Sanitary Department, assumed his duties in 1884, he found that government physicians administered vaccinations only in the fourteen principal cities and towns of Egypt; the country districts were all "left to their own devices." In areas where the government requirement for vaccination was poorly enforced for lack of personnel, the inhabitant reverted to "native customs." In Buhaira, Fayyum, and Upper Egypt, some "wise man" of the tribe would practice variolation by scratching the patient's skin with a knife, razor, or sharpened ostrich feather. The Bedouin were afraid of smallpox, according to Sandwith, but the Berberin tribes considered it a necessary evil, best gotten over with while young. They inoculated by a method probably learned from their ancestors long ago: "The barber scarifies the skin of the arm or the chest with a razor, dips cotton wool into smallpox pustules and applies it to the wound."[38]

Since the arm-to-arm method of public vaccinators in Alexandria and Cairo entailed the danger of transmitting syphilis and other infections, Sandwith urged standardizing calf lymph vaccinations throughout Egypt, and the National Vaccine Institute was established in 1896 for that purpose. Village barbers continued as the mainstay of the system until recent times, however. Writing in 1905, Sandwith reported that "country barbers are brought up to Cairo from time to time to learn the art, and when they return to their villages they receive one piaster for each successful vaccination; . . . their work is superintended by travelling inspectors."[39]

In 1926–27, one hundred years after the introduction of smallpox immunization, the village barbers and midwives were mobilized and retrained again for a general vaccination campaign; only subsequently were they replaced by medical personnel appointed by a central Ministry of Health.[40] In retrospect, training village barbers as vaccinators seemed a logical choice, but mobilizing women was one of Clot-Bey's most promising innovations. It was his felicitous idea to train women health officers who could function as physician auxiliaries primarily concerned with maternal and child health care.

7

Women Health Officers

While Egypt's School of Medicine followed the pattern of institutional development in Europe, the offshoot foundation of a school to train women health officers ran counter to a strong movement abroad to enforce a "single standard" in medical care by eliminating all traditional practitioners in favor of clinically trained surgeons and physicians. The thrust for registration and licensing in the British and French medical profession referred to in the introduction included a sustained effort to discredit and exclude midwives as an inferior class of practitioner.[1] Yet Muhammad Ali's sponsorship of a school to train women health officers, who would serve primarily as midwives, was a rational response to the persistent problem of underpopulation, which undermined his drive for economic and military power. He could not escape the logic of Dr. Clot's argument that concern for future manpower resources required active promotion of maternal and infant health care by female personnel.

The school was remarkable for two reasons: it was the first government educational institution for women in the Middle East, and it was an unprecedented experiment in drawing into social service women who appeared to be more secluded from public activity than women in any other part of the world. Peasant women labored in the fields with their menfolk, of course, but visitors from abroad rarely became acquainted with the countryside and they consistently remarked on the absence of women in town and city life. In the early nineteenth century, Egypt still had the appearance of a medieval Muslim society, where custom and tradition strictly circumscribed the activities of urban women. All European writers of the time were struck by the universal observance of the customs of veiling and seclusion in separate women's quarters in the home.

Nor was there any popular ideology in Egypt at that time, comparable to the nationalist movements of the twentieth century, to elicit public acceptance of new social roles or responsibilities for women. Women were indeed affected by the viceroy's mobilization of manpower, but their employment by the government was limited to work that could be performed in the home—spinning thread for the textile mills and sewing uniforms for the armed forces during peak periods of conscription. Muhammad Ali himself conceded that the feminine half of the population was virtually inaccessible to his modernization program; in conversation with the British consul general, he declared that the harems were sacred places that strangers could not enter.[2]

But faced by the evidence that disease was undermining the country's potential manpower, the viceroy accepted Clot's argument that women must be trained to help safeguard the health of Egypt's women and children. And in 1832, he approved the establishment of a school for midwives.[3] Muhammad Ali and Egypt were fortunate that Clot adopted a French model for the women's school, for there was a strong tradition in France of official regulation and instruction for midwives dating back at least to the Bourbon monarchy's concern about a population decline during the 1770s. A midwifery school founded in Paris in 1793 drew young women from all parts of France for a yearlong training program that included vaccination and bloodletting techniques as well as the study of anatomy, obstetrics, and pathological abnormalties of childbirth observed in postmortems. By the time Clot accepted an appointment to serve in Egypt, the Paris Maternité was awarding one hundred diplomas every year to young women to practice midwifery throughout the country.[4] The school founded to instruct women medical aides in Egypt is called the Midwifery School in most historical studies because it emphasized obstetrics and infant care.[5] However, this study uses the term *hakima*—"doctoress"—to distinguish the new corps of trained women from the untrained folk midwives, known as *dayas*. The distinction is analogous to that between hakim (doctor), which denoted a calling requiring book learning, and *jarrah* (surgeon), the related skill acquired by apprenticeship to a recognized practitioner.[6] The hakima's six years of training, which included at least rudimentary theoretical science, was an impressive amount of instruction for the majority of women in any part of the world at that time; for the Middle East, it was prodigious.

It should be pointed out that Clot was a strong supporter of Muhammad Ali, and his writings consistently presented the most positive picture possible of the enterprises he engaged in under the viceroy's patronage. Clot tended to minimize the formidable difficulties under which the new medical institutions struggled and to exaggerate their achievements. In this study, Clot's account has been matched against the Egyptian government archives, which often qualify his too-rosy account of the experiment in enlisting women in public health service.

The first and most redoubtable obstacle to developing a women's auxiliary health corps was the problem of finding candidates for training. As custom would not permit women to be treated by male physicians, it was inconceivable that respectable Egyptian parents would allow their daughters to receive instruction from male instructors for a dubious occupation outside the home. Even Muhammad Ali would not risk the consequences of drafting young women by force as he did young men.[7] To break the impasse, in 1832, Clot proposed and won the viceroy's approval for enlisting young slave girls as the first apprentice hakimas. In his request for funds, Clot assured the government that he would instruct the women in their own separate quarters near the military hospital outside Cairo. He reported the initial complement of personnel as follows: eight Sudanese and Abyssinian students, a pair of eunuchs from the palace harem to act as guards, a third eunuch to watch the first two, and a shaykh "of mature age" to teach the women reading and writing.[8]

According to Clot-Bey, within two years the girls had become literate in Arabic, they had acquired the techniques of dressing wounds, scarification, and cupping, and they had mastered the theory in a basic manual of obstetrics. The government then authorized the construction of a small, twenty-bed lying-in hospital adjacent to the students' quarters, where they could gain practical training.[9] When the men's School of Medicine moved to Cairo in 1837, the hakimas also transferred to the capital, and their quarters were annexed to the women's wing of the civil hospital.[10]

By that time, the hakima's course of study had been set at six years, beginning with two years of literacy training to enable them to read simple instructional texts in Arabic. Their four-year special training course consisted of the following: theory and practice of obstetrics; pre- and postnatal hygiene for mothers and care for new-born infants; principles and techniques for dressing simple wounds, treating inflammatory tumors, cauterization, and applying vesicatories or setons; techniques for vaccination, scarification, cupping, and the application of leeches; and identification and preparation of the most common medicines. As they progressed, the best students in the upper classes coached groups in the lower classes; they repeated and explained the classroom instructions and drilled their charges on the subject matter.[11]

Like other students, the apprentice hakimas were housed, fed, clothed, and instructed at state expense. During their two years of basic education, they received a monthly allowance of 10 piasters (about $0.50; one piaster was roughly equal to $0.05), which rose to 35 when they advanced to specialized training. Those students who passed examinations with distinction were appointed assistant instructors and received 75 or even 100 piasters a month. Students who failed examinations were removed from the school and assigned as aides in the Civil Hospital. Since the government was chronically in arrears in paying its employees, the hakima's allowance seems to have been most often an illusory credit on the state. Records indicate that payment of students' allowances usually were a year behind.[12]

In recognition of their mastery of the theory in Dr. Clot-Bey's instructional manuals, students who completed the six-year course of study were awarded licenses to administer vaccinations, perform deliveries, and treat women and children free of charge.[13] Those who did not remain as instructors in the school were assigned to duty in Cairo Civil Hospital and later in health centers in other parts of the country. As government functionaries, they received the rank of second lieutenant, with a salary of 250 piasters ($12.50) a month, and the title of Effendi.[14]

The phenomenon of women in a nineteenth-century Muslim society suddenly entering government service is doubly remarkable in view of the military context in which the hakimas functioned. Their training school was established under the jurisdiction of the Ministry of War, and they were subject to army regulations. It was hardly to be expected that Muhammad Ali's parsimonious administration would extend any preferential treatment to the students because they were women, but there were occasional concessions, like providing a "special" type of bread that was held to be more nutritious than that included in ordinary army fare. The government also approved engaging a bath attendant and hairdresser for the students' free days, stipulating, however, that her monthly pay of 40 piasters was to be deducted from the girls' allowances.[15]

As for clothing, the government apparently outfitted the student hakimas in the prevailing fashion for Egyptian women. Every year, each student received a tarboosh, two linen shirts, pantaloons and a belt, a broadcloth jacket trimmed with silk braid, two cotton dresses, Istambuli shoes, three meters of local muslin for a veil, and a bath towel. Every year and a half, they were issued slippers, a long gown for street wear, and the all-enveloping cloak called *habarah* (the typical feminine attire that Edward Lane sketched so effectively in *The Manners and Customs of Modern Egyptians*).[16]

Since nothing was left to chance or to private initiative in Muhammad Ali's all-embracing bureaucracy, the arrangement of marriages for hakimas became the subject of government communications as the students completed their training. In 1844, the director of the School of Medicine was ordered to submit the names of appropriate spouses among the male medical officers of Cairo for prospective graduates from the hakimas' school. Both husband and wife would be appointed second lieutenants, and the couple would receive a small house furnished at government expense. During the next few years, numerous exchanges of official correspondence dealt with authorizations for marriages.[17]

Generally, the hakimas seemed to remain in senior student status, without promotion in rank or advance in salary, until they were married.[18] This seems to have been in line with official policy to retain the women in government service after marriage as well as to maintain the pool of cheap labor of those still single. In the case of a student hakima who was engaged to marry a man employed in a textile mill, a government communication made this point clear. "You are well aware," it pointed out, "that the purpose of marrying off these women students to students at the School of Medicine is to enable both of them to practice their sciences together," so that the government would benefit from that practice. Since sending the woman medic to a textile factory would not serve that purpose, the government suggested that a more suitable partner be found for her.[19]

In spite of, or perhaps because of, such a heavy-handed paternalism, a serious dearth of students jeopardized survival of the hakimas' school during its early years and gave telling evidence of popular resistance to the idea of young women leaving the home for what was undoubtedly considered a menial occupation. As might be expected, Dr. Clot-Bey gave the impression that the school had a large number of candidates to choose from. "Orphans, the daughters of deceased servicemen or those still on active duty, are given preference in admission," he wrote.[20] The fact seems to have been that only orphans, paupers, and homeless girls volunteered, or were persuaded, to enter training. At least one was a runaway servant, and although the government declared in 1849 that all the students were Egyptian, one suspects that slaves and freedwomen continued to appear among the trainees after that date.[21]

According to Clot, the future of the new school for women was assured after 1836, when a government minister discovered the first Egyptian girls smuggled into the school two years earlier. These 16 (actually only six) students performed so brilliantly in their examinations that the minister immediately gave his blessings to the enterprise, Clot wrote. And the students, rewarded by several days leave in Cairo, returned with sisters, cousins, and acquaintances as candidates for the course, raising the enrollment to 60 students "at one stroke."[22]

Regrettably, government correspondence reveals that the school for hakimas enjoyed no such overnight flowering of popularity; the problem of recruiting students remained serious for many years and sometimes became acute. After its transfer to Cairo in 1837, the future of the school seemed assured: established by official statute and attached to a civil hospital, it could boast 22 students, a French directress of studies, its first Egyptian supervisor, and evidence of effectiveness in the first student instructor, Fatema. But by 1840, both the French directress and the Egyptian supervisor had died, and the number of students had dwindled to 11.[23] Thereafter, numerous communications dealt with the perennial problem of recruiting additional trainees. At the end of 1842, for example, the chief tax collector in Cairo was directed to enlist the local shaykhs in rounding up girls, preferably 12 or 13 years old, to fill the desired quota of 30 students.[24]

Dr. Clot had envisaged a corps of 100 women health officers as the opimum number, 20 to be recruited from Cairo and four from each of 20 provincial centers.[25] However, the government stipulated that the number of students in the school should not exceed 60, a goal that was achieved in 1846 and apparently never exceeded during the nineteenth century.[26]

There is virtually no information about the hakimas themselves— who they were and how they fared while in training or after graduation and marriage. A roster of seven senior students gives the only hint of the student body composition in 1844: Tarnajah, age 25; Khazuran, 23; Tamurhan, 23; Zaynab al-Kabira, 22; Zaynab al-Saghira, 22; Amina bint Husayn, 21; and Nafisa bint Bedawi, 21. The list indicates that, in view of the six-year duration of the course, hakimas must have entered training at 15, 16, or older. Also, the lack of patronymics among the names reveals that the school was acquainted with the fathers of only two of the seven women.[27]

In 1845 the *Egyptian Gazette* published a history of the school for hakimas in which the government not only expressed tolerance toward the enterprise but took some credit for its accomplishments. The *Gazette* specifically mentioned that the government had arranged marriages for the graduates with Egyptian physicians assigned as district health officers so that both man and wife would have close contact with the public. It claimed that local families relied on the women health officers for delivering babies and administering smallpox vaccinations, services they were licensed to perform free of charge.[28] Early in 1847, the *Gazette* also published a situation report on accomplishments among graduates of both the men's and the women's training schools. At this time, the hakimas had reached their peak— 60 students and 5 graduate women medics, all commissioned second lieutenants. One of the graduates, Mahbuba, had been posted to the women's ward at the Civil Hospital in Cairo, and three students were admitted to replace her at the school. An outstandingly clever and accomplished student, Tamurhan, had been assigned as assistant schoolmistress and promoted to first lieutenant. The *Gazette* pointed out that the number of students had risen from 25 to 60 in only recent years and the school was flourishing.[29]

The few European travelers who visited the Egyptian school for hakimas inevitably were impressed. One titled visitor, invited to attend an examination at the school only two years after its founding, professed himself "astounded" that former slave girls had mastered Arabic, as well as practical subjects, in two years. The pupils demonstrated "unbelievable" intelligence in their examinations, he said.[30] Another observer several years later mentioned examinations that required identifying the parts and functions of the body on a skeleton. He was struck by a 14-year-old "Arab peasant girl," he wrote, who demonstrated an "amazing" knowledge of anatomy, physiology, and embryology.[31]

A British physician, whose Victorian sensibilities apparently were affronted, noted only, "Several eunuchs and females are being initiated into the mysteries of the Obstetric Art . . . to attend the ladies of the Seraglie."[32] In contrast, a French traveler about the same time was elated by the spectacle of 30 girls, 12 to 20 years old, who were able to answer questions on the circulation of the blood and the functions of the heart and lungs and could demonstrate the technique of forceps delivery on a dummy. His final judgment was enthusiastic:

> The talent of his [Clot's] midwives had been speedily and universally appreciated by all; they have replaced routine with science and rationality . . . and they have begun to introduce vaccination into the harem. There is even a lying-in hospital where a great number of women among the common people go to be delivered, now that they know they will receive enlightened care there, free of charge, at the hands of women.[33]

The visitor's assertion that "a great number" of women were flocking to the hospital for maternity care demonstrates more faith in Clot-Bey's claims than power of observation. Ironically, there seemed to be no demand for the hakimas' training in midwifery, the skill that Clot-Bey hoped would prove the most likely avenue for introducing rational medical practice among women. He was militantly opposed to the daya and like most of his European colleagues, condemned what he considered the baneful effects of her untrained, irrational, and often superstition-motivated ministrations. To Clot-Bey, the daya was the symbol of the whole complex of "old-wives medicine" with its magic potions, charms, and incantations, and he did everything in his power to undermine her persistent popularity. To make matters worse, his detractors apparently challenged the entire raison d'être of the hakimas and their training school. In 1848, a government communication revealed this serious public relations problem: the students were being criticized for lack of effectiveness, since only three pregnant women had come to the Civil Hospital for delivery within the past two years. As incentives for expectant mothers to patronize the maternity care facilities, the government proposed to grant every woman who entered the hospital for delivery a 30-piaster bonus, plus clothing for her infant worth an additional 12 piasters. It was hoped that this expedient would attract patients and provide practice for the women medics. At the same time, the police were ordered to alert local shaykhs to urge poor women to go to the hospital by pointing out that they would receive these benefits as well as food and care free of charge during their confinement.[34]

In view of the public's consistent indifference to Muhammad Ali's new fangled corps of trained midwives, it appears remarkable that the school for hakimas survived at all. In spite of its precarious existence, however, the school gradually trained a group of women who came to function in a budding public health establishment. Evolution of the women medics' responsibilities was very slow. As long as their school was located near the military hospital, the radius of their operations was limited to the few army-related women who might come to its small maternity care center.

The scope of their activities broadened when the school was annexed to the Civil Hospital in Cairo, where hakimas could practice among indigent women who were treated in the outpatient clinic or among the few who entered the hospital's maternity ward. More important, the hakimas formed the nucleus of a municipal smallpox immunization service. A vaccine depot was set up at the hospital, which maintained a supply of vaccine sufficient to immunize 15,000 children each year. Twice a week, the hospital held an open clinic to which women brought their children to be vaccinated.[35] The first figures on vaccinations reported in the government gazette do not indicate what share of the total was administered in Cairo: an announcement stated simply that 61,000 children had been immunized against smallpox during the period from April 1837 to July 1940. In 1848, the *Gazette* published periodic returns on vaccinations at the Civil Hospital; during a six-month period, the hospital provided free immunization for 3,673 children, averaging more than 600 each month.[36] In addition, as the French visitor had observed in 1845, the hakimas were able to enter private homes to vaccinate the children of the city's upper classes.

The creation of a quarantine station to handle the rising traffic of people and goods in Alexandria in the 1830s eventually raised the problem of detaining women travelers and examining them for evidence of communicable diseases. The problem was delicate since a large proportion of travelers were Muslim pilgrims en route to or returning from Mecca. In 1843, government physicians in Alexandria submitted one of the first requests for hakimas to take over physical examinations of women at the quarantine station as well as treatment of women admitted to the Navy General Hospital. Within that month, two graduate women health officers, Halima Effendi and Zaynab Effendi al-Kabira, were on their way from Cairo to Alexandria.[37] As quarantine stations and hospitals opened in Damietta, Rosetta, and Suez, the need for women practitioners was recognized from the outset, and one or more hakimas were assigned promptly to those establishments.[38]

In the 1840s, student hakimas at the Civil Hospital also were called on to verify the deaths of women in Cairo. This function was extended to the entire country in 1846, when the government enacted procedures for collecting vital statistics. With the penny-pinching attitude characteristic of Muhammad Ali's administration, the government at first refused to fund transportation for the women medics' official rounds in the city but finally authorized the procurement of donkeys, stipulating, however, that the cost of the animals should be deducted from the women's salaries. Regulations issued in 1851 indicate that the graduate hakima who entered the government public health service received a monthly salary of 140 piasters ($7.50), plus allowances for food, clothing, and fodder for her donkey. However, the 400 piasters advanced to purchase the animal continued to be deducted from her salary in monthly installments.[39]

The hakimas' school apparently experienced severe fluctuations in operations and student body after its promising expansion at the end of the 1840s. A French physician who visited in 1862 found only 4 students. He remarked that there had been 17 two years earlier and 10 until only a few months before his arrival but did not explain the decline. The girls entered the school at 12 to 15 years of age and apparently remained in government service after training, for twelve years total residence at the school. They were kept secluded as in a harem and were married off when they left the school or government service. Although French had been dropped from their curriculum, the students' instruction followed the same lines it had twenty years earlier: reading and writing in Arabic and elementary mathematics were preparatory studies; minor surgery, basic physiology, gynecology and obstetrics, and "a little ophthalmology" constituted their specialized training. The professor of midwifery and female ailments, Sitt Tamurhan, the illustrious appointee reported in the *Gazette* in 1847, also lectured to the male students at the medical school. The hakimas received a modest salary from the government for registering births and verifying causes of death among women, but apparently they also received compensation from the families whose infants they delivered. Those in modest circumstances offered only a few coins, while wealthy families presented the hakima with a complete outfit of clothing and one to ten pounds in cash for the delivery and care during the customary 40 days postnatal confinement.[40]

Remarkably, the hakimas and their school survived and continued to function in the Egyptian public health establishment into the twentieth century. The women medics made a substantial contribution to health care in the government's broad-gauge immunization effort, which effectively kept Egypt free from smallpox for the remainder of the nineteenth century. In the provinces, village barbers carried out the major part of the immunization program, but in large cities, the hakimas were indispensable for introducing vaccination among upper-class women who would be slow to utilize the city's free medical facilities. The vaccination of 600 children a month in the Civil Hospital's outpatient clinic was a creditable record for the capital.[41]

In rural areas, the hakima performed a worthwhile function in verifying the cause of death among women, thus contributing to the registration of mortality statistics, a requisite for identifying endemic health problems and planning any program of preventive medicine.[42] Another of the women medics' contributions to public health in the countryside was the introduction of trained and rational practice. In 1872, forty-seven graduates of the hakimas' school were functioning within the framework of a provincial health service established thirty years earlier. About that time, a European physician serving in Egypt under contract with the government acknowledged that the hakima was performing an essential role, since women and children were virtually inaccessible to male physicians. "In this sort of emancipation," he concluded, "Egypt is already in advance of most Western countries."[43]

Unfortunately, although official and public indifference gradually changed to a more positive attitude, the government failed to create any recruiting ground for future trainees by providing general education for women. A Swiss pedagogue who surveyed the Egyptian educational system in 1872 was astonished to discover that the hakimas' training center was the only state school for women in the country.[44] The Khedive Ismail's ambitious expansion of education in the early

1870s included plans for a number of girls' schools, both state and privately sponsored, but they were abandoned in the retrenchment that followed the financial crisis. And yet, the need for women health officers and midwives increased rather than diminished. When the men's School of Medicine reopened in 1856, its previous connection with the hakimas' school was not reestablished, and the practice of obstetrics remained exclusively reserved to women.

Although the fate of the women health officers under the British occupation is beyond the scope of this study, the outlook for further development of the hakimas' potential as a corps of physicians' auxiliaries concerned primarily with infant and maternal health care was dim indeed.[45] Professional nursing, which Florence Nightingale had elevated to the level of a religious vocation and which emphasized hospital-based curative medicine, was introduced in Egypt and was dominated by Europeans. Education for women in Egypt continued to lag and, in keeping with Western disdain for paramedical personnel, the hakima's instruction was not encouraged to rise above the level of a trade school. Ultimately, her public image declined to the level of the daya whom she had been trained to supplant.

8

Urban and Rural Health Programs: Hospitals, Clinics, and Provincial Health Centers

During Muhammad Ali's time, the women health officers functioned in a system of agencies that evolved in response to the government's widening perceptions of national health and medical care requirements. The viceroy's concern to safeguard the health of those groups that were implementing his policies drew his attention, in turn, to military recruits, students in state schools, workers in state industries, and urban and rural communities related to any government activity. A significant step occurred when the Egyptian armed forces demobilized and the medical corps converted to peacetime duty in hospitals, clinics, and dispensaries. Muhammad Ali finally crowned all these efforts by authorizing a system of health centers in the provinces which extended health care to rural villages (see Appendix 1). As these public health agencies evolved, their gradual accumulation of records brought to light facts about Egypt's state of health which observers had identified only vaguely earlier.

Revelations of Conscription

As early as 1831, reports on the ailments prevailing among military recruits began to appear in government communications.

During the early days of conscription for the army, one extraordinary phenomenon went far to explain the desperate measures draftees continued to take to avoid induction into military service: an alarming number of recruits became physically incapacitated and in many cases died of nostalgia, or "homeache." With no apparent organic disorder, many would decline and succumb to "marasmus," or general debility, soon after being displaced from their home villages. The phenomenon appeared among conscriptees from all areas but most frequently among Nubians and Saidis from Upper Egypt. If death did not overtake them in the training camp, they would desert at the onset of illness to die in their home villages.[1] European military surgeons conditioned by two centuries of military service in their own countries were struck by this syndrome. An English officer found it hard to believe that Egyptian young men from 18 to 25 should regard leaving home as a hardship. He found an explanation for the Egyptian's invincible attachment to his village in "the indolent life" afforded by easily cultivated land, the ties of early marriages, and generally limited horizons.[2] Whatever the complex of causes, the Egyptian's fidelity to home and family remained a significant social factor. As late as 1947, public health authorities struggling with the last serious cholera epidemic were hard put to stop a mass exodus of stricken workers from the port cities who wished to die in their home villages in Upper Egypt.[3]

Apparently reflecting reports from the training camps, War Ministry communications indicated that the most prevalent ailments among early recruits were "Egyptian chlorosis" (anemia), scabies, syphilis, and eye disorders. In 1831, the ministry acknowledged a report from Dr. Clot revealing that many draftees had to be rejected because they were boys not more than 14 years old or because they were so emaciated they were unfit for military service. The latter were referred to the regimental physician to determine whether they required treatment for a specific illness; if not, they were assigned to the drummers' corps or other light duty. Recruits suffering from itch and scabies received an extra soap ration and an order to go to the public baths. Those afflicted with syphilis or eye ailments were ordered to report for treatment from the military medical staff and forbidden to seek cures from folk healers.[4] It would be enlightening to see the regimental field hospitals' sick lists, if such exist, at this time.

The two military hospitals established near Cairo and Alexandria in 1827 had begun from the outset to identify Egypt's endemic health problems since they introduced clinical medicine practices: physical examinations, postmortem autopsies, and records of patient traffic. In 1833, Clot submitted to a medical journal in Paris one of his first reports on the army general hospital at Abu Zabel, which he and others described as a model facility capable of accommodating 400 to 900 patients. In a brief summary of the hospital's operations, Clot pointed to the high incidence of ophthalmia and dysentery as evidence they were endemic in Egypt.[5] In 1837, the military hospital gained expanded facilities when it transferred to Qasr al-Ainy, a former palace with an estimated capacity of 1,200 to 1,600 beds.[6] Clot's summary of cases (table 3) treated during 1847 and 1848 indicates the hospital's scale of operations.[7]

The naval hospital in Alexandria, the Mahmudiya, which began operating in 1827 with only 300 beds, served 26,000 men in the coastal artillery corps, infantry and marine battalions, municipal guards, and 11,000 laborers at the Arsenal as well as navy personnel.[8] Visitors thus had the opportunity to observe a broad spectrum of cases. John Bowring[9] reported the following numbers for patients treated at the Mahmudiyah during 1837–38:

Fevers	2,861
Intermittent fever	352
Dysentery '	301
Wounds	760
Ophthalmia	663
Venereal diseases	283
Itch (scabies)	314
Circumcision	188
Total	5,822
Died	426

A few years later, Pruner collected some mortality figures at the Mahmudiya hospital which he used to illustrate the high death rate from "internal ailments," especially dysentery.[10] During 1843 and 1844, the hospital treated the following patients:

	Total	Internal Ailments
Treated	9,685	6,586
Died	402	348 (209, dysentery and diarrhea)

Table 3   Cases Treated at Qasr al-Ainy Military Hospital,
          1847 and 1848

Clinic	No. of Patients	Discharged	Died
Internal Medicine	5,949	5,592	357
Ophthalmology	1,846	1,846	
Surgery	2,387	2,350	37
Venereal Diseases	5,134	5,136 [sic]	
Total	15,216	14,822	394

Health Care in Schools

Since students in all government schools were housed, clothed, fed, and instructed at state expense and all were destined to serve in the armed forces or the civil bureaucracy, the Egyptian government became concerned to safeguard its investment in youth. As early as 1835, inspectors reported poor health conditions in the newly created primary schools: they were makeshift affairs set up in vacant premises without baths or latrines, hence many students were suffering from scabies; their bedding, clothing, and food were completely inadequate for the numbers of students they housed. Within a month, the ministry ordered medical personnel stationed in the provinces to circulate among the village schools to provide care for any sick students.

The following year, the ministry assigned Egyptian medical officers to each governorate specifically to inspect the schools in the area, to treat ailing students, to vaccinate all local children, and to forward an account of immunizations as well as of school conditions in general. Apparently because the need was greatest there, the first four medical officers from Abu Zabel were assigned to provinces in Upper Egypt and authorized to utilize supplies the government had dispatched earlier to local barber-surgeons.[11] Government orders dealing with primary schools in the provinces at that time specifically provided for health facilities. Each school in a provincial capital was to have an infirmary, pharmacy, and health office to treat emergency cases. In 1838, Bowring reported that secondary and special schools he visited had such health offices, each staffed with a physician, an assistant medical officer, a deputy assistant medical officer, a pharmacist, an assistant pharmacist, a clerk, and two orderlies.[12]

Headmasters also were held responsible for the health of their charges and were authorized to treat minor ailments on the premises and send any cases of surgery or serious illness to the nearest hospital immediately. A shortage of personnel made enforcement of the directives theoretical until the 1840s, when official correspondence began to prescribe penalties for government school supervisors' failure to carry out instructions. In 1844, for example, the Ministry of Education notified the Medical Council that the superintendent and the physician at the government school in Giza would be punished with 500 lashes of the *kurbaj* (a whip made of hippopotamus hide) for negligence of their charges' health. At the same time, the district administrative officer (*Nazir*) in Asyut was ordered jailed for ten days for neglecting the health of students under his jurisdiction. The year following, a series of communications reprimanded the superintendent of a primary school in Abu Zabel for failure to maintain clean premises and subsequently sentenced him to six days detention when twenty-two of his student charges who had been sent to the Civil Hospital were found to be suffering from scabies. Queries from the Medical Council regarding health problems among students continued to appear during the 1850s.[13]

Government Workers' Hospitals

Although most schools in the provinces closed during the retrenchment following 1841, numerous factories and cotton mills remained in operation and provided an incentive for founding small civil hospitals or clinics. Not surprisingly, the initiative came from the viceroy, according to the *Egyptian Gazette*. While touring Upper Egypt in 1846, the pasha was struck by the numbers of men employed in government factories, and he ordered small hospitals established in all principal cities to treat sick workers and the local poor people. Each hospital was to be staffed by a resident physician, a pharmacist, and orderlies. The government would supply all furnishings including iron bedsteads, mattresses, blankets, and shirts for the patients. Depending on the number of inhabitants in the district, each hospital would have 10 to 50 beds (table 4).[14]

Table 4   District Hospitals Established in 1846

Governorate or Province	Hospital Site	Beds	Estimated Population
Asyut	Asyut	30	20,000
Asyut	Jirga	10	8,000
Asyut	Tahta	10	
Qina	Qina	50	
Qina	Farshut	10	
Isna	Isna	10	10,000
Minia	Minia	30	12,000
Bani Suayf	Bani Suayf	30	12,000
Fayyum	Madinat al-Fayyum	10	15,000
Dakhaliya	al-Mansura	30	18,000
Dakhaliya	Mit Ghamr	10	
Dakhaliya	Nabaroh	10	
Buhaira	Rashid	50	18,405
Dimyat	Dimyat	50	28,922
Qalyubiya	Qalyub	30	9,050
Qalyubiya	Banha	10	
Gharbiya	Mahallat al-Kubra	30	22,238
Total		500	

Urban Hospitals

As Egypt's forced demilitarization caused the government to shift attention from the armed forces to the general population, the large service hospitals in Cairo and Alexandria converted gradually from military to civil institutions. The Mahmudiyah in Alexandria from the outset had included among its patients the families of men in the navy as well as civilian workers at the Arsenal and their families. Bowring even had claimed in the 1830s that pregnant women sought admission to Mahmudiya Hospital for delivery.[15] Ali Mubarak also referred to civilians in the Government Hospital in Alexandria, including 34 orphans housed there in 1831. The Government Hospital was open to all, he wrote, and in his day most poor people were treated there.[16] A French physician visiting in the early 1860s found the hospital still functioning in Alexandria, but its few inmates were lost in the huge facility built to accommodate 1,200 patients.[17]

In time, civil hospitals were constructed at Rosetta, Damietta, and Suez, but their operation fluctuated according to the degree of official concern with health problems. In Suez, for example, the government built a 900-bed hospital as early as 1847 to handle quarantinable cases among travelers through the Red Sea. We know that the number of travelers through Suez increased and that quarantine practices were regularized after the canal opened, but the government institution declined until new European hospitals built there posed an embarrassing contrast to the decrepit facility and the Khedive Ismail ordered a new building constructed.[18]

Cairo's first civil hospital, the Ezbekiyah, the garrison infirmary that Ibrahim Pasha ordered converted into a free municipal institution in 1837, continued to operate for at least a decade, but by 1861, Qasr al-Ainy was the only hospital serving the capital.[19] A French physician visiting about that time was impressed by the three divisions in the women's wing: one for surgical cases had 47 patients; another for venereal diseases had 26; and a third for internal ailments held 15 women.[20] By Ali Mubarak's time, Qasr al-Ainy had become commercialized; all patients except paupers had to pay for treatment there.[21]

In view of the lack of effective therapeutics for internal ailments during the early nineteenth century, it is not surprising that the majority of patients in Egyptian hospitals from the beginning were surgical cases. The preponderance of external operations like hernias, hemorrhoids, varicosities, and urological disorders also may help to explain the remarkably low mortality rate for surgery reported in Dr. Clot's military hospital statistics at that time.[22] From all accounts, Clot was an exponent of active surgical intervention, and his early annual reports on the medical school described with obvious pride the large number of cases at Abu Zabel which offered the students practical training in modern surgical procedures.[23] Apparently his frequent resort to surgery aroused some criticism, for Clot concluded his annual report in 1833 with a lengthy justification of surgical activism at Abu Zabel hospital.[24] Clot credited the felicitous results of surgery in Egypt primarily to the climate, which was extremely favorable for healing wounds, and to the Egyptians' "imperturbability," which enabled them to undergo serious operations without fear. In 1849, Clot thus reported very low mortality figures for surgery performed during the preceding year: only 37 deaths following 2,837 operations.[25] He also reported the first use of anesthesia in eight cases involving the removal of stones during 1847–48; the *Gazette* identified the first use of ether anesthesia at that time in two cases of cataract removal.[26]

Surgery remained an important function at Qasr al-Ainy hospital even after Dr. Clot retired to France, because the best-known Egyptian director of the School of Medicine, Muhammad Ali al-Baqli, had gained fame first as a surgeon. During the late 1840s when al-Baqli was chief surgeon and Muhammad al-Shafi'i was acting director of the medical school and hospital, the government chronicle carried a number of reports emphasizing the superiority of the new, trained medical practitioners over the old barber-surgeons and bonesetters. In 1847, the *Gazette* carried a long account of the skill of al-Baqli who had successfully set 85 fractured limbs of patients at Cairo's civil hospital over a fourteen-month period.[27]

Another report in the *Gazette* pointed out that patients with a wide variety of internal ailments had found relief and effective treatment in the civil hospital. Invoking the miasmatic theory of disease causation, the *Gazette* declared that the hospital was carrying out its mission to free people from the ills caused by evil-smelling locales, and it offered its readers the hospital director's recommendations for common ailments. Al-Shafi'i cautioned the readers to avoid exposure to seasonal complaints like skin eruptions during the hottest months, and he counseled awareness that fatigue and loss of appetite could indicate "marasmus" (perhaps anemia). He advised seeking treatment for chills and fever (perhaps malaria) and for smallpox, which the government was stamping out by systematically vaccinating 3,000 to 4,000 individuals every month.[28]

Underlying the *Gazette*'s buoyant reports of effective treatment at Cairo's civil hospital was a fact the government organ never acknowledged: except for setting broken bones, vaccination for smallpox, or corrective surgery, the majority of Egyptians avoided hospitals and resisted all attempts to draw them into the government's expansion of medical services. The *Gazette*'s last-mentioned report, however, reveals that government medical officers like al-Shafi'i were turning their attention to fatigue, loss of appetite, and chills and fever—signs and symptoms of chronic health problems more serious than the ailments that called for al-Baqli's surgical expertise.

In the same direction, some of the most promising responsibilities Egyptian army physicians assumed after demobilization were found in outpatient service in free municipal health centers.

Cairo's Free Clinics

As the official *Gazette* would have it, Muhammad Ali's solicitude for the health of the common people moved him in 1845 to create popular clinics in the capital and to charge the Ministry of Education to staff them with trained physicians who would provide free treatment to all, particularly the poor. The medical centers' major responsibilities were to safeguard public health by vaccinating children for smallpox and following up with booster immunizations and by taking appropriate steps to prevent plague outbreaks. The clinics also would treat common ailments like ophthalmia, scabies, syphilis, and dislocated or broken limbs, for which pharmacists at the Civil Hospital would supply adequate and appropriate remedies. Finally, people who were infirm and unable to go to the clinics could summon to their homes the physician on duty at the nearest medical center, according to the *Gazette*. Two years later, another decree spelled out similar responsibilities for municipal clinics in Alexandria: free consultation for all the city's inhabitants; emergency aid to victims of drowning or asphyxiation; dressing injuries; free vaccination; dispatching hakimas to confinement cases; verifying and certifying causes of death; and supervising the cleaning of streets and the premises of buildings.

The first clinics in Cairo were located in four of the most heavily populated quarters, and as demand increased, two additional centers opened in Old Cairo and Bulaq.[29] In 1848, the number of free clinics in Cairo rose to eight, apparently as part of extensive preventive measures adopted to avert the threat of cholera reported in the Hijaz.[30] The available records of outpatient treatment for the period from December 5, 1845, through December 8, 1847, offer evidence of popular patronage of the free clinics at mid-nineteenth century (table 5).[31] For example, the clinic serving the quarters of Khalifiya, Darb al-Jamamiz, and Old Cairo treated twice as many patients as the other centers; in fact, it treated three-fourths of the total number for the entire metropolitan area. These poor, or "popular," quarters were

*Table 5 Outpatient Treatment, December 5, 1845–
December 8, 1847*

Clinic	No. of Patients
Jamaliya and Bab al-Shar'iah	3,053
Darb al-Ahmar and Qaysun	4,346
Abdin, Bulaq, and Ezbekiyah	4,738
Darb al-Jamamiz, Khalifiya, and Old Cairo	9,331
Total	21,468

eager to take advantage of outpatient medical care, in contrast to their aversion to hospital care.

The limitations of diagnostic procedures at that time also are indicated in the breakdown of ailments treated.[32]

Ailment	No. of Cases Treated
First aid	198
Scorpion bites	327
Infectious diseases	456
Trauma or shock	534
Smallpox	607
Scabies	766
Venereal disease	958
Internal ailments	1,277
Injuries	3,111
Eye disorders or ailments	13,234
Total	21,468

There is no record of treatment for the ailments listed, except in the case of eye disorders, for which, as we shall see below, the government established special clinics.

Although the staffing pattern laid down by the government—a chief physician, assistant physicians, a woman auxiliary health officer, and orderlies—appears ample theoretically, it is not clear that trained personnel were available at all times.

Ophthalmological Clinics in Cairo

In the same way that the hakimas declined, ophthalmological clinics founded in the 1840s seem to have disappeared before the twentieth century. When we recall that almost two-thirds of the complaints for which people in Cairo sought relief at the municipal medical centers were eye ailments, it was logical for the government to sponsor clinics specializing in ophthalmology. Afflictions of the eye had figured routinely and prominently in historical and travel literature on Egypt from the fourteenth through the nineteenth century.[33] As noted earlier, Edward Lane's vade mecum for modern Egypt included simple remedies for the "Egyptian ophthalmia" that inevitably afflicted visitors to the Nile valley. Since the mechanism of infection was not yet understood, medical as well as lay observers in the nineteenth century assigned the cause of ophthalmia to dust, sand, sun glare, and suppression of perspiration during the chill of cool, humid nights.

The etiology of eye infections had not advanced appreciably beyond those views at the time the School of Medicine opened, and the study of ophthalmology was not included in the curriculum at the outset. Several graduates elected ophthalmology when they went abroad for specialized training, however. One of the first, Muhammad Ali al-Baqli, who later became director of the medical school, wrote a doctoral dissertation on ophthalmia at the Faculty of Medicine in Paris in 1837. In it, he described the etiology, symptomatology, course, duration, and sequelae for several types of ophthalmia common in Egypt.[34]

Another member of the graduate medical student mission, Mustafa al-Subki, specialized in ophthalmology and became the instructor in that field when he returned to the School of Medicine in 1838. In 1847, two additional medical school graduates returned from ophthalmological study in Austria, and the government was able to open three eye clinics in Cairo: one at Qasr al-Ayni directed by Mustafa al-Subki, another in al-Salibiya under Husayn Awf, and the third in al-Jamaliya headed by Ibrahim al-Dasuqi.[35] The *Gazette* occasionally published figures on the number of patients treated at these clinics which revealed that at that time the great majority of persons treated by medication were suffering from chronic trachoma or conjunctivitis. An equal number of patients underwent corrective surgery for eyelid abnormalities that are often sequelae of severe or prolonged infection.[36]

In the meantime, the study of ophthalmology had been incorporated into the medical school curriculum around 1840 when Shaykh Ahmad Hasan al-Rashidi completed a translation of Julius Sichel's classic textbook on the subject. A sufficient number of graduate medical students specialized in ophthalmology to maintain some continuity in teaching and practice.[37] And yet, like the municipal health centers, Cairo's ophthalmological clinics disappeared.

The Provincial Health Service

If Egypt's capital lost its clinical facilities, what of the countryside where the great majority of Egyptians lived? During Ismail's viceregency, Ali Mubarak paid tribute to Muhammad Ali's pioneering efforts to improve environmental health conditions and to provide medical care for the rural people in Egypt. Before Muhammad Ali's time, it had been rare to find a doctor in the villages, and medical treatment was left to barbers and old women, he wrote. During his own lifetime, however, every governorate had a hospital, a pharmacy, several physicians, and physicians' assistants. Stagnant pools were filled with earth and villages were cleaned up regularly. Ismail had resumed Muhammad Ali's public health reforms, Mubarak claimed, but he was hard put to cite any evidence besides widening and cleaning the streets of Tanta, where epidemics recurred regularly during the influx of visitors for religious festivals.[38]

As the majority of Egypt's population remained rural well into the twentieth century, the fate of the provincial public health service launched when Muhammad Ali shifted the military medical corps members to civilian duties is of significance.

Four factors facilitated the extension of health care personnel to the countryside: (1) Muhammad Ali's will to protect the health of government personnel who were implementing his policies; (2) the influence of European public opinion, which held graveyards, stagnant pools, and "filth" responsible for disease; (3) the quarantine administration in Alexandria which provided European personnel trained in quarantine practices and recordkeeping; and (4) the availability, albeit in limited number, of trained Egyptian staff, thanks to Clot's schools. The chronic shortage of trained personnel made extending public health services impossible until Egyptian members of the military medical corps returned from Syria for demobilization. The Quarantine Board in Alexandria first submitted plans for expansion which called for sending European and Egyptian physicians to key points in Lower Egypt to collect information on prevailing diseases and mortality and to enforce quarantine measures in case of communicable disease outbreaks.[39] Clot-Bey, however, saw the provincial health service as a channel for introducing preventive sanitary measures, active treatment of illness, and widespread immunization for smallpox. These aims were felicitously combined when decrees issued in 1842 and 1847 created a medical-sanitary service for all the provinces of Egypt. Each governorate capital was to have a resident European chief physician and a European deputy responsible to the quarantine administration in Alexandria; a European pharmacist would dispense medicines gratis to local inhabitants and supply physicians in the districts. Egyptian district medical officers would carry on routine health monitoring, sanitary policing, reporting, and medical services at the village level.[40]

Aside from quarantine responsibilities, which would arise only in the event of an outbreak of plague or cholera, the district medical officer faced a staggering list of duties and reporting requirements for an area of 25 to 30 villages.[41] Under the heading of medical services, he was charged with vaccinating all nonimmunized residents in the area, treating the sick, investigating prevailing illnesses to determine whether they were "sporadic" or epidemic, and investigating livestock diseases. In addition, he was to register all births and verify and record the cause of deaths in each community. The district medical officer was also required to recommend improvements in environmental conditions: removing cemeteries from towns and villages, draining swamps and pools of stagnant water, leveling heaps of refuse, and transferring from inhabited areas all industries considered nuisances like tanneries and brick or pottery kilns. Regulations also called for him to monitor the cleanliness of streets, markets, bazaars, inns, public baths, and private residences; to carry on regular inspection of comestibles; and to prohibit the sale of unripe or spoiled meat, fish, or produce.

Personnel for the provincial health service came from the military medical corps, which in 1849 numbered 421 men: 60 European physicians and 44 pharmacists, and 255 Egyptian physicians and 62 pharmacists. Clot admitted that the proportion of medical personnel to the population was still very low; some 400 physicians and pharmacists for four million people provided only a ratio of one per 10,000, whereas in countries like France the ratio was one per 1,000. However, he pointed out, this small number of Egyptian and European personnel had provided medical staff for the army, navy, schools, factories, shipyards, and physicians in each of the ten districts of Cairo. At least three times the number of medical officers then available was required for the country at large and the only answer was educating more Egyptian physicians. In the meantime, he proposed training village barbers as paramedical personnel. A three-month course of instruction including the elements of anatomy, physiology, public and personal hygiene, and emergency treatment for wounds, contusions, scorpion bites, asphyxiation, and drowning would make the local barber-vaccinator a useful auxiliary to the over-burdened district medical officer.[42] In his innovative plan to create paramedical personnel, as in training hakimas, or "doctoresses," Clot was ahead of his time.

The provincial health service in operation

There are few references to the Egyptian provincial health service in foreign observers' writings. In 1844, when government records indicated that 41 Egyptian physicians were serving in the provinces, Dr. Perron, who succeeded Clot as director of the medical school, casually mentioned a "sanitary service." By the end of the decade, the service had become well established and regularized, and a European visitor applauded the "civilizing influence" of a network of European provincial physicians who supervised a program of vaccinations and other health services.[43]

Hekekyan-Bey, the former director of the School of Engineering, found a functioning district health service during a trip through Upper Egypt in 1849. He particularly praised the public baths at Tahta and a prison recently constructed in Asyut. Well-built, spacious and airy, boasting baths and an infirmary, "it is the only prison in Egypt designed to prevent typhus," Hekekyan wrote. The town of Asyut and its hospital also were clean and well maintained, and the bazaar and warehouses were laid out better than any in Cairo or Alexandria. Hekekyan found sanitary regulations conscientiously observed in Manfalut as well; thoroughfares were kept clean, and the market was under strict surveillance. In conversation with the district medical officer, Hanafi Effendi Abd al-Tawab, Hekekyan confirmed his own observation that local government officials' cooperation was essential to enforce sanitary regulations in the provinces. Both men contrasted the scrupulous observance of public health regulations under officials named by Muhammad Ali with the indifference of functionaries who had taken office since the pasha's demise. The deputy governor of the province and the nazir of Manfalut "will not listen to any recommendations about cleanliness, public health, and so on," Hanafi Effendi told Hekekyan.[44]

The inability of Egyptian district physicians to function effectively without active support from local government officials appeared frequently in observations recorded by a Russian physician, Artemy Rafalowitch, who wrote a highly informative description of the provincial health service in 1847–48. The Russian government had commissioned Rafalowitch to investigate the trustworthiness of Egypt's quarantine administration, and he traveled the length of the Nile up to Wadi Halfa to observe public health conditions.[45] Rafalowitch's observations on the provincial health service operations are important as he shared neither French partisan admiration nor British hostility toward projects sponsored by Muhammad Ali. He visited the capitals of governorates in Upper, Middle, and Lower Egypt, and he visited some of the leading towns in districts where the seat of the governorate was not its principal city. His reports identify the agricultural specialization of the area, the principal industries, the number of medical personnel, and whether or not they were supported by a contingent of "sanitary police." He also noted the existence of civil hospitals established primarily for workers in various government factories, as table 6 indicates. His observations also provide a useful comparison with the theoretical and compendious description of Egypt's provincial public health establishment which the director of the quarantine service submitted to the first international quarantine conference in 1851; the table of organization is presented in Appendix 2.

Table 6   Governorate Health Units, 1847–48

	Governorate	European Physician	Egyptian District Physicians	Hospital Site
Upper Egypt	Bani Suayf and Fayyum	Chief—Castelli	5 1	Bani Suayf
	Minia	Chief—Folso	6	Minia
	Asyut	Chief—Capograsso	9	Asyut
	Qina Isnà	(Chief—Cuny)	6	Qina
Lower Egypt	Qalyubiya	Chief—Allasi	5	Qaliub
	Minufiya	Chief—Mariani and deputy	10	Shibn al-Kum
	Gharbiya	Chief—Cambi	?	Mahallat al-Kubra
	Dakhaliya	Chief—Colucci	14	Mansura
	Buhaira	Chief—Farfara	12	(Shibr-al-Khit)

Rafalowitch must have been acquainted with Egypt's sanitary regulations, for he checked each provincial city and district town for the following: location of graveyards in relation to habitation, cleaning and disposal of refuse from the streets, squares, markets, and bazaars; progress in filling stagnant ponds and covering the open drains of mosques' fountains for ablutions; leveling mounds of refuse; inspection of foodstuffs; and enforcement of the mandatory death certificate before burial. He was very critical of Muhammad Ali's government, and he observed repeatedly that the worst social conditions appeared to exist in those villages that were personal estates of the ruling family. He tried to appear unannounced in towns and villages, he wrote, so as to inspect the communities in their normal state, rather than cleaned up for an official visitor.[46]

Surprisingly, Rafalowitch reported in most cases fair, and in some cases admirable, progress toward improving and maintaining good sanitary conditions in governorate capitals and in some principal towns. In Minia, Qina, and Asyut, the streets were swept twice daily, the bazaar was kept clean, inspection of comestibles was enforced actively, and the death certificate requirement strictly observed. Christian and Muslim cemeteries, and in the case of Qina, pottery kilns and slaughterhouses as well, were distant from the city. Mina had a "decent" government pharmacy and a well-built civil hospital, although all the beds were empty.

The Russian physician found sanitary policing neglected in Bani Suayf and Fayyum provinces in spite of the presence of a European and an Egyptian resident physician and a contingent of military police; the people simply refused to carry out their orders to clean the canals and sweep the streets. But Mahallat Al-Kubra was found to be the best-maintained city in Lower Egypt after Alexandria; streets were amazingly clean, inspection of comestibles was carried out rigorously, drains from the mosques were being covered over, and most pools of water had been filled in. He also reported the streets, baths, and bazaar in Qalyub and Mansurah were kept in good condition under the chief physician's watchful surveillance.

In Minufiya, Rafalowitch observed a similar situation wherein the principal city, Minuf, with one resident Egyptian medical officer, was clean and well maintained while the seat of the governorate at Shibin al-Kum, with two European physicians, appeared extremely lax in enforcing sanitary regulations. He ascribed this situation to the *mudir*'s (governor's) hostility toward sanitary measures as well as to the European physicians' half-hearted efforts. Rafalowitch found the reverse in Buhaira province: the capital, Shibr al-Khit, a small village with 1,800 people and a resident European physician, was clean and well maintained, while the principal city, Damanhur, boasting a population of 20,000, a big cotton mill, and a resident Egyptian medical officer, appeared very neglected. In explanation, he suggested that the Egyptian medical officer received no cooperation from the local authorities because half of the city and the surrounding area belonged to Said Pasha.[47]

Local authorities' support and cooperation in carrying out the medical officers' recommendations appeared to Rafalowitch to be the key factor in the provincial health service operations. According to him, the hospital in Mahallat al-Kubra was the only one in which most of the beds were occupied; in other hospitals, the beds stood empty the year around except when local workers were ordered to report to the hospital. In addition to workers in the government factory, Mahallat al-Kubra's hospital admitted poor people among the local inhabitants; in other provinces, the mudirs did not permit them to enter the hospital.

Rafalowitch offered no explanation for this contravention of government regulations, but another traveler asserted that each governorate was obliged to pay the expenses of hospital care for the inhabitants from local administrative funds and to reimburse the central government for pharmaceutical supplies dispensed. Hence, he said, although the care of the poor theoretically was free, "there is not a soul who, having had recourse to the government doctors, has not been persuaded by the local administration, through lashes of the kurbaj, that he is rich enough to pay both the physician and the pharmacist." Neither the physician nor pharmacist received anything more than his salary, but the local treasury thus "recovered the money the central government snatched from it."⁴⁸

Rafalowitch and other observers also expressed the belief that the people shunned the personnel of the entire public health service because they represented the central authority and thus were viewed with suspicions.⁴⁹ "It is impossible to convince the fallah," Rafalowitch wrote, "that this arrangement of district medical officers, who must treat patients free of charge and dispense medicines to them at government expense, is not a camouflage for some trick to extract money."⁵⁰

Deep mistrust of the government continued to thwart the efforts of medical officers to reach the rural population in the provinces. In 1864, Lady Lucie Duff-Gordon mentioned meeting the Egyptian government physician from Qina, Ali Effendi, who although the son of a peasant in Lower Egypt, spoke both French and Italian because he had studied medicine in Pisa. The local people would have nothing to do with him, however, she wrote, because, they said, "He is a Hakim Pasha, he will send us to the hospital at Kena, and there they will poison us." Duff-Gordon did not make a connection, but she recorded at the same time that Ismail had reinstituted military conscription and the Saidis were up in arms about the draft.⁵¹

Although the people still avoided it, a visiting physician found a provincial health center functioning in Lower Egypt in the 1860s. It occupied a two-story building with the ground floor divided into offices and a well-organized laboratory run by an Egyptian chief pharmacist. The upper floor consisted of six rooms, each containing three to ten beds for patients. The rooms were sparsely furnished with iron bedsteads equipped only with a mattress and three thin blankets. The health center was under the direction of an Italian chief physician, Andrea Martini, who stated he had fourteen Egyptian physicians under his supervision in the districts. Few people availed themselves of the clinic's free facilities, the French visitor observed; only 23 patients appeared during his stay in the town, and he felt the center could accommodate many more.[52]

If we examine the common ailments listed and enumerated by War Ministry communications, military and civil hospital returns, clinics, and health centers for the 25 or so years following the first reference in 1831, three major afflictions stand out: trachoma, then mistakenly identified as "ophthalmia"; ancylostomiasis, or hookworm disease, which Griesinger incriminated as the cause of the severe anemia called "Egyptian chlorosis"; and "dysentery," the catchall term then applied to diarrhea caused by any gastrointestinal infections or infestations. With additions made possible by more accurate diagnosis (e.g., bilharziasis), the list has remained depressingly the same for the past 150 years. Basic improvement in sanitation was the countryside's most urgent health need, but it was overlooked during the headlong expansion of irrigation, which made possible Egypt's dramatic agricultural development.

9

The Continuing Evolution of Concepts of Disease and Medicine

We return to the question, were the medical institutions and technologies introduced by Muhammad Ali adaptable to local circumstances or did their Western origins make them inappropriate for Egypt? We have seen that a public health service was created in Egypt gradually and piecemeal, by Muhammad Ali's responses to specific problems. The viceroy first became alarmed about the number of military draftees who were unfit for service or who perished in the training camps, and he charged Dr. Clot to organize a military medical corps. In 1827, Clot, reasoning that European contractees would always be inadequate for the huge army Muhammad Ali had in mind, founded a medical school to train Egyptian physicians. Devastating cholera and plague epidemics in 1831 and 1835 further alarmed the viceroy, and he commissioned the European consuls to organize a quarantine service in Alexandria. Around 1836, Clot initiated a vaccination service by assigning Egyptian medical officers to the districts where government schools were located. In 1841, an outbreak of plague aroused Muhammad Ali's concern for ensuring the marketability of Egyptian commodities abroad, and he issued a comprehensive sanitary code for Alexandria. The year following, he united the agencies of the military Medical Council in Cairo and the Quarantine Board in Alexandria in a general urban and provincial health service. In 1846, the viceroy ordered civil hospitals established in all districts where government factories existed. A final decree in 1846 confirmed the provincial health service's functions and extended Alexandria's comprehensive sanitary code to cities, towns, and villages. Appendix 1 charts the ramification of these agencies from the original establishments of the School of Medicine and the Quarantine Board.

Although the *Egyptian Gazette* consistently reported these initiatives as evidence of Muhammad Ali's solicitude for the people, it is clear that he was motivated by reasons of state: concern to ensure the battle readiness of the armed forces and the free movement of Egyptian products in the world market, the two major instruments of his drive for power and wealth. Like the liberation of the serfs and the zemstvo medical system in Tsarist Russia, Egypt's small network of urban and rural health centers was a ruler's rational response to the demands of growing industrialization in the world and the expansion of international trade. Thus fortuitously created, did Egypt's public health establishment serve to protect and promote the health of the people?

Quarantine

Since maritime quarantines were strongly contested as efforts to contain communicable disease, it is appropriate to look again at claims for quarantine's efficacy in preventing plague epidemics. The great historian of plague, Jean-Noel Biraben, has proposed that the Ottoman Empire's adoption of the European maritime quarantine system in 1841 was the single most important factor in the elimination of plague from the entire Mediterranean basin. It is difficult to support unequivocal claims for the elimination of plague by maritime quarantines alone, for they were never observed universally. Yet plague mysteriously receded from Egypt for 55 years after a series of epidemics between 1834 and 1844.

To clarify the disappearance of plague from Egypt after 1844, we can draw comparisons from the voluminous literature on plague in Western Europe. In addition to allegedly more efficient quarantine procedures, epidemiologists and historians have suggested four possible explanations for plague's withdrawal from Western Europe after the seventeenth century: a gradual development of immunity to the bacillus among people subject to contact with plague-bearing rats and fleas; a gradual development of general resistance to disease gained from improved nutrition; improvements in housing, which separated flea-bearing animals from human habitation; and changes in the dominant rat and flea species.[1]

In the case of Egypt, the fourth factor may explain the establishment of a locus for plague in Upper Egypt in the twentieth century.[2] None of the other factors satisfactorily explains the disappearance of plague in Egypt after mid-century, however. A gradual development and, conversely, gradual decline of immunity may explain periodic fluctuations in epidemic outbreaks, but, as Pollitzer pointed out, immunity has been only relative and temporary. As for improved nutrition, housing, and general living standards, it is not clear that the masses of poor Egyptians enjoyed a higher level of living after 1844 than they had at the outset of the century. Egypt's population increased markedly during the second half of the century primarily because of the imposition of order in the country and the elimination of compulsory military service. Contemporary accounts indicate that because of growing population pressure in urban and seaboard communities, poorer Egyptians' living conditions probably deteriorated. Reports on housing in port cities at the time of the cholera epidemic in 1883 describe conditions that were as bad as, if not worse than, those of a half-century earlier.[3]

Quarantine procedures thus remain the most likely explanation for the disappearance of plague from Egypt. As we have seen, stringent isolation measures in schools, hospitals, army barracks, and other government installations during the plague epidemic of 1834–1836 did protect those groups that otherwise might have suffered mass mortality. In the same way, the combination of detention and isolation procedures at the Ottoman ports of debarkation as well as at ports of entry in Egypt—defied, evaded, and imperfectly applied as they were—must have intercepted rats and fleas and prevented the entry of infection.

Although their criteria for susceptible merchandise were arbitrary and illogically applied, Mediterranean quarantine authorities were justified in suspecting that cargo could be a source of infection. The chief threat came from commodities harboring plague fleas acquired in rat-infested warehouses or transport vessels. Trade in grain and cotton has historically been the most important vehicle for propagating plague.[4] And since recognizing the mode of transmission is more useful for disease control than identifying the causative agent—witness Snow's demonstration that cholera is primarily a waterborne disease almost thirty years before the discovery of the cholera vibrio—some procedures followed by quarantine administrators were sound practice, even if based on faulty theory.[5] Exposing suspected goods to strong sunlight in the Mediterranean lazarettos was reasonable. And although the methods were rule of thumb, the use of sulfur fumes for fumigation also was rational, as was the later use of chlorine gas and heat for disinfection, especially in Russia, where plague continued to break out periodically.[6]

As for cholera, the much-disputed maritime quarantine system was relatively effective in protecting the country from disease invasions *if* rigorously enforced. As we observed in the accounts of cholera epidemics in 1831, 1849, 1865, and 1881, in every case, it was the failure to require detention and isolation of suspected carriers at the outset which permitted the disease to spread throughout the country.

At the time Muhammad Ali sought expertise from European states to combat the diseases that threatened Egypt's manpower, Western medicine and public health were in a state of transition. Far from enjoying superiority in theory or practice for dealing with infectious disease, the Western world wrestled with mounting community health problems arising from runaway urbanization, accelerated transport, and expanded international trade. Everyone is familiar with the appalling health conditions in overcrowded port cities and factory towns, which remained neglected for a quarter of a century until Victorian reformers found a solution in the technology of sanitary engineering.

The importation of alien infectious diseases was more aggravating in its complexity. In the Americas, efforts to contain cholera were complicated by recurring yellow fever outbreaks, while Europe and Mediterranean Asia and North Africa were frustrated by the seemingly futile quarantine practices inherited from the fourteenth-century Black Death. In this prebacteriological era, the medical profession was baffled in attempting to identify common causes in epidemics carried by vastly different, and still unsuspected, agents: human beings, polluted water, mosquitoes, rats, and fleas.

Since physicians were powerless to cure or prevent outbreaks of the killer diseases, state authorities attempted to reduce panic, maintain order, and contain the epidemics by any action possible. Local governments revived old municipal boards of health or created new ones ad hoc; in some cases, the central government created a national agency to advise and coordinate action. Historians attribute Western nations' first faltering efforts to establish public health agencies to their traumatic experience with cholera epidemics.[7] As each crisis passed, the institutions languished and sometimes disappeared, until another epidemic aroused renewed official action. The pattern of alternating initiatives and neglect, with frequently appalling losses of life, demonstrated that crisis-generated action was insufficient; effective health protection required consistent effort with at least minimal government funding and administrative support.

But a wave of political liberalism following the repudiation of monarchical rule in France, reinforced by the success of economic liberalism in England's industrial transformation, rejected government intervention in society's affairs. The British government anxiously sought defense measures against cholera which would not require any increase in local taxes, while economic unrest added fear of possible uprisings to their planning for epidemic control. In 1832, France had just undergone a revolution; a cholera epidemic was rumored to be a royalist poison plot to undermine republicanism, and physicians calling on patients wore workers' clothing to avoid being mobbed as suspected poisoners. Popular violence flared quickly, and the Paris municipal council was helpless to prevent city scavengers from upsetting and destroying new covered night soil wagons introduced as a sanitary measure but seen as an intrusion into familiar working habits. In both countries, the lower orders fought hand-to-hand battles with police who tried to transport cholera victims to emergency hospitals set up during the epidemic. Regulations introduced by the British Board of Health provoked so much opposition that the board was allowed to expire, and the *Times* celebrated its demise by observing, "The British nation abhors absolute power. . . . We prefer to take our chance of cholera and the rest than be bullied into health."[8]

Smallpox Vaccination

In this connection, it is instructive to compare Egypt's relatively successful efforts to control smallpox with those of her two mentor states, England and France. In both countries, the government's immunization programs proceeded by fits and starts. Although Jenner's own nation made a promising beginning early in the century, specialists with a vested interest in inoculation soon led a broad front of antivaccination resistance. Libertarian sentiments reinforced the opposition to the mandatory Vaccination Act passed in 1853, and it was not enforced until a serious smallpox epidemic moved Parliament to approve funds for its implementation in 1871. France was even more laggard. Napoleon had attempted to reach the entire population when he introduced Jennerian vaccination in 1801; local government agencies trained health officers and midwives in the approved vaccinating technique, supplied rural practitioners with vaccine gratis, and manned free vaccination centers in municipalities. After 1815, however, frequent changes in administration combined with professional and popular hostility to defeat immunization programs, and the French government did not pass a compulsory vaccination act until 1902. In the meantime, the results of abandoning the Napoleonic model of military efficiency became evident in the Franco-Prussian War of 1870–71, when smallpox removed about 20,000 French troops from action while Prussian forces remained immune through vaccination.[9]

Comparison of the experience with smallpox vaccination in England, France, and Egypt suggests that in all three countries demonstrable good results did not automatically carry conviction. Facts do not necessarily speak for themselves; they are examined and interpreted to conform with the assumptions and concerns of the examiner.[10] For different reasons, during the nineteenth century, a large proportion of the population in all three countries resented or were mistrustful of government officials. All were suspicious of functionaries who most often represented either the detested tax collecting or police operations of government. But ideology—nineteenth-century individualism and libertarianism—played a stronger role in opposition to vaccination in France and England than alleged Muslim fatalism did in Egypt. Once the threat of military conscription had passed, Egyptian resistance to vaccination gradually disappeared.

Two positive factors facilitated the success of Egypt's immunization program. First, the use of local barbers as paramedics allowed the village people a certain degree of control and participation in the effort. But most important was government support of the program, of the health officers' "outreach" campaign, their monitoring of the results and enforcing accountability at the community level. As was noted earlier, when local functionaries no longer feared retribution from above, when they subverted funds and failed to make incentive payments to vaccinators, or neglected record-keeping, the program ground to a halt. These observations were confirmed by the WHO-sponsored program to eliminate smallpox in the 1970s when medical teams offered monetary incentives for immunization monitoring as they tracked the disease to its final hiding places in the villages of India and the tribal camps in Somalia. What has been overlooked in hailing the program's success as a Third World triumph is the half-century preceding, during which the Western world became resigned to public health administration: decades of compulsory vaccination of schoolchildren, public health bureaucrats distributing vaccine, and border functionaries all over the world examining yellow vaccination cards carried by obedient travelers.

Western-trained Professional Physicians

A third innovation imported from Europe was hospital-based clinical training for the aspiring professional physicians at Egypt's School of Medicine. Acquiring a European-style medical school at exactly the time when Western nations were transforming the character of medical practice from an aristocratic and scholarly calling to an autonomous profession should have been serendipitous for Egyptian physicians. But few among future generations of Egyptian medical practitioners would enjoy the European professional prerogatives because they evolved in the process of socioeconomic change accompanying industrialization, a process in which Egypt did not participate.[11]

European powers' intervention to remove Muhammad Ali from Syria in 1841 and ensure his capitulation to the Ottoman sultan had two important results: reduction of the Egyptian armed forces to 18,000 men and compliance with the Anglo-Ottoman trade conventions of 1838 which granted British merchants the right to engage in free trade throughout the Ottoman Empire. The trade agreement meant the end of Egyptian government export monopolies and the removal of any protection for native industries. To escape the consequences of his loss of monopoly control over the land, the viceroy granted large areas to family members and court favorites, creating a semifeudal system in private landownership. The modernization of agriculture for export brought about expansion of irrigation, development of transportation and communications, and establishment of financial links with the international community, which eventually led to the accumulation of a public debt. All of the service sectors of the economy—commerce, transport, and finance—were geared primarily to moving the cotton crop, with no spillover of investment into other sectors and little stimulus on social development.

The collapse of Muhammad Ali's ambitions for political and economic autonomy and the reduction of the armed forces removed the driving force in development, and it was taken up later by foreign capital and foreign enterprise. European development of Egypt's resources had two major flaws. First, development followed the path of least resistance—extension of irrigation and expansion of cotton exports. No attempt was made to diversify the economy by creating new forces of production in other fields. Second, the influx of foreign entrepreneurs, technicians, and professional people inhibited the development of native entrepreneurs and technicians and the incentive for education at all levels—mass, technical, and professional. Except for the Schools of Engineering and Medicine, the schools founded under Muhammad Ali were allowed to decline. The Khedive Ismail attempted to revive education by encouraging community support of primary schooling, by patronizing professional training, especially at the medical school, and by promoting secondary schools, the essential preparation for any higher education. But funds for education were among the first to be cut when Egypt's national budget came under Dual Control in 1876.

Neglect of education did not slow down economic growth, however, because imported personnel as well as imported capital built up and ran the economy, developing Egypt's natural resources with no corresponding development of human resources. The benefits of economic growth accrued mainly to foreigners or stimulated higher consumption by rich Egyptian landowners. Wealthy Egyptians bought more land; the educated entered the civil service; and the railroad and irrigation absorbed those few who were technically trained. The untrained majority could not compete for job opportunities with the growing number of Europeans resident in Egypt; only 5,000 in 1840, they had increased to 68,000 by 1878.

A flood of foreign goods followed imported personnel and capital into the country. European products abounded not only in Alexandria and Cairo but even in the more distant towns of Upper Egypt. In addition to the bazaar with local wares, every town had its smart Greek store where "Bass's ale, claret, curaçao, Cyprus, vermouth, cheese, pickles, sardines, worcester sauce, blacking, biscuits, preserved meats, candles, cigars, matches, sugar, salt, stationery, fireworks, jams, and patent medicines can all be bought at one fell swoop."[12] Trivial as the list of merchandise in a grocer's shop may seem, each item had symbolic significance, serving as a reminder that European products were desirable and superior; everything indigenous was rustic, "*baladi,*" not up to cosmopolitan standards.

This was the attitude the Egyptian physician had to overcome during the century-long apprenticeship he served under European domination. Many accounts in nineteenth-century literature referred to the gullibility of well-to-do patients who were swindled by charlatans, some native, but more often itinerant Europeans who exploited the popular notion that all European practitioners represented a superior level of the art. The mystique of European training influenced a greater number of Egyptians as the European presence became increasingly noticeable during the century. "These people will no longer consult an Arab hakim if they can get a European to treat them," Lady Duff-Gordon wrote during the reign of Ismail; "they ask if the Government Doctors have been to Europe to learn *Hikmah*; if not, they don't trust them."[13]

By any standard, the Egyptian medical graduates who entered government service had to perform under multiple disadvantages. As men of inferior rank in the military establishment, they were bullied by upper-echelon officers; channeled later into serving the civilian population, they were scorned by European practitioners and mistrusted or ignored by the Egyptian people. Yet they became the backbone of a rudimentary public health service for Egypt at a time when endemic and imported health hazards were about to multiply.

Muhammad Ali had sponsored the creation of a Western-style school of medicine with hospital-based clinical training in order to command a corps of trained physicians who could safeguard the health of target groups in the population drafted into government service. He later deployed those Egyptian physicians in the countryside to disarm European trading partners' mistrust of the country's state of sanitation and health. To repeat what we noted about the vaccination campaign, two features of the budding public health service that resulted promised potential positive development to address the changing needs of the people: the utilization of local personnel in administering the system and emphasis on sanitation and prevention of disease outbreaks.

We have already noted how the village barber became the chief agent in a national vaccination program. Sanitary regulations also were to be carried out by familiar minor officials or service personnel at community level: gendarmerie or military forces in local garrisons were charged with sanitary policing; the scavenger and water carrier corporations' street-cleaning duties were regularized under the supervision of the local shaykh; and the muhtasib, or market supervisor, was directed to broaden his surveillance to assist the district medical officer in pure food inspection. Thanks to the insistence of two rival groups of European physicians, the provincial health service specifically provided for two prophylactic measures, smallpox immunization and quarantine for infectious diseases. The local medical officers' duties also included sanitary regulation or "sanitary works"—street cleaning, refuse removal and disposal, filling in ponds, and relocating cemeteries. These would soon prove inadequate as the population grew, but the fact that they were statutorily specified as the local medical officer's responsibility established a healthy precedent for evolution in the future, when microbiology would provide a scientific rationale for sanitary procedures. The public health surveillance duties required of local functionaries also might have evolved later into new health care roles when guided by advances in the biomedical sciences.

But the evidence indicates that this promising beginning later was neglected in favor of the urban-based, curative medicine-oriented Western model that carried the prestige of the successful and prosperous leading nations of the world. Government policies assigned a low priority to rural health and welfare, and the provinces' health centers never received adequate support to realize their potential as channels for scientifically based preventive and curative medicine to the village population.[14] In neither England nor France was there official recognition of the health and sanitation needs of the rural population which might have served as a model for Egypt. The industrializing world in the nineteenth century opted for high-quality medical care for a few, rather than minimal health care for the many, and the twentieth century has been slow to reject that model.

Since the mid-nineteenth century, Western systems of medical care delivery have been hospital oriented, providing personal care for individual patients by private physicians. Today, the standard indicators used worldwide to assess health care resources are the number of physicians and hospital beds per capita. A popular reference work summarizing data on nations of the Third World offers an example in the chapter on Egypt, under the heading of "Health." "In 1975 there were 1,444 hospitals in the country with 77,611 beds or one bed per 464 inhabitants. In 1974 there were 7,495 physicians, or one physician per 5,000 inhabitants."

Without any attempt to link the two sets of data, the work goes on to state that in Egypt, "major health problems are bilharziasis, hookworm, trachoma, tuberculosis, dysentery, beriberi, and typhus."[15] Urban-based hospitals and physicians are ill-equipped to deal with this spectrum of environmental and deficiency diseases requiring preventive medicine or social welfare measures: improved nutrition, housing, sanitation, parasite control, or education in hygiene. But these measures have not been considered part of the practice of medicine in the Western world since nineteenth-century society separated medicine from public health and defined the roles of hospital and physician exclusively in terms of curing disease.

For some idea of what Egypt's provincial public health service might have become, we can look at the fate of zemstvo medicine in Russia. The Bolshevik Revolution's leveling of society inevitably eliminated the zemstvo physicians, members of the aristocratic intelligentsia who joined the "Narodniki," or populist movement, to bring the people the benefits of education and science; only 15 percent of the total medical profession at the turn of the century, they nevertheless had played a vital role as exemplars of the socially conscious physician devoted to the welfare of others without regard for his own compensation. To uphold the revolution's egalitarian principles, the Bolsheviks also attempted to dissolve the feldshers because they were considered second-class practitioners. But, like the Jacobins who had sought to abolish hospitals as symbols of the ancien régime's stultifying charity, they had to reverse their plans because of overwhelming need. By the 1920s, the government had to establish new schools to train feldshers, and, again like the Jacobins, Soviet officials tried to make them more useful socially by gradually upgrading their training.

Today more than 400,000 feldshers, many of whom are women, work in various physician-substitute or "physician-extender" roles in the Soviet health system. Some feldshers in Soviet cities have specialized roles as industrial hygienists or midwives, but more commonly they act as the primary screening health worker in polyclinics or hospital outpatient departments. In rural areas, primary care is provided by feldsher-midwife stations with a wide range of responsibilities including epidemic control measures, reduction of childhood morbidity and mortality, "predoctor" medical aid to adults and children, sanitary and hygienic measures to improve the living and working conditions of people engaged in farming, and health education.[16]

With the Russian system for comparison, it seems reasonable to conclude that the Western system imported to Egypt has proved inappropriate for the country's needs. The biomedical technology that developed within the matrix of a single patient-doctor transaction emphasized curative procedures required for individual ailments rather than preventive medicine measures for social and environmental health hazards threatening the majority in society.

Evolving Concepts of Health and Sickness

To return to the nineteenth-century squabble over disease causation, in view of the ineffectiveness of physicians' efforts to control epidemics, their self-confidence appears paradoxical. Considering the provisional, incomplete nature of their etiological knowledge at the time, how do we account for the dogmatism of champions of the two opposing theories, particularly the supporters of the miasmatic hypothesis, which we now recognize as dangerously inadequate in explaining the transmission of plague and cholera?

In the case of Great Britain, the obvious success of sanitary reform in reducing the incidence of waterborne diseases circumstantially seemed to vindicate the validity of the miasmatic theory. Although policy planners ignored John Snow's evidence incriminating water as the medium for disease transmission, by creating sewage systems to dispose of the human waste they believed the cause, they fortuitously protected the water supply and applied the proper remedy, if for the wrong reason. In addition, Great Britain's preeminent place in world affairs cannot be ignored as an important factor contributing to the medical profession's self-confidence. Physicians from British India especially, unaccustomed to having their opinions challenged, could see in Egypt all the features that guided their policies in South

Asia, and they believed they had the answers to what appeared to be analogous social and medical problems.[17]

Clot is an interesting example of the continental physicians committed to variations of the miasmatic, anticontagionist hypothesis. To his advocacy of "indigenous" institutions, Egypt owes its School of Medicine, the School of Hakimas, the promotion of universal smallpox immunization by village barbers, and the extension of Egyptian physicians into provincial health centers after demobilization of the military medical corps. The initial institutionalization and nationalization of Western medicine in Egypt is largely due to Clot's drive and organizing genius. But on the subject of disease transmission, he was dogmatic. In rebutting arguments for the contagiousness of plague, he loses sympathy when he asserts that by 1840 all enlightened men, "except Italians and Spaniards," had abandoned the idea of contagion for scrofula, scabies, leprosy, ophthalmia, phthisis, dysentery, typhus, yellow fever, and cholera as well as plague. He shudders at the "ridiculous and barbarous custom" of Romans who segregated pulmonary consumption patients from other patients in their hospitals.[18]

It was the cogency of the Morgagni paradigm that confirmed Clot's frequent diagnoses of "gastroenteritis" by revealing enteric lesions in corpses and strengthened his conviction, enhanced his self-confidence, and led him to doctrinaire attacks on his opponents. By the end of the century, the Morgagni paradigm had vindicated Clot's Italian and Spanish contagionist adversaries by identifying specific microorganisms as the pathogenic agents for the diseases over which they had quarreled. Although both sides believed they were dealing with definitive scientific truths, both theories were only limited, partial, and approximate descriptions of reality.

Concepts of the diesase process have evolved during the intervening century, and proposals for a new paradigm for medicine have appeared in recent decades.[19] The pathology- or disease-focused concept of sickness sharpened to the principle of etiological specificity, which was vindicated by the bacteriological discoveries of the late nineteenth and early twentieth centuries, provided the perfect key concept for understanding infectious diseases and opened the way for rational therapeutics. The clinical system worked, and by focusing on pathology as the core discipline in hospital training, it established accuracy in diagnosis as the medical practitioner's major aim and primary skill. The emergence of bacteriology next became the vehicle that first introduced the ideology of science into medicine, and paradoxically it led physicians away from the bedside to the laboratory.

More important for agrarian societies like Egypt, the ideology of science appears to have reinforced the idea that authentic medicine is curative medicine, a more serious pursuit than preventive or environmental control measures. No doubt Egyptian medical students and practitioners who are reluctant to practice in the countryside are influenced by the lack of social amenities, poor accommodations and facilities, inadequate supplies and assistance, and perhaps daunting social problems. But some of their dissatisfaction with rural practice may be attributed to training that encourages self-definition as scientists in the forefront of the latest discoveries. Confronting infectious diseases, the scientist-physician is concerned about the availability of broad-spectrum antibiotics; mounting a campaign of pest control or a program of hygiene education for villagers would be outside his area of responsibility.

The nineteenth-century divorce of the practice of medicine and community or public health concerns may be the most unfortunate aspect of the Western system transferred to the non-Western world. And Western leaders in medical science continue to insist, as one member of the elite of academic medicine declared, that "when the emphasis is shifted from sick individual human beings to people in the aggregate, clinical medicine becomes esoteric medicine, biochemistry and physiology become irrelevant, and the appropriate disciplines are more in the nature of economics and sociology."[20] As long as the West upholds urban hospital-based curative medicine for the individual as the ideal for "health care," the lives of rural Egyptians and many others may continue at risk.

Appendix 1: A Public Health Establishment in Egypt, 1825–1850

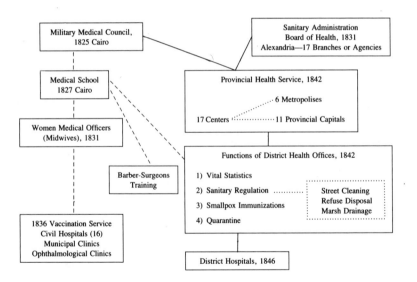

Appendix 2: Medical-Pharmaceutical Personnel in the Public Health Service in Egypt under the Direction of the Sanitary Administration Resident in Alexandria (1851)[a]

Table of Organization

City (Quarters)	No. of Personnel	Position or Function	Duties
Alexandria:			
4 Quarters	1	Chief Physician	Medical service of the lazaretto, confirmation of cases of plague, legal medicine, temporary inspector, interior health service
	1	Public Health Physician	Medical service of ports of Alexandria; confirmation of plague cases; verification of deaths; legal medicine; inspection of vaccinations of comestibles, and of municipal public health and hygiene; temporary inspector, interior health service

[a]Translation from Italian of Tavolo E appended to Francesco Grassi, *Sulla Peste e Sulle Quaranten* (Genova: R. I. de Sardo Muti, 1852). Grassi's book was based on a report he presented to the International Sanitary Conference in Paris in 1851.

City (Quarters)	No. of Personnel	Position or Function	Duties
	2	Deputy Public Health Physicians, Egyptian	Verification of decease of men; hygienic police and the city and environs
	1	Egyptian Vaccinator	Vaccinations in the city and environs; vaccine conservation
	1	Woman Aide	Verification of decease of women
	1	European Pharmacist	Service in the Lazaretto Hospital
	9		
Rosetta-Rashid: 2 Quarters	1	Public Health Physician	Verification of deaths, confirmation of plague cases; medical service in the civil hospital; legal medicine; vaccinations; inspection of comestibles; municipal hygienic service
	1	European Pharmacist	Pharmaceutical service of the Civil Hospital and free distribution of medicines to the city's needy
	1	Chief Orderly	Civil Hospital
	1	Orderlies	Civil Hospital
	1	Woman Aide	Verification of decease of women
	6		
Damietta-Dimyat: 2 Quarters	1	Public Health Physician	Medical service of the lazaretto and anchorage; verification of deaths, confirmation of plague cases, etc.
	1	Deputy Public Health Physician, Egyptian	Verification of deaths
	1	Woman Aide	Verification of decease of women
	1	Egyptian Pharmacist	Hospital Service
	1	Chief Orderly	Hospital Service
	3	Orderlies	Hospital Service
	10		

City (Quarters)	No. of Personnel	Position or Function	Duties
Al-Arish:			
1 Quarter	1	Public Health Physician, Egyptian	Medical service at quarantine; vaccinations; confirmation of plague cases; verification of deaths, etc.
	1	Egyptian Pharmacist	Distribution of medicines
	1	Woman aide	Verification of decease of women
	<u>1</u>	Orderly	Service at the pharmacy
	4		
Suez:			
1 Quarter	1	European Sanitary Physician	Direction of quarantine service; medical service of the hospital; other as above
	1	Deputy Sanitary Physician, Egyptian	Verification of deaths; vaccinations; etc.
	1	Pharmacist	Hospital Service, etc., as above
	1	Woman Aide	Verification of decease of women
	<u>3</u>	Orderlies	Hospital Service
	7		
Cairo:			
10 Quarters (i.e., 8 thumns in Great Cairo, plus Bulaq and Old Cairo)	1	Physician delegated by the Sanitary Administration	Direction of the Delegation's service
	6	Same; European chiefs of offices of each quarter	Medical service of each quarter of Cairo
	4	Same; Egyptian chiefs of offices of each quarter	

City (Quarters)	No. of Personnel	Position or Function	Duties
	12	Same; Egyptian deputies	Free treatment of illness; verification of deaths; confirmation of plague cases; hygienic inspection of their respective quarters
	1	Same: European assigned to local police for inspection of comestibles	
	1	Same; Egyptian chief of vaccination service	Besides vaccinating the citizens, the physician-vaccinator is responsible for that of all blacks arriving from the south
	1	Same	
	10	Women Aides	
	10	Orderlies	Assistants to the Chief Physician
	46		

Province	Districts	No. of Personnel	Position or Function
Dakhaliya			
Capital City: al-Mansur	14	1	Chief Physician, European
		1	Deputy Physician, European
		2	Egyptian Physicians, assigned to the two District hospitals
		14	District physicians, Egyptian
		1	Chief Pharmacist, European
		1	Deputy Pharmacist, Egyptian
		1	Chief Orderly, assigned to the provincial capital's hospital
		5	Orderlies assigned to pharmacies and three hospitals
		253	Sanitary Barbers responsible for vaccinations and verifications of deaths

Province	Districts	No. of Personnel	Position or Function
		250	Women Aides responsible for verification of decease of women
		529	
Gharbiyah Capital City: al-Mahallat al-Kubra	17	1	Chief Physician, European resident in the capital city
		1	Deputy Physician, European, resident in Fuah
		1	Deputy Physician, Egyptian, resident in the capital city
		17	District Physicians, Egyptian
		286	Sanitary Barbers
		279	Women Aides
		1	Chief Pharmacist, European
		1	Pharmacist, Egyptian
		1	Chief orderly, assigned to the capital city's hospital
		2	Orderlies
		590	
Giza Capital City: Giza	5	1	Chief Physician, European
		5	District Physicians, Egyptian
		1	Chief Pharmacist, European
		1	Deputy Pharmacist, Egyptian
		1	Orderly assigned to the Pharmacy
		106	Sanitary Barbers
		97	Women Aides
		212	
Qalyubia Capital City: Qalyub	5	1	Chief Physician, European
		5	District Physicians, Egyptian

Province	Districts	*No. of* Personnel	Position or Function
		1	Egyptian Physician assigned to the Civil Hospital
		1	Chief Pharmacist, European
		1	Deputy Pharmacist, Egyptian
		1	Chief Orderly of the Hospital
		3	Orderlies: two at the hospital; one at the pharmacy
		111	Sanitary Barbers
		<u>111</u>	Women Aides
		235	
Sharqiya Capital City: Zagazig	10	1	Chief Physician, European
		1	Deputy Chief Physician, Egyptian
		10	District Physicians, Egyptian
		1	Chief Pharmacist, European
		1	Pharmacist, Egyptian
		1	Orderly at the Pharmacy
		212	Sanitary Barbers
		<u>212</u>	Women Aides
		439	
Minufiya Capital City: Shibn al-Kum	10	1	Chief Physician, European
		1	Deputy Chief Physician, Egyptian
		10	District Physicians, Egyptian
		1	Chief Pharmacist, European
		1	Pharmacist, Egyptian
		1	Chief Orderly at Civil Hospital
		3	Orderlies
		343	Sanitary Barbers
		<u>312</u>	Women Aides
		673	

Province	Districts	No. of Personnel	Position or Function
Buhaira			
Capital City:	12	1	Chief Physician, European
Shubra Khit		1	Deputy Chief Physician, Egyptian
		12	District Physicians, Egyptian
		1	Chief Pharmacist, European
		1	Pharmacist, Egyptian
		1	Chief Orderly at Civil Hospital
		3	Orderlies
		127	Sanitary Barbers
		123	Women Aides
		270	
Middle Egypt			
Bani Suayf		1	Chief Physician, European
and *Minya*		1	Deputy Chief Physician,
Capital Cities:			Egyptian
Bani Suayf,			
Minya		11	District Physicians, Egyptian
		2	European Pharmacists in the two provincial capitals
		3	Chief Orderlies at the hospitals in al-Minya, Bani-Suayf and al-Fayyum
		7	Orderlies at the hospitals named above
		a	Sanitary Barbers
		a	Women Aides
		25	
Upper Egypt			
Asyut and	9	1	Chief Physician, European
Girga		9	District Physicians, Egyptian
Capital City:		1	Chief Pharmacist, European
Asyut		1	Chief Orderly at the Civil Hospital in Asyut

Province	Districts	No. of Personnel	Position or Function
		4	Orderlies
		*	Sanitary Barbers
		*	Women Aides
		16	
Upper Egypt			
Qina and	7	1	Chief Physician, European
Isna		7	District Physicians, Egyptian
Capital City:			
Qina		1	Chief Pharmacist, European
		2	Chief Orderlies at the two Civil Hospitals
		6	Orderlies
		*	Sanitary Barbers
		*	Women Aides
		17	

* Exact number undetermined.

Description of the Provincial Health Service

Provincewide Service

This service includes the verification of deaths and attendance on the sick, vaccinations, inspection of comestibles, internal and external sanitary policing of the towns and villages, and removal of every cause of ill health, including filling in of stagnant pools of water. Treatment of all sick is free of charge, as is the disbursement of medicines. Also included are observation and treatment of spizootics.

The ma'mur of the province, nazir of the department, the shaykh al-balad (village headman), the military commandant, and army surgeons are all obliged to offer aid and cooperation to the Sanitary Physicians in all parts of their service, including service in the quarantine operations in the event of plague, and purification of the locality infected with plague.

Specific Duties of the Chief Physician and His Deputy

In addition to the execution of what is noted above, and service at the Civil Hospital of the provincial capital, the chief physician and his deputy are to inspect the district physicians frequently and to report on their service to the central Administration. The Chief Physician shall correspond with the Mudir and with other provincial authorities for the execution of hygienic regulations. He shall refer all business to the central Administration for decision and shall keep it informed on the service and on the state of public health. He shall maintain registers of mortality and of illnesses treated in the provincial capital and districts, of vaccinations and their results, of population movements, returns from the provincial civil hospital, of sanitary works performed and those in contemplation. He shall report on these in his correspondence. He shall forward to the central Administration detailed figures for deaths, diseases, vaccinations, hospital returns and population returns, in the provincial capital and the districts, every month; and the same for sanitary works every three or six months. In time of plague he shall assume direction of the quarantine operations, calling upon the assistance of the civil and military authorities and of the army medical corps.

Specific Duties of the District Physicians

Every district physician must continually tour the villages in his district to insure proper execution of the service. He shall keep a daily register of illnesses treated, deaths verified, vaccinations he has performed, those performed by the Barbers, and whether they had positive results; also his medical observations, and observations on the hygienic state of the villages, sanitary works completed, and foodstuffs unfit for consumption found for sale in the markets. His injunctions to the local authorities on causes of ill health observed shall be recorded in another daily register kept by the chief authority in the village and furnished with his seal and that of the provincial capital. He shall forward to the Chief Physician in the provincial capital a copy of his journal every ten days.

Duties of the Barbers and the Women Aides

While the District Physician is touring other villages, in his absence the barber assigned to the Sanitary Administration in every village shall verify the deaths of men, and the women's aides those of women. Each visit shall be confirmed in the village sanitary register and supported by a separate declaration. Vaccinations shall be recorded in the same register. The barbers and the women aides shall receive one piaster as compensation for each verification of death, and for each vaccination.

Notes

The following abbreviations have been used in this text to designate the state archives consulted:

AE *CCC*   France, Ministère des Affaires Etrangères, Correspondence Consulaire et Commerciale, *Alexandrie*

ENA   Egypt, National Archives

FO   Great Britain, Public Record Office, Foreign Office Series, *Turkey*

Introduction: Evolving Concepts of Disease and Medicine

1. See chap. 3, n. 13, for a description of the effects of a cholera attack.

2. There was public concern about tuberculosis, of course, but until Koch discovered the causative mycobacterium, "consumption" was considered a common health hazard, especially for young adults, similar to the infectious "childhood" diseases and the degenerative ailments of old age. Cholera, however, terrorized the nineteenth century. See Susan Sontag, *Illness as Metaphor* (New York: Random House, 1978), where she contrasts the literary treatment of pulmonary tuberculosis with that of cancer in the twentieth century.

3. "Imbalance" is an important physiological concept in all the ancient civilizations' medical systems, including the Greco-Roman humoral system that remained in force in European practice until the late nineteenth century.

In the twentieth century, René Dubos became a major spokesman for an ecological perspective on sickness, proposing that man's bodily afflictions are caused by failure to adapt to his environment. See, especially, *The Mirage of Health* (New York: Harpers, 1959), pp. 85ff., and *Man Adapting* (New Haven: Yale, 1965).

4. Robert P. Hudson, *Disease and Its Control: The Shaping of Modern Thought* (Westport, Conn.: Greenwood Press, 1983), chaps. 4 and 6; Harris L. Coulter, *Divided Legacy: A History of the Schism in Medical Thought*, I (Washington, D.C.: Wehawken Books, 1975), especially the introduction. In this study, "Western" or "European" medicine refers to theories and practices defined and developed by medical scientists from the sixteenth century, when Vesalius's anatomical studies posed one of the first challenges to the authority of the Greco-Roman system, through the first three quarters of the nineteenth century, when clinical methods elaborated by the French schools and advances in the basic sciences of microbiology, physiology, and biochemistry had become normative for medical training throughout Europe and the British Isles. By the last two decades of the nineteenth century, when the theories and practices had been extended to colonies throughout Asia and Africa and new contributions to medicine in the basic sciences were coming from Russia and Japan, the system had become "cosmopolitan" medicine.

5. The distinction between *definitive* technologies for the prevention, cure, and control of disease, based on scientific understanding of the disease process, and *halfway* technologies, mainly palliative techniques, first appeared in the President's Science Advisory Committee in 1972; *Scientific and Educational Basis for Improving Health Care: Report of the Panel on Biological and Medical Science of the President's Science Advisory Committee* (Washington, D.C.: U.S. Government Printing Office, 1972). Lewis Thomas later expanded on the policy implications of these important concepts in *Aspects of Biomedical Science Policy: An Occasional Paper* (Institute of Medicine, Washington, D.C., November 1972). A graphic example is the contrast between the simple immunization offered today by the Salk or Sabin vaccine for poliomyelitis and the cumbersome and expensive iron lungs and hydrotherapies required earlier in the century. Jenner, of course, had not identified the causative microorganism for smallpox, but he empirically observed the immunizing action of cowpox vaccine, the definitive prophylactic that has not been superseded in spite of the discovery of the virus's complete life history during the twentieth century.

6. Most influential in refuting the claims for quarantines' efficacy advanced by their proponents was the British prison reformer, John Howard, who visited the principal lazarettos in the Mediterranean at the end of the eighteenth century and described appalling inconsistencies in mindless application of routine procedures; the testimonies of John Bowring, a close associate of Utilitarian Jeremy Bentham, in England and Dr. A. B. Clot in France also were effective in influencing public opinion's repudiation of the maintenance of quarantines. John Howard, *An Account of the Principal Lazarettos in Europe* (London: J. Johnson, C. Dilly, and T. Cadell, 1791), 20–21; John Bowring, *Observations on the Oriental Plague and on Quaran-*

tine as a Means of Arresting Its Progress (Edinburgh: n.p., 1838); A. B. Clot-Bey, *De la Peste* (Paris: Fortin, Masson et Cie., 1840), 374–407.

7. Erwin H. Ackerknecht, "Anticontagionism between 1821 and 1867," *Bulletin of the History of Medicine* XXII (1948): 589. See the discussion on plague in Egypt in chap. 4.

8. A number of recent works have analyzed the evolution of the British and French medical systems, including John Woodward and David Richards, eds., *Health Care and Popular Medicine in Nineteenth-Century England: Essays in the Social History of Medicine* (New York: Holmes and Meier Publishers, Inc., 1977); F. B. Smith, *The People's Health* (London: Croom Helm, 1979); Anthony S. Wohl, *Endangered Lives: Public Health in Victorian Britain* (Cambridge: Harvard University Press, 1983); M. Jeanne Peterson, *The Medical Profession in Mid-Victorian London* (Berkeley, Los Angeles, London: University of California Press, 1978); Toby Gelfand, *Professionalizing Medicine: Paris Surgeons and Medical Science and Institutions in the Eighteenth Century* (Westport, Conn.: Greenwood Press, 1980); Jacques Léonard, Roger Darguenne, Louis Bergeron, "Médecins et notables sous le Consulat et L'Empire," *Annales: Economies, Sociétés, Civilisations* (1977); Oliver Faure, "Lyons Doctors in the Nineteenth Century: An Exceptional Social Union," *Journal of Social History* 10 (1977); George D. Sussman, "The Glut of Doctors in Mid-Nineteenth-Century France," *Comparative Studies in Society and History* 19 (1977), and "Enlightened Health Reform, Professional Medicine, and Traditional Society: The Cantonal Physicians of the Bas-Rhin, 1810–1870," *Bulletin of the History of Medicine* 51 (1977); Matthew Ramsey, "Medical Power and Popular Medicine: Illegal Healers in Nineteenth-Century France," *Journal of Social History* 10 (1977); Michel Foucault, *The Birth of the Clinic: An Archaeology of Medical Perception* (New York: Random House, 1973).

9. It will be recalled that in the Greco-Roman humoral system, sickness was considered to arise from an excess of one of the body's four humors—blood, phlegm, yellow bile, and black bile—which required depletion, most commonly by bloodletting.

10. Erwin Ackerknecht, *Medicine at the Paris Hospital, 1794–1848* (Baltimore: Johns Hopkins University Press, 1967).

11. Mark G. Field, "The Health Care System of Industrial Society: The Disappearance of the General Practitioner and Some Implications," in Everett Mendelsohn et al., eds., *Human Aspects of Biomedical Innovation* (Cambridge: Harvard University Press, 1971), 168, 171–172.

12. In addition to the references in n. 8, information about hospitals in France is based on Erwin Ackerknecht, *Medicine at the Paris Hospital*; Charles Coury, "The Teaching of Medicine in France from the Beginning of the Seventeenth Century," in C. D. O'Malley, ed., *The History of Medical Education* (Berkeley, Los Angeles, London: University of California Press,

1970), 121–172; and Richard H. Shryock, "Nineteenth-Century Medicine: Scientific Aspects," *Journal of World History* III (1957): 881–907. For England, see also the references in n. 8 and the following: Thomas McKeown, "A Sociological Approach to the History of Medicine," *Medical History* 14 (1970): 350–351; George Rosen, *A History of Public Health* (New York: M.D. Publications, Inc., 1958), 147–149; F. N. L. Poynter and Kenneth D. Keele, *A Short History of Medicine* (London: Mills and Boon, 1961), 132–137; F. N. L. Poynter, *Medicine in 1815* (London: The Wellcome Trust, 1965), passim; John Anderson, "Medical Education and Social Change," in F. N. L. Poynter, ed., *The Evolution of Medical Education in Britain* (London: Pitman Medical Publishing Company, Ltd., 1966), 207–218; George Rosen, "The Hospital: Historical Sociology of a Community Institution," in *From Medical Police to Social Medicine: Essays on the History of Health Care* (New York: Science History Publications, 1974), 288–295; "Economic and Social Policy in the Development of Public Health," ibid., 185–189.

13. Ivan Waddington, "General Practitioners and Consultants in Early Nineteenth-Century England: The Sociology of an Intra-Professional Conflict," in John Woodward and David Richards, *Health Care and Popular Medicine in Nineteenth-Century England: Essays in the Social History of Medicine* (New York: Holmes and Meier Publishers, Inc., 1977). See references to France in n. 8.

14. Edwin Chadwick, *Report on the Sanitary Condition of the Labouring Population of Great Britain, 1842*; Great Britain, Poor Law Commissioners (Edinburgh: Edinburgh University Press, 1965), 396: "The great preventives, drainage, street and house cleansing by . . . supplies of water and improved sewerage, and especially removing all noxious refuse from the towns are operations for which aid must be sought from . . . the Civil Engineer, not from the physician, who has done his work when he has pointed out the disease that results from the neglect of proper administrative measures, and has alleviated the sufferings of the victims."

15. René Sand, *The Advance to Social Medicine* (London and New York: Staples Press, 1952), 1, 17–19.

16. George Rosen, *A History of Public Health*, 143–144.

17. George Rosen, "Cameralism and the Concept of Medical Police," 120–141, and "The Fate of the Concept of Medical Police," 142–148, in *From Medical Police to Social Medicine*; Erna Lesky, *The Vienna Medical School of the Nineteenth Century* (Baltimore: Johns Hopkins Press, 1976), 86–95, 248–260. The title of Frank's work, "System einer vollstaendigen medicinischen Polizei," has been translated most often as "A System of Complete Medical Police," but since "polizei" means policy as well as the machinery to enforce it, some writers have suggested that "State Medicine" is a more accurate denotation than "Medical Police." See also William H.

McNeill, *Plagues and Peoples* (Garden City, N.Y.: Doubleday, 1976), 269; Henry E. Sigerist, *Landmarks in the History of Hygiene* (London: Oxford University Press, 1956), 36–37; Rosen, *A History of Public Health,* 161–167.

18. Sussman, "Enlightened Health Reform," 566–567, 577; Faure, 510–511; Sussman, "The Glut of Doctors," 297–304; Ramsey, 562.

19. Roy M. McLeod, "The Anatomy of State Medicine: Concept and Applications," in F. N. L. Poynter, ed., *Medicine and Science in the 1860s* (London: Wellcome Institute of the History of Medicine, 1968), 199–227.

20. George Rosen, "Medical Care Social Policy in Seventeenth-Century England," 169–171, and "Economic and Social Policy in the Development of Public Health," 185–193, in *From Medical Police to Social Medicine.* Although England's seventeenth-century pioneers in statistics or "political arithmetic" proposed numerous reforms to satisfy the population's health needs, implementation would have required well-developed local administrative organs operating under centralized power.

21. Jeanne L. Brand, *Doctors and the State: The British Medical Profession, 1870–1912* (Baltimore: Johns Hopkins University Press, 1965), 83–135; Ruth G. Hodgkinson, *The Origins of the National Health Service: The Medical Services of the New Poor Law, 1834–1871* (London: Wellcome Institute of the History of Medicine, 1967).

22. Sand, *Advance,* 342–345; Rosen *History,* 154–157.

23. Henry E. Sigerist, *Landmarks in the History of Hygiene* (London: Oxford University Press, 1956), 67–68; *Medicine and Human Welfare* (New Haven: Yale University Press, 1941), 142; Sand, *Advance,* 28; Rosen, *History,* 445–446; Peter F. Krug, "The Debate Over the Delivery of Health Care in Rural Russia: The Moscow Zemstvo, 1864–1878," *Bulletin for the History of Medicine* 50 (1976): 226–241; Samuel Ramer, "Who Was the Russian Feldsher?" ibid., 213–225.

1: Muhammad Ali and the Egyptians

1. Muhammad Ali was born in 1769 at Cavalla, a port on the Aegean, of poor parentage. He had no formal schooling until late in life, but talent for business apparently provided him a comfortable living as a tobacco merchant. He enlisted as an officer in the Albanian contingent of the Turkish-British expedition to oust the French from Egypt, became an admirer of Napoleon Bonaparte, and tried to follow the same route to success. An early book-length biography in English is Henry Dodwell, *The Founder of Modern Egypt: A Study of Muhammad Ali* (Cambridge: Cambridge University Press, 1931). More analytical, Afaf Lutfi al-Sayyid Marsot's *Egypt in the Reign of Muhammad Ali* (Cambridge and New York: Cambridge University Press,

1984) makes clear the mercantilist character of Muhammad Ali's program to develop and exploit Egypt's resources.

2. Justin McCarthy, "Nineteenth-Century Egyptian Population," *Middle East Studies* XII, 3 (Oct. 1976): 17; Amin Sami, *Taqwim al-Nil (Almanac of the Nile),* 6 vols. (Cairo: Dar al-Kutub, 1916–1935), II, 585. Contemporary figures were generally underestimates.

Professor Marsot's study, *Egypt in the Reign of Muhammad Ali,* provides a comprehensive account of the viceroy's economic and administrative innovations; chap. 6, "Internal Policies," specifically details the impact of social changes on the Egyptians, particularly the peasantry. Other works consulted for this study are Gabriel Baer, *Studies in the Social History of Modern Egypt* (Chicago: University of Chicago Press, 1969), and *Egyptian Guilds in Modern Times* (Jerusalem: Israel Oriental Society, 1964); Helen Rivlin, *The Agricultural Policy of Muhammad Ali* (Cambridge: Harvard University Press, 1961); Moustafa Fahmy, *La Révolution de l'industrie en Egypte et ses conséquences sociales au 19ᵉ siècle (1800–1850)* (Leiden: E. J. Brill, 1954); J. Heyworth-Dunne, *An Introduction to the History of Education in Modern Egypt* (London: Luzac and Co., 1938).

3. Among the contemporary sources drawn on for this sketch of early nineteenth-century Egyptian society are Edward Lane's *The Manners and Customs of the Modern Egyptians* (London: Dutton, Everyman ed., 1966); Antoine B. Clot-Bey, *Aperçu Général sur l'Egypte,* 2 vols. (Paris: Fortin, Masson et Cie., 1840); John Bowring, "Report on Egypt and Candia," House of Commons, Sessional Papers 1840, XXI: *Reports from Commissioners,* VI (London: Her Majesty's Stationery Office, 1840); and *Description de l'Egypte: Ou recueil des observations et des recherches qui ont été faites en Egypte pendant l'expédition de l'armée française: Etat Moderne,* 2 vols. (Paris: Imprimerie Impériale, 1809–1822).

4. René Cattaui, *Le règne de Mohammed Aly d'après les archives russes en Egypte,* 4 vols. (Rome and Cairo: Société royale de géographie d'Egypte, 1931–1936), II, Pt. I, 267.

5. C. Rochefort Scott, *Rambles in Egypt and Candia,* 2 vols. (London: Henry Colborn, 1837), II, 218.

6. *Egyptian Gazette,* no. 184, 6 August 1830, 4; no. 191, 20 September 1830, 1.

7. Lane, 199; P. S. Girard, "Mémoire sur l'Agriculture, l'Industrie, et le Commerce de l'Egypte," in *Description de l'Egypte, Etat Moderne,* II, pt. 1 (Paris: Imprimerie Impériale 1812), 512–513, 553–555.

8. M. Jomard, "Description de la ville et de la Citadelle du Kaire, accompagnée de l'explication des plans de cette ville et de ses environs, et de reseignements sur sa distribution, ses monuments, sa population, son commerce et son industrie," in *Description del'Egypte, Etat Moderne,* II, pt. 2 (Paris: Imprimerie Impériale, 1822), 580. Marcel Clerget, *Le Cairo: Etude*

de géographie urbaine et d'histoire économique, 2 vols. (Cairo: E. and R. Schindler, 1934), I, 187; II, 68. Lane, p. 4, also estimates Cairo's area at three square miles in the 1830s.

9. Clot-Bey, *Aperçu Générale,* I, 306–310; De Chabrol de Volvie, "Essai sur les moeurs des habitants modernes de l'Egypte," in *Description de l'Egypte, Etat Moderne,* II, pt. 2, 371, 379; Jomard, 584; Lane, 343–350. Jomard and De Chabrol observed 100 public baths in 1800; Clot and Lane refer to about 70 in the 1830s.

10. De Chabrol, 410.

11. Clot-Bey, *Aperçu Générale,* II, 344–345; M. le Baron Dominique Larrey, "Mémoire et observations sur plusieurs maladies qui ont affecté les troupes de l'armée francaise pendant l'expédition d'Egypte et de Syrie et qui sont endémiques dans ces deux contrées," in *Description de l'Egypte, Etat Moderne,* (Paris: Imprimerie Impériale 1809), I, 510, 513; René Desgenettes, *Histoire Médicale de l'Armée d'Orient* (Paris: Firmin Didot Frères, 1830), 12–15, 172–173, 236.

12. J. Christoph Buergel, "Secular and Religious Features of Medieval Arabic Medicine," in Charles Leslie, ed., *Asian Medical Systems: A Comparative Study* (Berkeley, Los Angeles, London: University of California Press, 1976), 44–62. Frederick L. Dunn, "Traditional Asian and Cosmopolitan Medicine as Adaptive Systems," in Leslie, 133–158, points out the continuing importance of two indigenous systems—local or folk practices deriving from preliterate society and the regional literate or scholarly traditions in China, India, and the Islamic world—in addition to the prevalent urban system of cosmopolitan medicine. Peter Gran, "Medical Pluralism in Arab and Egyptian History: An Overview of Class Structures and Philosophies of the Main Phases," *Social Science and Medicine* 13B (1979): 339–348, further proposes that, rather than a simple duality of folk and literate traditions, multiple systems coexisted, corresponding to a variety of cultural orientations and socioeconomic experience.

Needless to say, nineteenth-century observers were unaware of the wide spectrum of needs and relevant procedures underlying the practices they dismissed as "superstition." Pluralism has continued to characterize the total health care system in Egypt to the present day, but the older indigenous practitioners, now recognized as "the informal sector," have never been legitimized officially. The focus of this study is the institutionalization of Western medical practice in Egypt.

13. Peter Gran, *The Islamic Roots of Capitalism: Egypt, 1760–1840* (Austin: University of Texas Press, 1978), chap. 4.

14. Clot-Bey, *Aperçu Général,* II, 383; Christian G. Ehrenberg, "Ueber die Krankheiten in Aegypten und die jetzige arabische Heilkunde," *Literarische Annalen der gesammte Heilkunde* (1827), VII, 8, 9; Richard Strong Sargent, "Observations on the State of Medical Science in Egypt,

Ancient and Modern," in *The Dublin Journal of Medical Science* XX (1842): 93–95; Franz Pruner, *Topographie Médicale du Caire* (Munich: n.p., 1847), 57.

15. Larrey, 516–517.

16. Antoine Barthèlme Clot-Bey, *Mémoires*, ed. Jacques Tagher (Cairo: Imprimerie de l'Institut Français d'Archéologie Orientale, 1949), 56.

17. Charles Cuny, "Propositions d'hygiène, de médecine, et de chirurgie, relatives à l'Egypte." Thèse pour le doctorat en médecine présentée et soutenue le 31 août, 1853, in *Thèses de la Faculté de Médecine de Paris* (Paris: Rignoux, 1853), 5.

18. Pierre-Charles Rouyer, "Notice sur les médicamens usuels des Egyptiens," in *Description de l'Egypte, Etat Moderne* (Paris: l'Imprimerie Impériale, 1809), I, 219.

19. Ibid., 220–221.

20. J. Worth Estes and LaVerne Kuhnke, "French Observations of Disease and Drug Use in Late Eighteenth-Century Cairo," *Journal of the History of Medicine and Allied Sciences* 39 (April 1984): 121–152.

21. Desgenettes, *Histoire Medicale*, 322–323.

22. Larrey, 431ff.; Desgenettes, 18, 32; Clot-Bey, *Aperçu Générale*, II, 368–378; Aly Heybah, "Quelques mots sur les trois principales maladies endémiques de l'Egypte," thèse présentée et soutenue à la Faculté de Médecine de Paris le 16 août 1833, pour obtenir le grade de Docteur en médecine (Paris: l'Imprimerie de Didot le Jeune, 1833).

23. Antoine Barthèlme Clot-Bey, "Esquisse des Maladies les plus graves en Egypte," in *Introduction de la Vaccination en Egypte en 1827* (Paris: Victor Masson et Fils, s.d.), 1–4.

24. Pierre Nicolas Hamont, *L'Egypte sous Mehmet Ali*, 2 vols. (Paris: Léautey et Lecointe, 1843), I, 492–505, 512–518.

25. Pruner, 57, 73.

26. Besides references to medical men in the foregoing paragraphs, the following laymen mentioned dysentery and ophthalmia as the most prevalent diseases in Egypt: Jomard, 586, 697; De Chabrol, 382–383; Lane, 2, 3.

27. Ibid., 583.

28. Antoine Barthèlme Clot-Bey, *Mémoires*, passim.

2: Response: Establishment of the Egyptian School of Medicine

1. There is one history of the Egyptian medical school in English: Naguib Bey Mahfouz, *The History of Medical Education in Egypt* (Cairo: Government Press at Bulaq, 1935), 23–70. Also in English are J. Heyworth-Dunne, *An Introduction to the History of Education in Modern Egypt* (London: Luzac and Company, 1938), 122–131, 235, 237, 240–242, 355–357; and

F. M. Sandwith, M.D., "The History of Kasr el-Ainy, A.D. 1466–1901," in *Records of the Egyptian Government School of Medicine*, I (1901), 3–23. In French, the best sources are Antoine Barthèlme Clot-Bey, *Mémoires* (Cairo: Imprimerie de l'Institut Français d'Archéologie Orientale, 1949), passim; *Aperçu Général e sur l'Egypte*, 2 vols. (Paris: Fortin, Masson et Compagnie, 1840), II, 409–437; and various "Comptes rendus" in the *Annales de la médecine physiologique*, 1827–28, 1833, 1849, passim. Another contemporary account by an Egyptian physician who subsequently became director of the school is Hassan Effendi Mahmoud, "La Médecine en Orient: L'Ecole de Médecine d'Egypte," *L'Union Médicale* 30, no. 63 (1866): 393–403, 409–415. The best source in Arabic is Ahmad Izzat Abd al-Karim, *Tarīkh al-Ta ῾alīm fi ῾asr Muhammad ῾Ali* (Cairo: Maktab al-Nahda al-misriyah, 1938), 251–286. Two short summaries are Muhammad Sharaf, "Hazz al-bilad min al-ta῾alīm al-tibbīy," *Journal of the Egyptian Medical Association* 3 (1920): 392–421; and "Tashyīd al madāris al-tibbīyah al-hadītha," *Journal of the Egyptian Medical Association* II (1928): 337–356, 827–858.

2. Richard Shryock, "European Backgrounds of American Medical Education (1600–1900)," *Journal of the American Medical Association*, vol. 194, no. 7 (1965): 710–712; Erwin H. Ackerknecht, *Medicine at the Paris Hospital*, passim.

3. Clot-Bey, *Mémoires*, 42–45, 56, 59–60.

4. Ibid., 64–65. This translation is the writer's; another version in English will be found in Mahfouz, 27–28.

5. *Egyptian Gazette*, no. 8, 20 February 1828, 1. All histories of education in Egypt mention the medieval classical training in Islamic sciences still current at al-Azhar in the nineteenth century. Besides Heyworth-Dunne and Ahmad 'Izzat 'abd al-Karim, see Yacoub Artin Pasha, *L'Instruction Publique en Egypte* (Paris, Ernest Leroux, 1890); V. Edouard Dor, *L'Instruction Publique en Egypte* (Paris: A. Lacroix, Berboeckhouen et Cie., 1872), 117–178; Bayard Dodge, *Muslim Education in Medieval Times* (Washington, D.C.: Middle East Institute, 1962), 29, 114; and Edward W. Lane, 216.

6. Antoine Barthèlme Clot-Bey, "Compte rendu des travaux de l'école de Médecine d'Abou Zabel et de l'examen générale des élèves pour la première année de sa fondation, 1242–43 (1827–28)," in *Annales de la médecine physiologique* 23 (1833): 427; *Mémoires*, 86. A visitor in 1836 remarked that the school was well furnished with natural history specimens, anatomical models and drawings, physics and chemistry apparatus, etc.; C. Rochefort Scott, *Rambles in Egypt and Candia* (London: Henry Colburn, 1837), 242.

7. Jules Planat, *Histoire de la régénération de l'Egypte* (Paris: J. Barbezat, 1830), 153–154. The picture appears in Naguib Bey Mahfouz, *The History of Medical Education in Egypt* (Cairo: Government Press, 1935), 31.

8. Clot-Bey, *Mémoires,* 86; "Compte rendu . . . (1827–28)," *Compte rendu de l'état de l'enseignement médical et du service de santé civil et militaire de l'Egypte au commencement de mars 1849* (Paris: Masson, 1849), 2, 6. Premedical studies later were standardized as French, mathematics, geography, history, physics, chemistry, botany, and zoology.

9. Although Clot gives the impression that he created a military medical corps and a medical school de novo, Italian physicians staffed the medical corps before his arrival, and a Piedmontese, Del Signore, preceded him as chief physician and surgeon of the Egyptian army and director of the military hospital from 1822 to 1825. See E. Verruci Bey e A. Sammarco, *Il contributo degl'Italiani ai progressi scientifici e pratici della medicina in Egitto sotto il regno di Mohammed Ali* (Cairo: A. Lenciani and Co., 1928), 13–15; and Angelo Sammarco, *Gli Italiani in Egitto* (Alessandria: Edizioni del Fascio, 1907), 92, 99, 101.

The faculty of the Medical School for the first ten years was as follows:

General Anatomy	Prof. Gaetani, 1827–1829
	Prof. Cherubini, 1829–1831
	Prof. Pruner, 1831–1833
	Prof. Fischer, 1833–
Physiology	Prof. Seisson, 1833–
Pathology	Prof. Duvigneau, 1827–
Hygiene and Forensic Medicine	Prof. Bernard, 1827–
Materia Medica and Toxicology	Prof. Barthelmy, 1827–1829
	Prof. Riviere, 1829–
Pharmacy	Prof. Pachtod, 1827–
Botany	Prof. Figari, 1827–
Chemistry	Prof. Celesia, 1827–1833
	Prof. Perron, 1833–1839
Physics	Prof. Celesia
Surgery	Prof. Clot, 1827–1833
	Prof. Fischer, 1833–

10. Clot-Bey, "Compte rendu . . . (1827–28)."

11. Bayard Dodge, *Al-Azhar: A Millennium of Muslim Learning* (Washington, D.C.: Middle East Institute, 1961), 95, 96.

12. Clot-Bey, *Mémoires,* 70–74. Mahfouz (p. 9) claimed that the notion that the dead can feel derived from ancient Egyptian beliefs. Another writer cited it as a Muslim belief, supported by a well-known *hadith*: "al-mayyitu yatallamu kama yatallamu al-hayyu—the dead suffer like the living suffer," Mahmoud, op. cit., 396. Visitors to the school in 1837–38 remarked that anatomical dissection was practiced regularly; e.g., Baptistin Poujoulat, *Voyage en Asie Mineure . . . et en Egypte,* 2 vols. (Paris: Ducollet, 1841), II, 513–14; Hermann von Pueckler-Muscau, *Egypt under Mehmet Ali,* 2 vols. (London: Henry Colburn, 1845), I, 231; Planat.

13. Clot-Bey, *Mémoires*, 80, 325; *Compte rendu . . . au commencement de mars 1849*, 3.

14. Lester S. King, *The Medical World of the Eighteenth Century* (Chicago: University of Chicago Press, 1958), passim; Foucault, 184–192; Shryock, "Nineteenth-Century Medicine . . . ," 888–889.

15. M. L. Labat, "De l'hôpital d'Abou-Zabel et de son organization médicale, considerée sous le point de vue de l'application des principes de la médecine physiologique, aux diverses maladies qu'on observe fréquemment en Egypte," *Annales de la médecine physiologique* 24 (1833): 137–152.

16. Wilhelm Griesinger, "Klinische und anatomische Beobachtungen ueber die Krankheiten von Egypten," *Archiv fuer physiologische Heilkunde* (1853), 61.

17. Clot-Bey, *Mémoires*, 122–123; Abd al-Karim, 260; Sandwith, 14.

18. *Egyptian Gazette*, no. 350, 11 February 1832, 2; no. 376, 27 April 1832, 4.

19. Letter from C. Gaillardot, Aleppo, 1839, in Gabriel Guemard, *Les Réformes en Egypte* (Cairo: Paul Barbey, 1936), 434.

To recruit European physicians, the Egyptian government also granted a 500 piaster clothing allowance twice a year and authorized an advance of 700 piasters for a horse and saddle. *Egyptian Gazette*, no. 345, 31 January 1832, 3; 377, 30 April 1832, 3; 380, 7 May 1832, 3; 393, 17 June 1832, 4; 494, 19 June, 1832, 2; 395, 21 June 1832, 4; 421, 27 August 1832, 2; 424, 4 September 1832, 3. The table following indicates that the Egyptian medical corps retained its military character long after limitation of the armed forces had redirected its efforts toward the civilian population. It also indicates that Europeans still held the top-ranking posts.

Medical Personnel in Egypt, 1849 [a]
(Staffing Pattern for the Military Medical Corps)

Rank	Doctors		Pharmacists	
	Europeans	Egyptians	Europeans	Egyptians
Inspector General	1			
Inspector, I Class	3		2	
Inspector, II Class	4	1	1	
Chief Surgeon/ Physician	11	5	3	1
Medical Officer I Class	32	4	6	4
Medical Officer II Class	6	32	6	

Rank	Doctors		Pharmacists	
	Europeans	Egyptians	Europeans	Egyptians
Assistant Medical Officer	3	62	12	15
Deputy Assistant Medical Officer		120	8	36
Aspirant[b]	—	31	6	—
Total	60	255	44	62

[a] Antoine B. Clot-Bey, *Compte rendu de l'état de l'enseignement médical et du service de santé civil et militaire de l'Egypte au commencement de mars 1849* (Paris: Fortin, Masson et Cie., 1849), 23.

[b] Aspirant (Turkish-Arabic usage "Spiran") was the lowest officer rank, equivalent to midshipman in the navy.

20. Ibid.; Letter from Dr. D. to X. S., Cairo, 7 October, 1835; from "Kronika Emigraciji Polskiej," IV, 73–74; in Adam Georges Benis, *Une Mission Militaire polonaise en Egypte,* 2 vols. (Cairo: Société royale de géographie d'Egypte, 1938), II, 246; Clot-Bey, *Mémoires,* 141, 148, 165, 167–168; Victor Schoelcher, *L'Egypte en 1845* (Paris: Pagnerre, 1846), 43; William Holt Yates, M.D., *The Modern History and Condition of Egypt,* 2 vols. (London: Smith, Elder, and Co., 1843), I, 509.

21. In 1832, the *Gazette* reported that the executive council of the War Ministry had approved a request from the Medical Council to transfer two medical officers from field duty to Abu Zabel to finish their studies; *Egyptian Gazette,* no. 404, 16 December 1832, 3.

An official communication to the commander-in-chief of the armed forces in 1840 acknowledged his complaints about Egyptian medical officers reporting for active duty inadequately prepared; it further described a joint ministry-medical school program of continuing education and annual examinations for medical officers; ENA, *Ministry of Public Instruction,* register no. 2061, 72; orig. no. 474, in series 604; Communication to the Sir Askar dated 22 Rabi' al-awwal 1256 (25 May 1840). D. M. Perron, letter to the editor, *Gazette des hôpitaux,* 3 December, 1844, 565–566, also referred to the annual examination and continuing education program.

22. Antoine B. Clot-Bey, *Relation de l'Epidémie de Choléra qui a Regné en Arabie et en Egypte* (Marseille: Arnaud Cayer et Cie., 1866), 14–16, 20–28; *Mémoires,* 162–163. Dr. Clot was granted the title of Bey, denoting civil status equivalent to the rank of colonel in the military forces, in recognition for his dedicated service during the cholera epidemic in 1831.

23. Clot-Bey, "Compte rendu . . . (1829–1830)," 651, 655; *Mémoires*, 67, 83.

24. Ibid., 147–149, 166. The English translation following is from Mahfouz, 38–39.

"I swear by the Name of God the Most High and of His Revered Prophet Muhammad, whose glory may God increase, to be faithful to the codes of honor, honesty and benevolence in the practice of Medicine. I will attend the poor gratuitously, and will never exact too high a fee for my work. Admitted into the privacy of a house, my eyes will not perceive what takes place therein; my tongue will guard the secret confided in me. My art shall not serve to corrupt, nor to assist crime, and I will not yield, under any pretext or persuasion, to prescribing any poison to anyone. I will neither give, nor prescribe to any pregnant woman dangerous drugs, capable of provoking or producing an abortion. Ever respectful and grateful to my masters, I will hand on to their children the instruction which I received from their fathers.

May I be respected by men if I remain faithful to my vow. If not, may I be covered with shame and despised. God is witness to what I have said."

25. Clot-Bey, *Mémoires*, 80, 141–142, 146–147, 325; "Compte rendu . . . (1829–1830)."

26. Clot-Bey, *Mémoires*, 175.

27. ENA, *Maʿiya*, register no. 61, Extract of Order no. 281: From the Wali to the deputy minister of war, dated 20 November 1835. Perron to Mohl, 26 September 1839. Yacoub Artin Pasha, ed., *Lettres du Dr. Perron à M. Jules Mohl, 1838–1854* (Cairo: F. Diemer, Finck and Baylaender, 1911), 58.

28. ENA, *Ministry of Public Instruction*, carton 49, register no. 125, pt. 2, correspondence no. 65, p. 421, Communication to the School of Medicine dated 10 October 1848. Amin Sami, *Taqwīm al-Nīl*, II, 414.

29. Clot-Bey, *Mémoires*, 276; *Compte rendu . . . 1849*, 57–60; Mahfouz, 38; "Tashyīd al-madāris al-tibbīya al-hadītha," 349–352.

30. ENA, *Ministry of Public Instruction*, register no. 2022, Records of Minutes of the Ministry of Public Instruction: Translation of a Memorandum to the Inspector of Government Buildings, dated 6 April 1837; Clot-Bey, *Mémoires*, 313.

31. Clot's portrait in the resplendent attire of an Ottoman bey appears in Mahfouz, 24. The Turkish title "Bey" held by high-ranking civilian officials corresponded to colonel in military rank, while the title "Pasha" was the equivalent of general. Civilians in public service generally were addressed as "Effendi," a polite designation similar to "Esquire" in English.

32. Schoelcher, 43; Michaud, 89; Scott, II, 247.

33. René Cattaui Bey, *Le Règne de Mohamed Aly d'après les Archives Russes en Egypte*, 4 vols. (Rome and Cairo, 1931–1936), II, pt. 2, 395–396.

34. The problem of preparatory premedical education was not solved in

Russia either until well after the revolution of 1917. In the immediate post-revolutionary period, evening courses in medical schools provided a temporary solution for urban workers; Mirko Grmek, "The History of Medical Education in Russia," in O'Malley, 323.

35. Abd al-Karim, 221–250; Mahfouz, 33–34.

36. Theodor Puschmann, *A History of Medical Education from the Most Remote to the Most Recent Times,* trans. and ed. Evan H. Hare (London: H. K. Lewis, 1891), 613–619.

37. Schoelcher, 43.

38. Moreover, the scholastic tradition at al-Azhar was not completely inimical to experimental investigation. The works of classical Islamic scholars included not only the Aristotelian deductive rationalism of Ibn Sina but the empirical approach of al-Razi as well. There is some evidence that a few scholars recognized the epistemological advantages of pursuing both methods. Shaykh Hasan ibn Muhammad al-Attar, for example, is said to have invoked al-Razi's writings to justify dissection of cadavers for anatomical investigation. Al-Attar's references to thirteenth-century scholar-physician Ibn al-Nafis's hypothesis on pulmonary circulation of the blood also indicates that the theory was not lost to posterity, as had been assumed. It was known in medical circles in Istanbul, and at least some of the *'ulama* in Cairo were in touch with intellectual activities in the Ottoman capital. Some of his colleagues and students at al-Azhar may have shared al-Attar's relatively free-thinking approach as well. See Peter Gran, *Islamic Roots of Capitalism: Egypt, 1760–1840* (Austin: University of Texas Press, 1979), 164–177.

39. ENA, *Ministry of Education,* portfolio 50, Subject: Instruction; register 129, document 482, 2162, 29 July 1848; register 143, document 38, 659, 6 December 1849.

40. Wilhelm Griesinger, *Gesammelte Abhandlungen* (Berlin: Hirschwald, 1872), II, 479–728. Kamal Sabri Kolta, "Die Gründung der Kairoer medizinischen Schule im 19. Jahrhundert und die Mitwirkung deutscher Aerzte," *Medizinische Monatsschrift* 30, no. 4 (1976): 171; Ernst Senn, *Theodor Bilharz: Ein deutsches Forscherleben in Aegypten, 1825–1862* (Stuttgart: Ausland u. Heimat Verlags Aktiengesellschaft, 1931), 24–49. Bilharz's biographer tells us that in spite of international pressures and intrigues, a severe case of typhus fever during an epidemic in 1855, and chronic nonpayment of his salary—which was 28 months in arrears at the time of his death—Bilharz was too enthusiastic about research possibilities in Egypt to return to Europe. He never realized his wish to be assigned to the Red Sea coast as a medical officer but died, apparently of typhus fever, while accompanying a German hunting expedition in East Africa.

41. According to Sandwith, p. 17, Saïd suspected that the medical school administration was trafficking in fraudulent certificates of ill health that exempted the purchaser from military service.

42. Ernest Godard, *Egypte et Palestine: Observations médicales et scientifiques* (Paris: Victor Masson et Fils, 1867), 9–17.

43. Heyworth-Dunne, 301–307, 324–330.

44. Ibid., 348–352, 358–380, 393–395.

45. Ali Mubarak, *Al-Khitat al Tawfiqiya al-Jadida,* 20 vols. (Cairo: Bulaq, 1306 A.H./1888–89), XI, 85–86. See the following table for Egyptian staff under al-Baqli.

The School of Medicine[a] Staff, Winter 1871–72

Position	Incumbent
Director of the School and of Surgery Clinic	Muhammad Ali Bey al-Baqli
Full Professors	
Internal Pathology and Director of Clinic	Salem Bey Salem
Ophthalmology	Husayn Bey Awf
Obstetrics	Hasan Bey Hashim
Associate Professors	
Anatomy	Hasan Effendi
Physiology	Abd al-Rahman Hirawi
Therapeutics and Materia Medica	Muhammad Badr
Minor Surgery	Muhammad Effendi Fawzi
Instructors and Assistants	
Internal Pathology and Clinic, Assistant	Kattawi Effendi
Ophthalmology, Assistant	Muhammad Bahagat Awf
Hygiene	Mahmud Effendi
Forensic Medicine	Ibrahim Effendi Hasan
Anatomy, Assistant	Muhammad Dawri
General Surgery and Surgical Anatomy	Ahmad Hamdi

[a]V. Edouard Dor, *L'Instruction Publique en Egypte* (Paris: A. Lacroix Verboeckhouen et Cie., 1872), 385.

46. "Modern Medical Schools," *Journal of the Egyptian Medical Association* XI, no. 10 (1928): 356J through Q; Naguib Mahfouz, *The Life of an*

Egyptian Doctor (Edinburgh and London: E. and S. Livingston, Ltd., 1966), 22.

3: Cholera: The Epidemic of 1831 and Later Invasions

1. The standard monograph on cholera, which includes a brief history, is Robert Pollitzer, *Cholera* (Geneva: World Health Organization, 1959). Outstanding studies of the social effects of the pandemics include the following. France: Louis Chevalier, ed., *Le Choléra: La première épidémie du 19ᵉ siècle* (La Roche sur Yon: Imprimerie Centrale de l'ouest, 1958); Albert Colnat, ed., "L'âge du Choléra," in *Les Epidémies et L'Histoire* (Paris: Editions Hippocrates, 1937), 162–181; Paul Delaunay, *Le Corps Médical et le Choléra en 1832* (Tours: Imprimerie Touranelle, 1933). Great Britain: Norman Longmate, *King Cholera: The Biography of a Disease* (London: Hamish Hamilton, 1966); Robert J. Morris, *Cholera 1832: The Social Response to an Epidemic* (New York: Holmes and Meier, 1976). United States: Charles E. Rosenberg, *The Cholera Years: The United States in 1832, 1849, and 1866* (Chicago: University of Chicago Press, 1962). Russia: Roderick E. McGrew, *Russia and the Cholera, 1823–1832* (Madison: University of Wisconsin Press, 1965). George Rosen, *A History of Public Health* (New York: MD Press, 1958), is still a standard study of the subject.

2. Dr. Abdel Gawad Hussein Bey, "Epidemiology of Cholera in Egypt," *The Medical Press of Egypt* 60 (Dec. 1949): 1–9; Muhammad Khalil Bey, "The Defense of Egypt against Cholera in the Past, Present, and Future," *Journal of the Egyptian Medical Association* 30, no. 12 (Dec. 1947): 616–619; Abd al-Wahid al-Wakil Bey, "The History of Cholera in Egypt," *JEMA* 30, no. 11 (Nov. 1947): 409–413. There was no serious epidemic of cholera between 1902 and 1947.

3. Hussein, 17–19.

4. Robert Pollitzer, "Cholera Studies: Epidemiology," *Bulletin of the World Health Organization* 16 (1957): 805–806. Under "intelligence," Dr. Pollitzer also includes laboratory diagnostic tests, which were not common practice until the last quarter of the nineteenth century.

5. Hussein, 1; Khalil, 618. Although the population of Egypt in the nineteenth century has been much debated, Hussein's epidemiological study gives the mortality figures during the 1831 epidemic as 150,000 for all of Egypt, i.e., 50/1000 of the population, and 36,000 for Cairo, i.e., 129/1000 of the population. This death toll of one person in twenty was matched only in Imperial Russia, where 400,000 of the estimated eight million inhabitants died. As for single cities, Cairo's mortality far exceeded that of Paris, one of the hardest-hit European cities: 18,400 of a total population of 760,000 died during the epidemic; Chevalier, 4, 30.

6. Pollitzer, 14, 19–20; "The Cholera," 200; John Barker, *Syria and*

Egypt under the Last Five Sultans of Turkey, 2 vols. (London: Samuel Tinsley, 1876), I, 331. Clot believed that the Egyptians called cholera "the yellow wind" because it coincided with the appearance of low-hanging gray or yellowish fog, common at the high point of the Nile flood (*Mémoires,* 163–164). Dr. Khalil has pointed out that high humidity often contributes to the spread of cholera, hence its association with meteorological phenomena (612, 614–615, 617).

7. France, Ministère des Affaires Etrangères, *Correspondence et Commerciale, Alexandrie,* vol. 21, Drovetti, 10 November 1824, 13 February, 22 November, 1825; Ministry to Drovetti, 14 August 1824, 8 April, 24 September 1825.

8. Ibid., vol. 24, Mimaut, 16 July 1831; FO 78/202, Barker, 21 July 1831; Cattaui, I, 432; "Extrait d'une lettre addressé a M. Felix d'Arcet par M. Mimaut, consul-general de France in Egypte," *Annales de l'Hygiène Publique et de Médecine Légale* VI, no. 1 (1831): 476–478; Pollitzer, 25.

9. AE, *CCC Alexandrie,* vol. 24, Mimaut, 9 August 1831.

10. Cattaui, I, 223–224, 428, 433.

11. FO 78/202, Barker, 10 August 1831; A. B. Clot-Bey, *Relation de l'Epidémie de Choléra qui a Regné en Arabie et en Egypte* (Marseilles: Arnaud Cayer et Cie, 1866), 44 (hereafter referred to as *Relation*).

12. FO 78/202, Barker, 18 August 1831.

13. Clot-Bey, *Relation,* 14–16; *Mémoires,* 162. "The Cholera," 171. In cholera attacks, the development of the microorganism (vibrio) was accompanied by ptomaine, which attacked the epithelium of the intestinal mucous membrane; hence, the classic diagnostic sign was tiny particles of the intestinal lining in copious "rice-water" discharges. Violent vomiting and diarrhea brought about sudden and extreme dehydration, while the ptomaine, entering the bloodstream, attacked the red corpuscles and disturbed the nervous system, especially the vasomotor and respiratory centers. The signs were so spectacular that French writers described the action of cholera as "cadaverizing" the patient. Edward Shakespeare, *Report on Cholera in Europe and India* (Washington, D.C.: U.S. Government Printing Office, 1890), 885–888; Pollitzer, 684–708.

14. AE, *CCC, Alexandrie,* vol. 24, Mimaut, 22 August, 24 August 1831; FO 78/202, Barker, 18 August, 23 August 1831.

15. FO 78/202, Barker, 2 September 1831; AE, *CCC, Alexandrie,* vol. 24, Mimaut, 2 September 1831, 10 September 1831; William Holt Yates, *The Modern History and Condition of Egypt,* 2 vols. (London: Smith, Elder and Co., 1843), I, 136–137.

16. Cattaui, I, 440.

17. AE, *CCC, Alexandrie,* Mimaut, 24 August, 10 September 1831. Under normal circumstances, Muslim burials were extremely simple, but belief and practice made it mandatory that the deceased be laid in the earth

with his face toward Mecca. Destruction of the body by burning or caustics was forbidden to Muslims; it was strongly opposed in Europe and the Anglo-Saxon countries at this time as well since practicing Christians shared the Muslim belief in resurrection of the body on the day of judgment.

18. Felix Mengin, *Histoire Sommaire de l'Egypte* (Paris: Firmin Didot Freres, 1839), 31. Cattau, I, 441. *Egyptian Gazette* (al-Waqā'ī' al-Misriyah), no. 303, jumadi al-awwal 1247 (8 October 1831), 1.

19. AE, *CCC, Alexandrie*, vol. 24, Mimaut, 22 August 1831.

20. *Egyptian Gazette*, no. 303, 8 October 1831, 2, 3; no. 305, 13 October 1831, 1; no. 329, 19 December 1831, 2; no. 332, 26 December 1831, 2; no. 333, 28 December, 1831, 2; Yates, I, 136.

21. AE, *CCC, Alexandrie*, vol. 24, Mimaut, 2 September 1831; Clot-Bey, *Mémoires*, 163.

22. FO 78/202, Barker, 2 September 1831, AE, *CCC, Alexandrie*, vol. 24, Mimaut, 2 September, 10 September, 26 September 1831.

23. Ibid., vol. 24, Mimaut, 23 October and 18 November 1831. In 1848, Francesco Grassi wrote that 12,000 to 15,000 were buried in and around Alexandria during September 1831; FO 78/759, Gilbert, 30 December 1848.

24. AE, *CCC, Alexandrie*, vol. 24, Mimaut, 22 October, 18 November, 28 November, 8 December 1831.

25. The viceroy no doubt had heard all the noncontagionist arguments against quarantine procedures which would hold Egypt's poor environmental sanitation responsible for epidemic disease outbreaks. He probably was aware that the Ottoman Board of Health also had experienced difficulty in gaining European compliance with domestic quarantine regulations. The British ambassador had protested strongly against rulings that would permit Turkish health officers to enter the houses of British subjects because, he instructed the Ottoman government, plague could be combated more effectively "by introducing cleanliness and ventilation in Constantinople"; FO 78/352, FO to Ponsonby, 18 February 1839.

26. FO 78/260, Campbell, 16 October 1835; ENA, Index Cards: Health, *Maʿīya,* register 139, doc. no. 627, akhkhar rajab 1251 (November 1835); portfolio 5, doc. no. 75, 23 rajab 1252 (4 November 1836); portfolio 5, doc. no. 131, 7 Ramadan 1252 (16 December 1836).

27. "General Regulations Concerning the Public Health at Alexandria to be Put into Execution According to the Order of His Highness the Viceroy, dated 15 Rajab 1257 (30 August 1841)," enclosure with FO 78/502, Barnett, 23 December 1842. The regulations were divided into four chapters: I, "Exterior Quarantine"; II, "Interior Quarantine"; III, "Sanitary Police of the City and Environs"; IV, "Cleanliness of Houses and Airing of Effects."

28. The muhtasib, or market inspector, checked commodities quantitatively, ensuring that they met standard weights and measures; this area of

responsibility offered a natural framework for the functions of a pure food inspector.

29. "Statement of the General Mortality in Cairo and Alexandria during the Prevalence of the Cholera Morbus," enclosure in FO 78/759, Gilbert, 30 December 1848. One visitor in Egypt during the epidemic accepted the official mortality figure for Cairo but claimed that 70,000 died in all Egypt; Friedrich Dieterici, *Reisebilder aus dem Morgenlande,* 2 vols. (Berlin: Wiegandt und Grieben, 1853), I, 152.

30. *Egyptian Gazette,* no. 49, 27 January 1847, 1; no. 51, 10 February 1847, 1; no. 88, 27 October 1847, 1; no. 101, 24 January 1848, 1.

31. Francesco Grassi, "A Relation and Reflections on the Indian Cholera which Raged in Egypt in the Year 1848," translation from the Italian enclosed with FO 78/759, Gilbert, 30 December 1848. Grassi's account was forwarded to the Sanitary Commission of London, then collecting information on the disease that caused the worst epidemic of the century in the British Isles. He was somewhat defensive because Great Britain had abolished quarantines as useless, and he was no doubt aware of all the criticisms directed at the service in which he functioned.

A Russian physician, Artemis Rafalowitch, in "Briefe eines russischen Artztes (Rafalowitsch) aus der Turkei," *Das Ausland* 22 (1949): 59, described the nine-day quarantine required of all travelers from Syria, which he underwent in September 1847, as useless. He claimed that the ships' passengers were not examined by anyone before they entered the lazaretto and the physician in charge only glanced at them in a cursory fashion before releasing them from detention.

32. Dieterici, I, 144; Rafalowitch, 508; Grassi. Grassi gave the population of Tanta as only 8,000 to 10,000, but Rafalowitch's figure, 17,630, appears to be that of the census of 1846. Grassi may have wished to minimize the number of deaths in Tanta, which are not reported anywhere.

33. FO 78/757, Murray, 26 July, 6 August, 14 August 1848; Dieterici, I, 145, 147.

34. *Egyptian Gazette,* no. 124, 26 July 1848, 1. The *Gazette* contains frequent references to directives from the chief physician forbidding the sale and consumption of green, unripe fruits, e.g., no. 7, 3 July 1845, 3; no. 20, 7 July 1846, 1.

35. ENA, *Ministry of Public Instruction:* Carton 49, Study No. 1, Subject: Education, register no. 100, Pt. VIII, doc. no. 696, 3283, dated 24 July 1848. By this time, government communications were beginning to refer to cholera as "Haida," the local Coptic term for diarrhea. Dieterici, I, 144.

36. *Egyptian Gazette,* no. 124, 26 July 1848, 1. See chapter on the Provincial Health Service.

37. FO 78/757, Murray, 26 July, 14 August 1848; AE, *CCC, Alexandrie*, vol. 32, Barrat, 6 September 1848; Grassi.

38. *Egyptian Gazette*, no. 124, 26 July 1848, 1; no. 126, 7 August 1848, 1; no. 130, 5 September 1848, 1; no. 131, 12 September 1848, 1; no. 132, 19 September 1848, 1.

39. FO 78/757, Murray, 26 July, 6 August, 14 August 1848; Legros, 19 September 1848; Dieterici, I, 145–148.

40. ENA, *Ministry of Public Instruction*: Carton 49, study no. 1, Subject: Education; register no. 91, par. 10, doc. no. 235, 3523, dated 26 Ramadan 1264 (26 August 1847); Clot-Bey, "Quelques réflexions nouvelles sur les épidemies de choléra du Caire de 1834, 1840, 1848," in *Mélanges*, XXVI (Paris: Faculté de Médicine, 1866), 43.

41. See n. 13 preceding; also, Dieterici, I, 142, 143, and 145, who mentioned encountering resignation and fatalism as well.

42. Paul Cassar, *Medical History of Malta* (London: Wellcome Historical Medical Library, 1964), 196. According to Cassar, this ruling was adopted during a cholera epidemic in 1837; presumably, it remained in force until the Maltese Medical Society's investigation of the epidemic in 1850 concluded that cholera was contagious; 199–201.

43. Grassi.

44. Serious cholera epidemics broke out in Egypt in 1850–51 and 1855, but according to the president of the Quarantine Board, they followed the same pattern as that in 1848; circular no. 633 dated 21 June 1865 from Dr. Colucci Bey, President of the international Quarantine Board, enclosed with AE, *CCC Alexandrie*, no. 24, Gazay, 24 June 1865.

45. *Proceedings of the International Sanitary Conference, 1866* (Calcutta: Office of the Superintendent of Government Printing, 1868), 528–533; Firmin Duguet, *Le Pelerinage de la Mecque* (Paris: Rieder, 1932), 126–129; Circular No. 633 dated 21 June 1865 from Dr. Colucci Bey.

46. FO 78/1885, Alexandria no. 23, 23 June 1865; FO 78/1887, Cairo no. 21, 28 June 1865; AE, *CCC, Alexandrie*, no. 26, 5 July 1865.

47. Lady Lucie Duff-Gordon, *Letters from Egypt* (London: Routledge & Kegan Paul, 1969), 270.

48. Colucci-Bey, circular no. 633; John C. Peters, "Cholera in Egypt in 1883," chap. 10, in Edmund C. Wendt, ed., *A Treatise on Asiatic Cholera* (New York: William Wood and Company, 1885), 61–62.

49. FO 78/1885, Alexandria no. 23, 23 June 1865; James C. McCoan, *Egypt as It Is* (London: Cissell, Petter, and Galpin, 1889), 36.

4: The Plague Epidemic of 1835: Background and Consequences

1. The standard monograph on plague, which includes a brief history, is Robert Pollitzer, *Plague* (Geneva: World Health Organization, 1954).

L. Fabian Hirst, *The Conquest of Plague: A Study of the Evolution of Epidemiology* (Oxford: Clarendon Press, 1953), is particularly enlightening for the nonspecialist. More general are Charles E. Winslow, *The Conquest of Epidemic Disease* (Princeton: Princeton University Press, 1943); and Hans Zinsser's classic, *Rats, Lice and History* (Boston: Little, Brown and Co., 1935). The old, classic histories of epidemics include details on individual outbreaks: H. Haeser, *Lehrbuch der Geschichte der Medizin und der Epidemischen Krankheiten*, Vol. II: *Geschichte der Epidemischen Krankheiten*, 2d ed. (Jena: Friedrich Mauke, 1865); August Hirsch, *Handbook of Geographical and Historical Pathology*, I: *Acute Infective Diseases* (London: New Sydenham Society, 1883), 494–544; George Sticker, *Abhandlungen aus der Seuchengeschichte und Seuchenlehre*, I: *Die Pest*, Pt. I: *Die Geschichte der Pest*, Pt. II: *Die Pest als Seuche und als Plag* (Giessen: Alfred Toepelmann, 1908, 1910). There is a voluminous literature on the fourteenth-century Black Death and the persistence of plague in individual areas of Europe into the early modern period, particularly for the Italian states, France, and England. For the Middle East, two works are indispensable: Alfred von Kremer, "Ueber die grossen Seuchen des Orients nach arabischen Quellen," *Sitzungsberichte der Kaiserlichen Akademie der Wissenschaften* (Philosophisch-Historische Classe), 96, Bk. 1, Vienna 1880, 69–156; and Michael W. Dols, *The Black Death in the Middle East* (Princeton: Princeton University Press, 1977). This inquiry has benefited from the impressive comparative study by Jean-Noel Biraben, *Les Hommes et la Peste en France et dans les Pays Européens et Méditerranéens,* 2 vols. (Paris and The Hague: Mouton, 1975–76).

2. Hirsch, 525; Hirst, 284.

3. Etienne Pariset, *Mémoire sur les causes de la peste et sur les moyens de la détruire* (Paris, 1847), quoted in P. et H., *L'Egypte sous la domination de Méhémet Aly,* 99–100.

4. A. B. Clot-Bey, *De la Peste* (Paris: Fortin, Masson et Cie., 1840), 213–223, 233–234.

5. Hirst, 288.

6. Pierre Nicolas Hamont, "Sur l'état hygiènique de l'Egypte," *Annales de l'hygiène publique* VI, no. 1 (1831): 481. See Louis Aubert-Roche, *De la Peste ou Typhus d'Orient* (Paris: n.p., 1840), passim; and Victor Schoelcher, *L'Egypte en 1845* (Paris: Pagnerre, 1846). British physicians who held similar views were R. R. Madden, *Travels in Turkey, Egypt, Nubia and Palestine,* 2 vols. (London: Henry Colburn, 1829), and William H. Yates, *The Modern History and Condition of Egypt,* 2 vols. (London: Smith Elder and Co., 1843).

7. Clovis René Prus, *Rapport a l'Académie Royale de Médecine sur la Peste et les Quarantaines* (Paris: J. B. Bailliere, 1846).

8. Dols, 93–94; Winslow, 100–101; Hirst, 25, 40, 46–50.

9. Ahmad ibn ʿAli al-Maqrizi, *Kitab al-Suluk li-maʿrifat Duwal al-*

Muluk, 2 vols. (Cairo: n.p., 1936–1958); M. Quatremère, trans., *Suluk, histoire des Sultans Mamelouks d'Egypte,* 2 vols. (Paris: n.p., 1837–1842), II, 772–787.

10. Dols, 23–25, 109–121. For some of the traditions, see Muhammad ibn Ismai'il Al Bukhari, *Sahih: Les Traditions Islamiques,* trans. O. Houdes (Paris: Ernest Leroux, 1914), Bk. LXXVI, *Medicine,* 69, 72, 82–83, 88, 89.

11. Dols, 121–142. Among the illustrations in Biraben, op. cit., II, 160ff., is a magic formula in Arabic which was used as a protection against plague. Such inscriptions were suspended around the neck in a locket; or, inscribed on a wooden tablet, the inscription was washed off and the rinse water swallowed as a preventive or cure.

12. Ahmad Issa Bey, *Histoire des Bimaristans (Hôpitaux) a l'Epoque Islamique* (Cairo: Paul Barbey, 1928), 31–37, points out that the best-equipped hospitals in Cairo in the fourteenth century and following included wards for fevers, but there is no mention in contemporary accounts of seg-regated facilities for plague patients.

13. Pollitzer, 483–518; Hirst, 28–34. Several writers, including Hirst, distinguish a third type of plague, septicemic, wherein the infection im-mediately enters the bloodstream, buboes have no time to form, and the course of the disease is rapid and invariably fatal.

Bubonic plague is characterized by the bubo, a swelling of the lymphatic gland located nearest the point of inoculation by a flea bite. The other form of the disease, pneumonic or pulmonary plague, is spread from person to person by airborne droplets of sputum coughed or sneezed by the infected person. Pneumonic plague is nearly always fatal, whereas a substantial pro-portion of bubonic plague cases—as high as 40 percent—have recovered in past epidemics.

14. Michael Dols, "The Second Plague Pandemic and Its Recurrences in the Middle East: 1347–1894," *Journal of the Economic and Social History of the Orient* 22 (1979): 183.

15. Ahmed Mohammed Kemal, ed., *Epidemiology of Communicable Diseases* (Cairo: Anglo-Egyptian Bookshop, 1958), 233–268; James S. Sim-mons et al., *Global Epidemiology,* 5 vols. (Philadelphia: J. B. Lippincott, 1951), 20–21.

16. To explain the anomaly of pneumonic plague in Upper Egypt, it has been suggested that extreme aridity may cause irritation of the respiratory system and pulmonary susceptibility to infection. When men from the Saïd who worked in the port cities returned to their native villages infected with plague, they might arrive home, according to Wakil, with pneumonic plague complications caused by the long journey; in overcrowded, poorly ventilated housing, the infection would spread like wildfire. Abd al-Wahid al-Wakil, *The Third Pandemic of Plague in Egypt: Historical, Statistical and Epi-demiological Remarks on the First Thirty-two Years of Its Prevalence* (Cairo:

Egyptian University, 1932), quoted and referenced in Pollitzer, 32–34, 513: Hirst, 221; J. Davis, "Plague in Africa," *WHO Bulletin*, IX (1953): 665–700. Fleming M. Sandwith, *The Medical Diseases of Egypt*, 2 vols. (London: Henry Kimptom, 1905), I, 172–174.

17. Patrick Russell, *A Treatise of the Plague* (London: G. G. J. and J. Robinson, 1791), 266–267; P. et H., 99. According to Lane, p. 495, the feast of *laylat al-nuqta* or "Night of the Drop [of Dew]" referred to an old belief that a miraculous drop of dew fell into the Nile and caused it to rise.

18. Russell, 2; Madden, I, 218–219; Constantin-François Volney, *Voyage en Egypte et en Syrie* (Paris: Volland et Desenne, 1787), 143; de Salle, II, 187; Belzoni, 1.

In addition to an adequate rat and rat-flea density, the propagation of plague requires optimum meteorological conditions—a temperature range between 68°F and 78°F in a moderately moist atmosphere—in which *Xenopsylla cheopsis* may breed and efficiently transmit plague. This is the temperature range that has been found to prevail during the plague "season" in nearly all parts of the world subject to severe epidemics of bubonic plague, according to Hirst, 263, 272, 301–303.

The meteorological conditions favorable for optimum proliferation of rat fleas thus moved slowly down the Nile, accompanying warmer and more humid weather, in the progression suggested by Wakil as follows (Pollitzer, *Plague*, 33):

The Plague Season in Egypt

Region	Onset	Peak	End
Upper	March	April	May
Middle	April	May	June
Delta and Suez	April	June	July
Mediterranean ports	May	July	October

19. Dr. Paolo Asalini in Clot-Bey, *De la Peste*, 417–419; also Madden, I, 252–257; Kinglake, 161; and Volney, 142.

20. Clot-Bey, *De la Peste*, xxii, 361, 416.

21. John Bowring, *Observations on the Oriental Plague and on Quarantine as a Means of Arresting Its Progress* (Edinburgh: n.p., 1838), included as Appendix F in *Report on Egypt and Candia*, 213.

22. Dominique J. Larrey, "Mémoires et observations sur plusieurs maladies qui ont affecté les troupes de l'armee française pendant l'expédition d'Egypte . . . ," *Description de l'Egypte, Etat Moderne* (Paris: Imprimerie Imperiale, 1899), I, 465; René Desgenettes, *Histoire Médicale de l'Armée*

d'Orient (Paris: Firman, Didot, Frères, 1830), 16. Virtually all members of the French medical corps wrote that their experience in Egypt confirmed their view that plague was contagious.

23. Al-Jabarti, VI, 45–46, 53, 155.

24. Ibid., VI, 106–107.

25. Ibid., VI, 282–283.

26. Desgenettes, 206–210.

27. Al-Jabarti, VI, 307–308.

28. Ibid., VIII, 341; IX, 9, 78, 83, 119, 137, 297–299, 330.

29. Ibid., IX, 18.

30. Ibid., IX, 19–20, 22, 83–84, 106.

31. Ibid., IX, 297–299.

32. Madden, I, 252–257.

33. Clot-Bey, *Aperçu Générale sur l'Egypte*, I, 192, 188–194; II, 327, 328; Bowring, 80–81; Arthur E. Crouchley, *The Economic Development of Modern Egypt* (London: Longmans, Green and Co., 1938), 82, 90, 92, 93, 96.

34. French translation enclosed in FO 78/376, Campbell, 9 May 1839.

35. ENA, Index Cards: Health; *Ma'īya*, register no. 59, doc. no. 670, 12 Sha'ban 1250 (15 December 1834), French translation enclosed in FO 78/376, Campbell, 9 May 1839.

36. Order to Zaki Effendi, *chef du cabinet* of the Khedivial Divan dated 14 Sha'ban 1250 (16 December 1834), French translation enclosed in FO 78/376, Campbell, 9 May 1839.

37. Order to Zaki Effendi dated 14 Ramadan 1250 (14 January 1835), French translation enclosed in FO 78/376, Campbell, 9 May 1839; AE, *CCC, Alexandrie*, vol. 26, De Lesseps, 20 January 1835.

38. FO 78/260, Thurburn, 9 March 1835; Clot-Bey, *De la Peste*, 409.

39. AE, *CCC, Alexandrie*, vol. 26, De Lesseps, 18 February 1835.

40. Order to Zaki Effendi dated 12 Shawwal 1250 (11 February 1835), French translation enclosed in FO 78/376, Campbell, 9 May 1839.

41. FO 78/260, Thurburn, 9 March 1835, AE, *CCC, Alexandrie*, Vol. XXVI, De Lesseps, 14 March 1835; Cattaui, II, 265.

42. ENA, Index Cards: Health: *Ma'īya*, register 806, doc. no. 135, 22 Sha'ban 1250 (25 December 1834).

43. Clot-Bey, *Mémoires*, 286–287. At the end of March, Ibrahim Pasha could no longer tolerate the confinement of three months' isolation and left for Syria; he had been preceded by Muhammad Ali who fled the capital for Upper Egypt and at the end of March set up a temporary court at Isna. Cattaui, FO 78/257, Campbell, 24 March, 29 March 1835.

44. ENA, Index Cards: Health: *Ma'īya*, register no. 798, doc. no. 107, 26 Shawwal 1250 (25 February 1835).

45. Ibid., register no. 62, doc. no. 551, 26 dhi al-hijja 1250 (25 April

1835); register no. 54, doc. no. 485, 17 dhi al-hijja 1250 (16 April 1835); register no. 57, doc. no. 559, 28 dhi al-hijja 1250 (27 April 1835); Summaries; *Ma'īya*, portfolio 61, register no. 62, order no. 414, 19 Shawwal 1250 (18 February 1835); register no. 60, order no. 44, 5 dhi al-qu'da 1250 (5 March 1835); portfolio 7, register no. 61, order no. 19, 4 Sha'ban 1250 (7 December 1834).

46. Clot-Bey, *De la Peste*, 427–428. Since schools were not staffed with physicians, the acting director of schools, Muharram Bey, was instructed to provide care for any students who might fall sick. ENA, Summaries, *Ma'īya*, portfolio 62; register no. 60, order no. 8, 11 Shawwal 1250 (10 February 1835).

47. Clot-Bey, *De la Peste*, 299–300, 310, 330, 428–429.

48. ENA, Index Cards: Health, *Ma'īya*, register no. 57, doc. no. 559, 28 dhi al-hijja 1250 (27 April 1835); Louis Aubert-Roche, letter to the *Gazette Médicale de Marseilles* dated 10 June 1836, quoted in Clot-Bey, *De la Peste*, 298–299; ibid., 343.

49. FO 78/260, Thurburn, 9 March 1835; Campbell, 23 March 1835; Thurburn, 1 April 1835; Campbell, 25 November 1835; AE, *CCC, Alexandrie*, vol. 26, De Lesseps, 14 March 1835; Mimaut, 31 March 1835; Cattaui, II, 256–266, 281; Dr. Koch, chief physician for the Egyptian fleet, letter to Dr. Clot, quoted in Clot-Bey, *De la Peste*, 319.

50. ENA, Index Cards: Health, *Ma'īya*, register no. 59, doc. no. 78, 13 muharram 1251 (11 May 1835); register no. 57, doc. no. 58, 3 Safar 1251 (31 May 1835).

51. Clot-Bey, *De la Peste*, 316.

52. ENA, Index Cards: Health, *Ma'īya*, register no. 60, doc. no. 161, 20 dhi al-hijja (19 April 1835); Summaries, *Ma'īya*, portfolio 7, register no. 61, order no. 114, 20 dhi al-hijja 1250 (19 April 1835); ibid., portfolios 61, 62, register no. 60, order no. 44, 5 dhi al-ga'ida 1250 (5 March 1835); order no. 162, 20 dhi al-hijja 1250 (19 April 1835).

53. FO 78/257, Campbell, 15 April 1835; Cattaui, II, 288–289; Clot-Bey, *De la Peste*, 301.

54. AE, *CCC, Alexandrie*, vol. 26, De Lesseps, 8 April 1835, Mimaut, 10 April 1835.

55. Alexander W. Kinglake, *Eothen* (London: J. M. Dent and Sons, Ltd., 1908), 155–173. Ceremonies following death, like ritual purity, were important to the people of Cairo. Although burials were simple, funeral ceremonies were often elaborate and prolonged for prominent persons; see the description in Lane, 516–534.

56. Cattaui, II, 299, 321–322, 334.

57. ENA, Summaries, *Ma'īya*. portfolio 7, register no. 61, order no. 162, 19 safar 1251 (17 June 1835), order no. 174, 29 safar 1251 (27 June 1835); ibid., portfolios 61, 62, register no. 60, order no. 328, 20 safar 1251

(21 June 1835); ibid., portfolio 7, register no. 61, order no. 182, 6 rabi al-awwal 1251 (2 July 1835); order no. 186, 8 rabi al-awwal 1251 (4 July 1835).

58. Cattaui, II, Pt. I, 338–339; AE, *CCC, Alexandrie*, vol. 26, De Lesseps, 20 May, 5 June 1835.

59. AE, *CCC, Alexandrie*, vol. 26, De Lesseps, 20 May 1835, 26 June 1835; FO 78/257, Campbell, 25 June 1835; Cattaui. Clot-Bey, *De la Peste*, 310, wrote that the government had expropriated 600 houses left vacant; Campbell reported the number as 1,200. De Lesseps cited the governor of Cairo as announcing that 75,000 had perished in the capital and that the government had taken over 1,200 houses. Edward Lane wrote (p. 3) that Cairo had lost one-third of its population, i.e., 80,000 people, and that 200,000 died in all Egypt; Lane claimed that it was government policy to report only one-half of the actual mortality during the epidemic. Justin A. McCarthy in "Nineteenth-Century Egyptian Population," *Middle East Studies* XII, no. 3 (October 1976): 13–15, suggests a total death toll of perhaps 500,000 by adopting the twentieth-century pattern of plague distribution and projecting 55 percent of the total mortality to Upper Egypt, where the present-day locus of the disease exists. This is not a valid assumption for the nineteenth century because while basin irrigation still prevailed, the annual Nile flood periodically flushed out rats in the irrigation dikes, preventing the rat-flea concentration required to trigger and sustain an epidemic. It is true that the temperature and humidity were the same then as they are now, but the requisite rat, flea, and human populations were not in place in 1835.

60. FO 78/257, Campbell, 25 June 1835; FO 78/260, Campbell, 16 October 1835; AE, *CCC, Alexandrie*, vol. 26, De Lesseps, 26 June 1835; Cattaui, II, Pt. I, 339, 344, 359, 411.

61. ENA, Summaries, *Maʿīya*, portfolio 62, register no. 66, doc. no. 9, 19 rabi al-awwal 1251 (16 July 1835). ENA, *Maʿīya*, portfolio 51, report no. 3, Subject: Education; register 64, doc. no. 64, 9 Ramadan 1251 (30 December 1835); Summaries, *Maʿīya*, portfolio 61, register no. 64, order no. 138, 19 Ramadan 1251 (9 January 1836).

62. FO 78/321, Campbell, 7 November 1837.

63. *De la Peste*, 352–357; *Mémoires*, 288–290. Of four condemned criminals who slept in plague victims' beds, wore their clothing, or were inoculated with plague patients' blood or bubo pus, two developed symptoms and one died. Although Clot referred to Desgenettes's similar experiment in autoinoculation in 1799, he did not include his conclusion (pp. 87–88) that the failure of the inoculation to produce plague "simply indicated that the conditions necessary for its occurrence are not well determined."

64. In 1855, Clot claimed that his "proof" of the nontransmissibility of plague twenty years earlier had resulted in the virtual abolition of quarantines in France and England, i.e., in Marseilles and Malta; Nassau W. Senior,

Conversations and Journals in Egypt and Malta, 2 vols. (London: Sampson Low et al., 1882), II, 197. Clot must share the credit, however, with John Bowring, who did much to publicize the views of Dr. James Laidlaw, surgeon to the European Hospital in Alexandria, who also became convinced that plague was not communicable during the epidemic in 1835; Bowring, 222–223.

65. Clot-Bey, *Mémoires,* 287, 292. ENA, Summaries, *Maʿīya,* portfolio 7, register no. 61, orders no. 189, 190, 8 and 9 rabiʾ al-awwal 1251 (4 and 5 July 1835). After the epidemic had passed, Muhammad Ali honored all four members of the Medical Council for "meritorious service." Dr. Clot was promoted to brigadier general and awarded the title of Bey.

66. Clot-Bey, *De la Peste,* 411–412.

67. ENA, Summaries, *Maʿīya,* register no. 59, doc. no. 567, akhkhar muharram 1251 (May 1835).

68. Bowring, 30–33.

69. Clot-Bey, *De la Peste,* 318–320.

70. ENA. Index Cards, Subject: Health, *Maʿīya,* register 64, doc. no. 182, 26 Ramadan 1251 (16 January 1836); Summaries, *Maʿīya,* portfolio 62, register no. 64, order no. 182, 26 Ramadan 1251 (16 January 1836). The weight was 32 uqqah; 1 uqqah = 1.25 kilograms or 2.75 pounds. It is possible that the guilty physician or physicians were Egyptian, but since all Egyptians in the army or navy were in subordinate posts, it is not likely they would take the initiative in contravening regulations.

71. Clot-Bey, *De la Peste,* 410. Clot probably was referring to "l'affaire Aubert-Roche"; the French consul general had to order Aubert expelled from the country because he resisted quarantining one of his patients who was suffering from plague, insulted the president of the Board of Health (the British consul general), and struck the health warden; AE, *CCC, Alexandrie,* vol. 26, Mimaut, 28 October, 24 November 1835.

72. A. F. Bulard de Meru, *De la peste orientale d'après les matériaux recueillis à Alexandrie, au Caire, à Smyrne et à Constantinople pendant les années 1833–1838* (Paris: n.p., 1839), gives full details of all the establishments that escaped plague during the epidemic in 1835. Unfortunately, the book was not available to the writer, who had to confine these observations to sites specifically mentioned in the European consuls' reports. Bulard, another member of the Plague Commission, became as convinced that plague was communicable as Clot was certain that it was not; they became bitter enemies and attacked each other personally in their writings.

73. Clot-Bey, *De la Peste,* 301; Cattaui, II, Pt. II, 9.

74. Louis Aubert-Roche, letter to the *Gazette Médicale de Marseille,* dated 10 June 1836, quoted in Clot-Bey, *De la Peste,* 299.

75. FO 78/260, Campbell, 25 November 1835; FO 78/271, Campbell, 12 December 1836. ENA, Index Cards: Health, *Maʿīya,* register no. 64, doc.

no. 12, 2 Ramadan 1251 (23 December 1835). ENA, Summaries, *Ma'īya*, portfolios 60, 61, register no. 67, doc. no. 333, 15 Sha'ban 1251 (7 December 1835).

76. Cattaui, II, Pt. I, 314.

77. Notification of the Board of Health dated 23 November 1835; translation from Italian enclosed in FO 78/260, Campbell, 25 November 1835.

78. The director of the first British Board of Health in Egypt observed that in the plague epidemic of 1899–1904, resistance against removal of the sick for hospitalization caused both Egyptians and Europeans to conceal the early cases of an outbreak; the rural Egyptians were especially clever in hiding their sick in the fields or their dead in boxes under beds or even in unused ovens. To encourage notification, the government found it effective to enforce isolation of contacts of all *undeclared* cases of plague. Fleming M. Sandwith, *The Medical Diseases of Egypt,* 2 vols. (London: Henry Kimpton, 1905), I, 195, 199.

79. Cattaui, II, pt. 2, 3–4.

5: The International Quarantine Board

1. To avoid confusion with the Board of Health in Cairo, this study uses only the title Quarantine Board to denote the agency in Alexandria, although it had many name changes. From 1831 to 1835, it was called the Consular Commission of Health; from 1835 to 1839, the Consular Committee of Health; from 1840 to 1843, Magistrate of Public Health; from 1843 to 1849, Health Administration; and in 1849, it became the General Sanitary Administration of Egypt resident in Alexandria. There may have been intervening changes of title, but in 1880, the board still was called the General Sanitary Administration of Egypt, and in 1881, it became the Sanitary, Maritime, and Quarantine Council of Egypt, as the two histories of this agency indicate: Dr. Tassos Demetrios Neroutsos-Bey, *Aperçu Historique de l'Organization de l'intendance Générale Sanitaire D'Egypte* (Alexandrie: Imprimerie Française A. Mourès, 1880), and Dr. C. E. Bérard, *Le Conseil Sanitaire, Maritime et Quarantenaire d'Egypte* (Alexandrie: Ve. Penasson, 1897), both written by former functionaries of the sanitary administration. Apparently, the latter title remained in force in the twentieth century, for one of the histories of the pilgrimage to Mecca written in 1932 refers to the agency in Alexandria under that name: Firmin Duguet, *Le Pèlerinage de la Mècque* (Paris: Rieder, 1932).

Muhammad Ali's initiative in establishing an international quarantine board in Alexandria was the first move in that direction but the Ottoman sultan and the bey of Tunis also invited Europeans to create and administer maritime quarantine systems at this time, all early-nineteenth-century examples of developing states soliciting Western technical assistance.

2. Dr. Minot, *Memoria sul Renascemento a stato atticale della medicina in Egitto* (Livorno: n.p., 1838), quoted in Arne Barkhuus, "The Dawn of International Cooperation in Medicine," *Ciba Symposia* V, no. 7 (Oct. 1943): 1560.

3. Hirst, 418; Sticker, II, 309–310, 344. French usage, which was adopted in Egypt, recognized three categories of bills of health: clean, suspect, and unclean.

4. See the introduction, n. 6, for reformers who criticized the antiquated practices of the maritime quarantine system.

5. Sir George Buchanan, C.B., M.D., F.R.C.P. London, "International Cooperation in Public Health; Its Achievements and Prospects," *The Lancet,* April 28, 1934, 879–884; May 5, 935–942.

6. ENA, *Ma'īya,* register no. 35, doc. no. 91, dated 12 Ramadan 1233 (28 March 1828); register no. 750, doc. no. 321, dated 14 dhi al-qa'da 1244 (18 May 1829); AE, *CCC, Alexandrie,* Vol. XXIV, Mimaut, 8 June 1831; Amin Sami, *Taqwīm al-Nīl,* II, 383.

7. Cattaui, I, 46, 89.

8. AE, *CCC, Alexandrie,* Vol. XXIV, Mimaut, 22 October 1831, enclosure "Note des Consuls Européens"; Cattaui, I, 452, 499–500, 502–504, 506, 510, 515, 518–519, 521–522, 525.

9. FO 78/260, Campbell, 16 October 1835.

10. In 1835, the British consul in Beirut reported that the trading community was pleased that the city had been named the quarantine station for the whole coast of Syria and had been endowed with a lazaretto; FO 78/264, N. Moore, Commercial Report, 16 November 1835. Following the plague epidemic, however, all the European consuls reportedly opposed Sulayman Pasha's directive forbidding travelers to enter or leave quarantined premises without authorization; those who did so would be challenged by the guards and fired on if they persisted; Cattaui, II, Pt. II, 8, 10–11. In 1839, Campbell observed that British businessmen strenuously opposed everything connected with quarantine in Beirut; FO 78/376, Campbell, 29 April, 13 June 1839.

11. Neroutsos, 24, 30–31, FO 78/360, Pt. I, Ponsonby, 5 November 1839.

12. Ibid., 35; Bérard, 6. Consuls' dispatches are not communicative about the circumstances of their ouster from the board; the British consul general mentioned only that the board's abolition was caused chiefly by "partial jealousies and petty intrigues"; he preferred not to involve himself in the matter. FO 78/407, Hodges, 6 February 1840.

13. Neroutsos, 33–35; Bérard, 6–7. It appears that when the European consuls refused to accept their exclusion, Muhammad Ali abolished the board completely. Local merchants petitioned for reinstatement of the quarantine agency, and an outbreak of plague in Alexandria gave the viceroy an opportunity to reverse his decision without losing face. AE, *CCC, Alexan-*

drie, Vol. XXVIII, Cochelet, 23 January 1840; FO 78/407, Hodges, 6 February 1840; Cattaui, III, 356–357, 359–360.

14. Neroutsos, 36–40; Bérard, 8; Sami, II, 501.

15. FO 78/407, Hodges, 6 February 1840; FO 78/502, Barnett, 3 December 1842, 20 December 1842; FO 78/541, Barnett, 16 January 1843, 19 March 1843, 6 April 1843, 17 April 1843, 22 April 1843, 4 July 1843, 20 July 1843, 25 September 1843; FO 78/542, Barnett, 17 May 1843, 20 May 1843, 18 October 1843; Cattaui, III, 355, 358–359, 360–363, 732–733, 737–738.

16. FO 78/542, Barnett, 13 November 1843; Cattaui, III, 682–684, 713, 725–726, 744–746; Neroutsos, 49–50; Bérard, 10.

17. Sticker, II, 344; Hirst, 383–384, 387. France did not relax quarantine regulations to the same extent as Great Britain; to appease the advocates of quarantine, the minister of commerce in 1847 commissioned the national health council to survey and report on sanitary regulations in all Mediterranean countries; this documentation of the wide variations in statutes as well as practices ultimately led to the first International Sanitary Conference in Paris in 1851. The minister also appointed sanitary physicians to all the principal ports of the Mediterranean—Constantinople, Smyrna, Damascus, Beirut, and Alexandria—charged with scrupulous surveillance of conditions on all vessels bound for France. *Bulletin de l'Académie Royale de Médicine,* 13 (1847–1848): 233–248, 985–991, 1392–1394.

18. Bowring, 116. Bowring's address to the British Association of Science in August 1838, "Observations on the Oriental Plague and on Quarantines as a Means of Arresting Its Progress," was considered quite authoritative. Clot-Bey's criticism of the quarantine system is included in his work on plague, *De la Peste,* 374–407, 434–436.

19. Dr. Prus visited Egypt in 1844 for the French Academy of Medicine inquiry mentioned earlier; Dr. Rafalowitch, whose writing is referred to in this study, took a tour of observation for the Imperial Russian government in 1847–48; an unidentified envoy from the Austrian government visited Egypt for the same purpose in 1849; Neroutsos, 60.

20. FO 78/1885, Alexandria, Colquhuon Cons. no. 11, 22 April 1865.

21. Following are the numbers of ships, listed according to the flag under which they sailed, that carried pilgrims between Suez and Jiddah during two pilgrimage seasons:

	Departures	
	1879–80	*1880–81*
Egypt	29	33
England	27	24

	Departures	
	1879–80	*1880–81*
Austria	5	5
France	2	6
Italy	3	11
Ottoman Turkey	1	5
Zanzibar	–	2
Serbia	1	–
Total	68	86

	Returns	
	1879–80	*1880–81*
Egypt	29	15
England	6	14
Austria	5	–
France	2	3
Ottoman Turkey	2	3
Italy	–	5
Serbia	1	–
Total	45	40
Caravans	7	8

From FO 78/3331, encl. to Cairo, san. no. 45, Cookson, 17 November 1881. There is a discrepancy between the number of ships that transported pilgrims to the Hijaz and the number that returned them to Suez; this may be partly explained by the fact that the Quarantine Board had authorized pilgrims to return to Egypt and the Maghrib overland by caravan as well as by sea. The difference between departures and returns also may have resulted from the fact that some of the ships proceeded to the Indian Ocean after debarking passengers at Jiddah. We have no numbers for the vessels that arrived from South Asia and Southeast Asia, but a list of southward-bound ships departing the two principal Red Sea ports suggests that supposition.

Southward Bound Departures from Jiddah		*Southward Bound Departures from Yanbu*	
Nov. 10, 1880–Jan. 12, 1881		Dec. 6, 1880–Jan. 30, 1881	
England	36	Egypt	5

Southward Bound Departures from Jiddah		Southward Bound Departures from Yanbu	
Italy	2	Ottoman Turkey	5
Zanzibar	2		
France	1		
Austria	1		—
Total	42		10

22. Following is a recapitulation of arrivals at Jiddah and Yanbu which indicates the origins and numbers of pilgrims and ships during the pilgrimage season of 1880–81.

Arrivals at Jiddah and Yanbu, 20 April–10 November 1880

Ships		Pilgrims	
Egyptian	38	Javanese	13,594
English	61	Indian	13,113
Austrian	8	Persian	3,390
Italian	10	Arab	902
Dutch	1	Yemeni	840
Ottoman	6	Sudanese	1,083
French	7	Ottoman	7,679
Russian	1	Egyptian	9,541
Zanzibar		Maghribi	6,805
(Small craft)	–	Various	2,712
Total	135 [*sic*]		59,659

From FO 78/3331, encl. to Cairo, san. no. 45, Cookson, 17 November 1881.

23. Only estimates of the total number of pilgrims visiting Mecca annually are available until the twentieth century. One estimate for the period between 1807 and 1873 suggested a range between 30,000 and 160,000 pilgrims per year. "Hadjdj," *Encyclopedia of Islam*, ed. by M. Th Houtsma and others, 4 vols. (Leiden: E. J. Brill, 1913–1936), III, 34.

24. Duguet, 38–41. The other five caravan routes followed by pilgrims were (1) Damascus-Ma'an-Medina-Mecca, for pilgrims from Anatolia, Con-

stantinople, and Syria; (2) Meshed-Kermanshah-Baghdad-Hail-Medina-Mecca, for pilgrims from Persia; (3) from the Persian Gulf to Riyadh and Mecca via the Najd Desert; (4) the Yemen route via Sana'a-Sa'ada and Taif; and (5) Jiddah to Mecca for pilgrims arriving by sea from the Arabian coast, India, Malaysia, and the east coast of Africa.

25. Dispatch of the Dutch consul at Singapore to the Hague dated 14 March 1866; excerpted in *Proceedings of the International Sanitary Conference, 1866* (Calcutta: Office of the Superintendent of Government Printing, 1868), 651–653.

26. Marc Armand Ruffer, "Measures Taken at Tor and Suez against Ships Coming from the Red Sea and the Far East," *Lancet,* December 30, 1899, 1803.

27. Duguet, viii.

28. The implications of some of these observations pointed to the Arabs of the Hijaz who worked assiduously to gain their year's livelihood during the pilgrims' few months or few weeks in Arabia. It was commonly suggested that even the pilgrim who arrived with ample means for his stay would be thoroughly fleeced by the time he departed. David Long, *The Hajj Today: A Survey of the Contemporary Pilgrimage to Makkah* (Albany: State University of New York, 1979), 34–35, has summarized present-day and historical accounts of the holy cities' allegedly extortionate service industries.

29. AE, *CCC, Alexandrie,* vol. 24, Mimaut, 16 July 1831; FO 78/202, Barker, 21 July 1831; FO 78/3331, Moncrieff, 29 October 1888, encl. to Cairo, san. no. 45, 17 November 1881. Above all, nineteenth-century Europeans were appalled by their mental image of the slaughter of tens of thousands of animals in a confined area. If, as they believed, epidemic disease was transmitted by a toxic principle in noxious smells from putrefying organic matter, then the sacrifice at Mina must generate sufficient poison to carry infection to all quarters of the world. From the time of the first cholera epidemic in the Hijaz in 1831, observations during the pilgrimage invariably referred to the presumed threat emanating from the feast of the Sacrifice at Mina. The sacrifice of an animal is not absolutely obligatory, and it is ritually permissible to offer the money value of the animal to charity instead. Nevertheless, most hajjis today, as in the nineteenth century, prefer to sacrifice the animal on the first day of the feast; Long, 86.

30. To provide a scientific basis for and standardize quarantine regulations, fourteen international sanitary conferences were held between 1851 and 1938. The third meeting, the Constantinople Conference in 1866, achieved a remarkable degree of agreement both in theoretical principles and practical measures. Participating nations did not sign a binding convention, however, until the eleventh conference in 1903. The convention was updated to conform with advances in biological science at a conference in 1911–12,

shelved during the First World War, and finally ratified in 1926. With the exception of the fifth conference convened by the United States in 1881 (which was concerned primarily with yellow fever), the first nine conferences dealt with the threat of cholera. The tenth was spurred by the plague epidemic that had broken out in China in 1894. The standard account is by a former official of the World Health Organization, Neville M. Goodman, *International Health Organizations and Their Work* (Philadelphia and New York: The Blakiston Co., 1952); a very useful summary is Arne Barkhuus, "The Sanitary Conferences," in *Ciba Symposia,* V, no. 7 (Oct. 1943), 1563–1579. A brilliant analysis of the conflict among etiological theories that delayed agreement for so many years is N. Howard-Jones, "The Scientific Background of the International Sanitary Conferences, 1851–1938," in six parts, *WHO Chronicle,* vol. 28 (1974).

Countries participating in the Third International Sanitary Conference held in Constantinople in 1866 were Austria-Hungary, France, Great Britain, Greece, Italy, the Papal States, Portugal, Russia, Turkey, Belgium, Denmark, the Netherlands, Persia, Prussia, and Sweden/Norway.

31. Goodman, 52–54; Duguet, 129–134; Howard Jones, 236–237. Although the conference delegates acknowledged that before 1865 cholera had spread to Europe overland via Persia, Russia, Poland, and Germany, it was not possible to win agreement on any border controls in central or northwestern Asia. Whenever the Mediterranean nations broached the question, they were solidly opposed by Persia, Turkey, Russia, and Great Britain.

The fact that there were no outbreaks of cholera in the Hijaz during the pilgrimages between 1867 and 1872 was credited to the vigilance of local sanitary and administrative personnel. During this time, a routine was established: before the pilgrimage, inns and resthouses were whitewashed, streets were cleaned, a hospital with a disinfecting service was set up, ambulances were provided for those who fell ill, and public assistance was organized for pilgrims who arrived in need in spite of efforts at prior control. By 1878, the Hijaz Sanitary Commission assigned physicians to travel with the caravan from Syria as well as to posts in Mecca, Medina, and Jiddah. The physicians also accompanied the pilgrims during the prescribed rituals.

32. AE, *CCC, Alexandrie,* vol. 45, no. 35, Gazay, 1 January 1878; *The Times,* July 1, 1874, quoted in Barkhuus, 1571.

33. Both vessels reportedly were discovered by Egyptian steamships and towed to Suez; Duguet, 141.

34. Dr. Bartoletti, Inspector General of the Ottoman Sanitary Department and a member of the Superior Board of Health at Constantinople; *Proceedings . . . 1866,* 651.

35. AE, *CCC, Alexandrie,* vol. 45, no. 37, Gazay, 8 January 1878, no. 43, 4 February 1878, Guillois, no. 78, 8 August 1878, no. 49, 23 February 1978.

36. Ibid.

37. Ibid., de Cazotte, san. no. 163, 5 January 1880; no. 164, 16 January 1880; no. 167, 28 January 1880; no. 170, 8 February 1880; Paris, no. 686, 7 May 1880; comm. no. 4, 21 May 1880; comm., unn., 3 July 1880. This heavy exchange of communications between Paris and Alexandria on the subject of pilgrim traffic apparently was because the French first entered pilgrim transport in 1880; hence the Khedivial Line violations constituted a "disadvantage in unfair competition."

38. Filippo Pacini (1812–1883) of Florence, a microscopist, anticipated Koch by 30 years with the description of cholera vibrios in an Italian publication in 1854. Like the London anesthetist, John Snow (1813–1858), who published investigation findings correlating cholera incidence and water supply in 1849 and 1855, his work was ignored.

39. Barkhuus, 1573; Howard-Jones, 379.

40. Gavin Milroy, "The International Aspects of Quarantine Legislation," *Transactions of the National Association for the Promotion of Social Sciences* (London, 1863), 871.

41. *Bulletin de l'Académie Royale de Médecine* XIII (1847–1848): 233, 236–248, 990–991.

42. AE, *CCC, Alexandrie,* Guillois, unn., 1 May 1878; unn., 1 June 1878; san. no. 19, 13 August 1878; no. 91, 17 October 1878.

43. Dr. S. V. De Castro, "Le Service sanitaire Egyptien dans la mer Rouge et le Canal de Suez," *Journal d'Hygiène,* 8th year, Vol. VII, no. 291, 20 April 1882, 52–55; Duguet, 144–145; Telegram, unno. (Jiddah), 27 September 1881; Cairo, san. no. 39, 1 October, no. 41, 1 October, no. 45, 17 November 1881.

44. FO 78/3458, Cairo, Malet, san. no. 23, 3 March 1882; Vatiokitis, 149.

45. Comte Ferdinand de Lesseps, "Notes sur les quarantaines imposées à Suez aux provenances maritimes de l'extrême orient," *Journal d'Hygiène,* 8th year, vol. 7, no. 291, 20 April 1882.

46. A. M. Fauvel, "Sur les quarantaines à Suez," *La France Médicale,* 20th year, Vol. I, no. 49, 27 April 1882, 577–594; no. 51, 2 May 1882, 601–604.

47. FO 78/3483, Paris, Comm'l., no. 17 (confidential), 7 March 1882; Paris Comm'l., no. 8, 7 February 1882.

48. FO 78/3457, London, san. no. 29, 4 September 1882; FO 78/3458, Alexandria, san. no. 44, 13 September 1882; Cairo, san. no. 48, 28 October 1882.

49. By the time the Sixth International Sanitary Conference opened in Rome in 1885, British delegates were declaring as an article of faith that cholera had never been imported to any country from India. FO 78/3458, Cairo, Malet, san. no. 15, 21 February 1882; Howard-Jones, 245–247.

6: The Conquest of Smallpox:
Variolation and Vaccination

1. Joel Shurkin, *The Invisible Fire: Story of Mankind's Triumph Over the Ancient Scourge of Smallpox* (New York: G. P. Putnam's Sons, 1979), 182–184; Donald R. Hopkins, *Princes and Peasants: Smallpox in History* (Chicago and London: University of Chicago Press, 1983), 93–95; Brand, 46; Anthony S. Wohl, *Endangered Lives: Public Health in Victorian Britain* (Cambridge: Harvard University Press, 1983), 132–135; Morris C. Leikind, "Vaccination in Europe," *Ciba Symposium* III, no. 10 (1942), 1111–1115.

2. Most historians agree that the Ethiopians' Siege of Mecca, during the so-called War of the Elephant in A.D. 568, was broken by a sudden, virulent outbreak of smallpox. Ar-Razi, Abu Bacr Mohammed Ibn Zacariya (Abu Bakr Muhammad Ibn Zakariya al-Razi), *A Treatise on Smallpox and Measles*, William Alex Greenhill, trans. (London: Sydenham Society, 1848).

3. John Lewis Burckhardt, *Travels in Nubia*, 2 vols. (London: John Murray, 1822) II, 379; Antoine Barthèlme Clot-Bey, *Introduction de la Vaccination en Egypte en 1827: Organization du service médico-hygiènique des provinces en 1840: instructions et règlements relatifs à ces deux services* (Paris: Victor Masson et Fils, n.d.), 9, 23 (hereafter referred to as *Introduction*); Charles Cuny, "Propositions d'Hygiène, de Médecine, et de Chirurgie, Relatives a l'Egypte," Thèse pour le doctorat en Médecine, présentée et soutenue le 31 août 1853 (Paris: Rignoux, 1853), 25.

4. Rosen, *A History of Public Health*, 184.

5. Clot-Bey, *Introduction*, iii.

6. Arnold C. Klebs, M.D., "The Historic Evolution of Variolation," *Bulletin of the Johns Hopkins Hospital* XXIV (1913): 69. Genevieve Miller, *The Adoption of Inoculation for Smallpox in England and France* (Philadelphia: University of Pennsylvania Press, 1957), offers a comprehensive study of the pre-Jennerian practice of smallpox inoculation. Miller avoided the term "variolation" because eighteenth-century writers used only the terms "smallpox inoculation," "insertion," "engrafting," or "transplantation"; preface, i, ii. In view of the wider connotation of the term "inoculation" in the post-Pasteur era of immunization, this study uses variolation, i.e., inoculation with *variola major* or smallpox, to denote the earlier practice.

7. Miller, 42–44, 51–63. Adde-Margras de Nancy, *Manuel du Vaccinateur des Villes et des Campagnes* (Paris: Labe, 1856), 37–51; Muhammad Ali Bey and Ahmad Zaki al-Hakim, "History of Smallpox and Vaccination," *Journal of the Egyptian Public Health Association* XXIV, no. 2 (1949): 40; Ahmad Hilmy-Bey, *Smallpox in Egypt: Its History and Control* (Cairo: Government Press, 1933), 3; Charles Creighton, *A History of*

Epidemics in Britain, 2 vols. (New York: Barnes and Noble, 1965), II, 463–468, 471–477; James Moore, *The History of Smallpox* (London: Longman, Hurst, Rees, Orme and Browne, 1815), 218–229; Klebs, 70; William L. Langer, "Immunization Against Smallpox Before Jenner," *Scientific American*, vol. 235 (1976): 112–117.

8. Larrey, I, 519. Burckhardt, 211–212, reported a similar practice among the Nubians called "tattooing smallpox" (*duqq al-jadari; dugg*—to strike, hammer, therefore also tattoo). "Tattooing smallpox" remained the common folk term for variolation or vaccination in Egypt until recently. Current Egyptian usage includes both Arabic terms *talqih* and *tat'im*, corresponding to inoculation and vaccination, respectively.

9. Cuny; Bowring, 6; Rafalowitch, 520.

10. ENA, *Ma'iya*, register no. 3, doc. no. 247, 23 March 1819; Sami, II, 278, Hilmy, 4.

11. ENA, Index Cards: Health, *Ma'iya*, register 9, doc. no. 30, 8 October 1821.

12. Paul Mouriez, *Histoire de Muhammad-Ali, vice-roi d'Egypte*, 4 vols. (Paris: Louis Chappe, 1855–58), III, 113.

13. ENA, *Ma'iya*, carton 51, study no. 3, Subject: Education, register no. 17, doc. no. 423, 22 July 1824; ibid.; doc. no. 595, 22 December 1824; ibid., Index Cards: Health, *Ma'iya*, register no. 25, doc. no. 153, 9 August 1826; register 22, doc. no. 12, 9 July 1826.

14. Clot-Bey, *Introduction*, 9.

15. Ibid.; ENA, *Ministry of Education*, carton 49, register no. 13, correspondence no. 626, p. 2772, 22 July 1845.

16. Cuny; Clot-Bey, *Introduction*, 10.

17. Ibid., 17–18. The instructions specified that the vaccine collected in arm-to-arm variolation should be deposited in containers of nonoxidizable materials such as glass, ivory, shells, or feather quills to safeguard it from exposure to air, light, heat, or humidity: (1) the vaccine should be dried, then inserted between two strips of glass, ivory, or shell and their edges sealed with wax; (2) a smaller goosefeather quill should be dipped in the vaccine, dried, and inserted into a larger quill; (3) fluid vaccine could be collected in a capillary tube and sealed with wax or by firing; (4) to protect the containers from light, glass plates or quills were to be wrapped in dark-colored paper or sheets of lead, and capillary tubes were to be packed in boxes with powdered charcoal. In 1856, the same procedures for collecting, preserving, and transporting vaccine were current in France, according to a manual published in Paris; Adde-Margras, 167–170.

18. ENA, Translations, *Ma'iya*, register no. 74, doc. no. 466, 5 May 1836.

19. A series of dispatches forwarded by the British consul general in

Alexandria in 1849 indicates that the consular missions acted as intermediaries for procuring vaccine lymph for the quarantine service in Alexandria. FO 78/806, Gilbert, 8 March, 6 June, and 7 August 1849.

20. ENA, *Ministry of Education*, register no. 2021, minutes of a session
of the Consultative Council of Public Instruction held on June 25, 1836,
p. 8. The regulations are identified only as the results of the council's de-
liberations; however, Clot-Bey refers to them (p. 26) as having been enforced and appends a sample of the register called for in paragraphs 4 and
5. The articles omitted in this text dealt with extension of the regulations to
Egypt's dependencies in Syria, the Hijaz, Sennar, and Crete.

21. Clot-Bey, *Introduction*, 22–23.

22. ENA, *Ministry of Education*, carton 49, register no. 3, Pt. III, correspondence no. 48, p. 839, 25 January 1845.

23. *Egyptian Gazette*, no. 619, 13 July 1840, p. 3; nos. 101, 109, 113,
119, 123, 128, January–July 1848. The writer could not locate figures for
the missing month of April 1848 (Jumadi al-Awwal 1264).

The breakdown of the total number of vaccinations by each month was
reported as follows:

A.D. 1848—1264 A.H.

Month	Boys	Girls	Total
January (Safar)	125	125	250
February (Rabi' al-Awwal)	622	390	1,012
March (Rabi' al-Akhar)	636	617	1,253
May (Jumadi al'Akhar)	247	220	467
June (Rajab)	270	269	539
July (Sha'ban)	73	79	152
	1,973	1,700	3,673

24. See n. 8, above. Tattooing was very common in Egypt, for identification as well as for decorative effect (see Lane, 42). Parents were said to
tattoo their children's arms for identification should they be lost or stolen,
slaves were marked by their masters for recognition in case of desertion,
and Christians often had tattooed the sign of the cross on their chest or arm;
less often, Muslims might have a crescent marked on themselves; Yates,
235–237. Around 1848, government communications began to refer to vaccination as "duqq" (tattooing) as well, reverting to local usage as they did
in referring to cholera as "haida."

25. ENA, *Sammarco Papers*, box 6, 1831 to 1868, doc. no. 6793;
Charles Cuny, "Mémoire sur les services rendus par M. Cuny en sa qualité

de médecin, depuis l'année 1837 jusqu'en 1851, qu'il a servi le Gouvern-
ment Egyptien," 4 (hereafter referred to as "Mémoire"). It is possible that
he exaggerated his accomplishments, but until memoirs or other writings by
Egyptian medical officers are uncovered, Cuny's account may serve as a useful description of the experiences of provincial health officers in Egypt in
the 1840s.

26. Hamont, I, 507–509.
27. Cuny, "Mémoire," p. 6.
28. Hamont.
29. Cuny, "Mémoire," 10, 12.
30. *Egyptian Gazette*, no. 59, 7 April 1846, 1.
31. Artemis Rafalowitch, "Briefe eines russichen Artztes (Rafalowitsch)
aus der Turkei," *Das Ausland* XXII (1849), 496, 512, 520. Rafalowitch did
not offer any figures for Buhaira or Minufiya governorates. He only observed
that the Bedouins in Buhaira, like the nomads in the Sinai desert, were very
receptive to vaccinating their children. Nor did Rafalowitch give any particu-
lars on vaccination in Upper Egypt, except to remark that the fallah's old
fear of "marking" children for conscription was dying out, and vaccination
was getting under way around Asyut and Minia.
32. ENA, Index Cards: Health, *Ma'iya*, register no. 284, doc. no. 124,
24 March 1841.
33. Clot-Bey, *Introduction*, 23.
34. Ibid., iv; *Mémoires*, 157.
35. See n. 2, chap. 3, for population statistics for Egypt in the early
nineteenth century.
36. B. Schnepp, "Considérations sur le mouvement de la population en
Egypte," *Mémoires de l'Institut Egyptien* I (1862), 551.
37. Frank G. Clemow, *The Geography of Disease* (Cambridge: Cambridge University Press, 1903), 421.
38. Sandwith, I, 134.
39. Ibid., 135–136.
40. Hilmy-Bey, op. cit., 7, 19–22. In the interim, Bedouin who had
sought out government vaccinators a century earlier had felt the restraints
of the state on their freedom of movement and no longer welcomed official
functionaries. In 1933, a public health official reported that the persistence
of smallpox among the nomads resulted from the difficulty of enforcing initial vaccination; they resisted it as they opposed registering the births of their
children, to avoid military service.

7: Women Health Officers

1. The early history of midwifery in both England and France is
punctuated by the names of outstanding women, particularly those who attended the royal court and the nobility. The old regime in France initiated

systematic training for midwives several times, but it was the revolutionary government's 1803 enactment that regularized and expanded instruction at the Paris Maternité. Trained midwives in France held their own against strong pressure from the male medical profession until late in the nineteenth century. In England, the male medical profession generally shunned the lowly manual craft of midwifery until after the Napoleonic Wars, when it became evident that obstetrical practice could be respectable and lucrative. Because men consistently and strongly opposed any instruction and licensing for midwives, untrained women like Dickens's Sairy Gamp continued to dominate the practice during the nineteenth century. Irving S. Cutter and Henry R. Viets, *A Short History of Midwifery* (Philadelphia and London: W. B. Saunders Co., 1964), 91–95; James Hobson Aveling, M.D., *English Midwives, Their History and Prospects* (London: Hugh K. Elliot, 1872, rep. 1967); Jean Donnison, *Midwives and Medical Men: A History of Inter-Professional Rivalries and Women's Rights* (New York: Schocken Books, 1977), 116–133; Shryock, *The Rise of Modern Medicine*, 50, 77, 83–84.

2. FO/285, Campbell, 24 December 1836.

3. Clot-Bey, *Mémoires*, 158.

4. Cutter and Viets.

5. See references for the Egyptian School of Medicine in chap. 2.

6. Max Meyerhoff, "Djarrah," in *Encyclopedia of Islam*, new ed., fasc. 30 (Leyden: E. J. Brill), 481–482; B. Carra de Vaux, "Tibb," ibid., Vol. IV (Leyden: E. J. Brill, 1927), 740–741; both authors point out that, in common Arabic usage, *Hakim* (Doctor) was the term applied to the scholar versed in the medical classics, while *Tibb* generally referred to a practicing physician. Government correspondence consistently referred to the women health officer as "hakima" in the nineteenth century.

7. Clot-Bey, *Mémoires*, 158.

8. Ibid., 159, ENA, *Ma'īya*, register no. 87, 85.

9. Clot-Bey, *Mémoires*, 158; Abdal-Karim, 296.

10. ENA, *Ministry of Education*, register no. 2027, unn. commun. to the Khedivial Ministry, 17 May 1837.

11. Clot-Bey, *Mémoires*, 161, 281, 320, 322–333; "Institutions médicales au Caire," *Gazette des Hôpitaux* XII (1838): 3–4; Abd al-Karim, 303–304.

12. Ibid., 305. ENA, *Ministry of Education*, register no. 13, pt. 6, 6749: To the School of Medicine, 17 July 1845; register no. 2095, 104, 20 November 1844: Results of the Annual Examination at the School for Hakimas; register no. 2140, 10: Khedivial Order to the Ministry, 1 November 1851; portfolio 49, register no. 46, pt. 4, 1317, no. 298: To the Khedivial Ministry, 13 January 1847; portfolio 50, register no. 108, 147, no. 18: From the Medical Council, 9 October 1849. In the 1830s, the currency equivalents were one pound sterling = 100 piasters; one franc = 30 piasters; one dollar (U.S.) = 20 piasters.

13. *Egyptian Gazette,* no. 1, 3 March 1845, 1–2.

14. Abd al-Karim, 305; ENA, *Ministry of Education,* portfolio 50, register no. 163, 1054, no. 124: From the School of Medicine, 9 April 1851.

15. Ibid., portfolio 49, register no. 2099, 148: From the School of Medicine, 30 May 1844; portfolio 49, register no. 13, pt. 6, 2749, no. 608: To the School of Medicine, 17 July 1845.

16. Abd al-Karim, 306.

17. ENA, *Ministry of Education,* portfolio 49, register no. 2096, 184: To the School of Medicine, 18 December 1844; register no. 2098, 169: Khedivial Order to the Ministry, 20 January 1845; portfolio 49, register no. 3, pt. 3, 844: To the School of Medicine, 17 January 1845; register no. 4, pt. 4, 2187: To the Medical Council, 1 April 1845; register no. 11, pt. 4, 4032: To the School of Medicine, 15 April 1845; register no. 13, pt. 6, 2799: To the School of Medicine, 1 August 1845.

18. Abd al-Karim, 305.

19. ENA, *Ministry of Education,* portfolio 49, register no. 27, pt. 2, 777: To the School of Medicine, 27 January 1846.

20. Clot-Bey, "Institutions médicales au Caire," 4; *Mémoires,* 321.

21. Abd al-Karim, 309; ENA, *Ministry of Education,* portfolio 49, register no. 10, pt. 3, 2028, no. 281: To the School for Hakimas, 10 October 1845; portfolio 50, register no. 143, 772, no. 28: To the School of Medicine, 13 December 1849.

22. Clot-Bey, *Mémoires,* 160–161.

23. ENA, *Ministry of Education,* portfolio 49, register no. 2058, 39, 16 February 1837: Results of the Annual Examination at the School for Hakimas; portfolio 49, register no. 2068, 48: To the Khedivial Ministry, 24 December 1840. The first French directress, Suzanne Voilquoin, a member of the St. Simonian group, died in the plague epidemic in 1835. Clot then recruited Palmyre Gault, a graduate of the midwifery program at the Maternité in Paris; Guémard, *Les Réformes en Egypte,* 233.

24. Ibid., portfolio 49, register no. 2081, 119: To the Chief Tax Collector, 17 January 1843. The results of this initiative apparently left something to be desired, for six months later another government directive ordered that girls brought in from the streets should not be admitted to the school; they were unsuitable, being either too young or not virgins. Ibid., portfolio 49, register no. 2083, 92: To the School of Medicine, 18 July 1843.

25. Clot-Bey, "Institutions médicales au Caire," 4; *Mémoires,* 321.

26. ENA, *Ministry of Education,* portfolio 49, registers no. 2090, 2099, Khedivial Orders to the Ministry, 8 and 9 July 1844; *Egyptian Gazette,* no. 27, 24 August 1846, 1.

27. ENA, *Ministry of Education,* portfolio 49, register no. 2098, 106. From the School of Medicine, 18 November 1844.

28. *Egyptian Gazette,* no. 1, 3 March 1845, 1–2.

29. Ibid., no. 46, 5 January 1847, 1–2.

30. Duc de Raguse, *Voyage de Maréchal Duc de Raguse* (Paris: Chez l'Avocat, 1837), 307–309.

31. Herman von Puckler-Muscau, *Egypt under Muhammad Ali,* 2 vols. (London: Henry Coburn, 1845), I, 232–233.

32. Yates, I, 509.

33. Schoelcher, 44–45.

34. ENA, *Ministry of Education,* portfolio 50, register no. 108, 147, no. 25: From the Medical Council, 3 December 1848; register no. 144, 821, no. 27: To the Chief of Police, 22 December 1849.

35. Antoine B. Clot-Bey, *Introduction de la vaccination en Egypte en 1827* (Paris: Victor Masson et Fils, n.d.), 22–23.

36. *Egyptian Gazette,* no. 619, 13 July 1840, 3; nos. 101, 109, 113, 119, 123, 128; 21 February, 21 March, 21 April, 19 June, 18 July, 21 August, 1848, 1.

37. ENA, *Ministry of Education,* portfolio 49, register no. 2083, 18, 19: From the Medical Council, 26 February, 19 March 1843.

38. *Egyptian Gazette,* no. 84, 29 September 1847, 1.

39. ENA, *Ministry of Education,* portfolio 49, register no. 11, pt. 4, 3017, no. 348: To the School for Hakimas, 9 March 1845; portfolio 49, register no. 11, pt. 4, 3050, 3083, nos. 372, 390: To the School of Medicine, 21 and 31 March 1845; portfolio 49, register no. 94, pt. 2, 749, nos. 120, 122: To the School of Medicine, 17 and 18 November 1847; portfolio 50, register no. 163, 1054, no. 124: From the School of Medicine, 9 April 1851.

40. Godard, 17–21; "Modern Medical Schools," *JEMA* (1928), 356D and E; Hassan Effendi Mahmoud, "L'Ecole de Médecine d'Egypte," 399–400. According to Umar Tusin's study of Egyptians who studied abroad (p. 500), Tamurham married a pharmacist, Saleh Ali al-Hakim, who had completed undergraduate training at the School of Medicine in Cairo. Their daughter, Galila, also was educated at the school for hakimas and published a students' manual, *A Guide to Obstetrics,* in 1869.

41. See chap. 6, "The Conquest of Smallpox."

42. Said Abdou, "Preventive Medicine," in *Health and Human Relations* (Cairo: Ministry of Public Health, 1952), 9–18.

43. Karl B. Klunzinger, *Upper Egypt, Its People and Its Products* (London: Blackie and Son, 1878), 81.

44. V. Edouard Dor, *L'instruction publique en Egypte* (Paris: A. Lacroix, Verboeckhouen et Cie., 1872), 226.

45. Florence Nightingale failed to act on her good intentions to raise the professional status of midwifery as she had for nursing. Trained midwives then had no patron with sufficient social standing and political influence to challenge the medical establishment's implacable opposition to any reform in midwifery practice. Dr. James Aveling, one of the few nineteenth-century male advocates of improvement in midwifery, wrote in 1872 that, during

the 325 years since the first attempt in 1547, the Royal College of Physicians had defeated twenty organized efforts to license, regulate, and instruct midwives. Both on the continent and in the British Isles, midwives were disadvantaged by the fact that the professional class of general practitioners emerging in the nineteenth century continued to invoke medieval guild regulations that restricted the use of instruments to surgeons, and they were able to enjoin midwives from using forceps. British midwives faced the additional handicap that the upper classes promoted the snobbish fashion of patronizing male "accoucheurs," preferably French, like male coiffeurs, as a superior class of practitioner. The Colleges of Physicians and Surgeons responded to this competition by abolishing the membership bar against man-midwives when these practitioners adopted the title of "obstetrician" in the 1850s; Donnison, 57, 62, passim.

8: Urban and Rural Health Programs: Hospitals, Clinics, and Provincial Health Centers

1. Franz Pruner, *Topographie Medicale du Caire* (Munich: n.p., 1847), 85; John Bowring, 84, 89, 91; Puckler-Muscau, II, 310. Dr. Clot wrote in 1833 that Muhammad Mansur would have to abandon his studies in Paris because he was mortally afflicted with nostalgia as well as phthisis (Letter to Mr. Briggs, dated 26 March 1833, in *Mémoires,* 264).

Johannes Hofer, an Alsatian medical student, made the first identification of nostalgia as an ailment in 1688. He described the symptoms as anorexia, insomnia, slow fever, irritability, anxiety, and a general wasting away of the organism. Nostalgia was first associated with the Swiss as they were identified with professional military service early in Europe's modern history. In his study of occupational disorders, the seventeenth-century Italian clinician, Bernardino Ramazzini, identified "homesickness" as one of the most common disabling diseases in Europe's armed forces. Later studies have proposed a psychosociological, rather than physical, basis for the ailment: military recruits from close-knit, isolated communities rarely visited by outsiders have a greater disposition to nostalgia than urban youth; Willis H. McCann, "Nostalgia: A Review of the Literature," *Psychological Bulletin* 38 (1941): 165–182.

2. Scott, II, 218.

3. Dr. Muhammad Khalil Abd al-Khaliq Bey, "The Defense of Egypt against Cholera, Past, Present, and Future," *JEMA* 30 (November 1947): 546–547.

4. *Egyptian Gazette,* no. 334, 29 December 1831, 2.

5. Clot-Bey, "De l'hôpital d'Abou-Zabel: Indication des maladies qu'on y observe fréquemment; et aperçus rapides des principales opérations pratiquées en Egypte," *Annales de la médicine physiologique* 23 (1833): 566;

"Notice sur l'hôpital d'Abou-Zabel," *Annales de la médecine physiologique* 25 (1833): 393–398; Yates, II, 583; Scott, II, 240.

6. Clot-Bey, *Mémoires*, 314, 315; Felix Mengin, *Histoire Sommaire de l'Egypte* (Paris: Firmin Didot Frères, 1839), 147; Schoelcher, 37.

7. Clot-Bey, "Compte rendu . . . , 1849," 75–79.

8. *ENA, Maʿīya*, register no. 1, doc. no. 52, 8 March 1827; register no. 731, doc. no. 269, dated 8 March 1827: summaries in *Index Cards, Subject: Health.*

9. Bowring, 56.

10. Franz Pruner, *Aegyptens Naturgeschichte und Anthropologie als Einleitung zu den Krankheiten des Orients* (Erlangen: Palm-Enke, 1847), 87.

11. ENA, *Maʿīya* (Summaries), register no. 63, doc. no. 75, 25 September 1835; register no. 66, doc. no. 825, 16 October 1835; *Ministry of Education,* portfolio 54, report no. 6, register no. 2012, 3, "Resolution of the Consultative Council on Education, June 1836."

12. Abd al-Karim, 155–156, 160–172, 497, 505–506; Bowring, 128, 194.

13. ENA, *Ministry of Education,* portfolio 49, register no. 8, pt. 1, 224, comm. no. 4, dated 20 September 1844; register no. 1, pt. 1, 117, comm. no. 15, dated 11 October 1844; register no. 9, pt. 2, 634, comm. no. 153, dated 21 November 1844; register no. 13, pt. 6, 2746, comm. no. 110, dated 17 July 1845; 2778, comm. no. 121, dated 4 August 1845, 2881; comm. no. 139, dated 1 September 1845; register no. 50, pt. 9, 3243, comm. no. 173, dated 10 June 1847; register no. 143, 659, doc. no. 28, dated 6 December 1849; portfolio 50, register no. 163, 1138, doc. no. 140, dated 30 April 1850.

14. *Egyptian Gazette,* no. 11, 10 May 1846, 2. Population figures are those of the government census of 1846, as reported in Rafalowitch, passim, and Lane, Appendix on p. 584, 1860 ed. The village of Nabaroh, as far as we know, was not populous and had no factory, but it belonged to the viceroy. Rafalowitch mentioned (p. 520) that in 1846 Shibr al-Khit, with a population of 1,800, was the capital of Buhaira province because it was the site of a huge government warehouse.

15. Bowring, *Report on Egypt and Candia.*

16. Ali Mubarak, VII, 71–72.

17. Godard, 32–35.

18. *Egyptian Gazette,* no. 91, 16 November 1847, 1; Mahfouz, *The Life of an Egyptian Doctor,* 56–57; Ali Mubarak, XII, 94.

19. Clot-Bey, *Mémoires,* 316; Amin Sami, II, 518; ENA, *Ministry of Education,* register no. 2027, unn. comm. to the Khedivial Ministry, 17 May 1837, *Egyptian Gazette,* no. 91, 16 November 1847, 1.

20. Godard, 35–36. Godard observed that women from Said Pasha's harem occupied half of the beds in one ward.

21. Ali Mubarak, I, 96.

22. Clot-Bey, "De l'hôpital abou-Zabel," 567.

23. Clot-Bey, "Compte rendu . . . 1830–1832," 66–67.

24. Clot, "De l'hôpital Abou Zabel," 570.

25. Ibid.; "Compte rendu . . . 1849," 82–85. The 20 percent mortality Clot concedes for lithotomies is quite likely, but the overall mortality rate of 0.0125 percent for surgery can only be explained if most of the operations were minor procedures like circumcisions, draining fluid, and incision of abcesses.

All morbidity and mortality figures from Egyptian hospitals during the nineteenth century are dubious because recording was not systematic and diagnosis was imprecise. Also, the *Gazette* most often interpreted all information on government enterprises in the most favorable light possible.

26. Clot-Bey, "Compte rendu . . . 1849," 85–87; *Egyptian Gazette*, no. 69, 15 June 1847, 1; no. 73, 4 July 1847, 1. The following year, the *Gazette* also reported that two Paris-trained Egyptian dentists, Mustafa al-Wati and Uthman Ibrahim, had used chloroform successfully for teeth extraction; no. 114, 17 May 1848, 1.

27. *Egyptian Gazette*, no. 20, 7 July 1846, 1; no. 57, 24 March 1847, 1; no. 67, 3 June 1847, 1.

28. *Egyptian Gazette*, no. 61, 1 May 1846, 1–2; no. 58, 31 March 1847, 1.

29. Ibid., no. 627, 5 February 1845, 2–3; no. 81, 7 September 1847, 1. It is not clear whether the medical centers were established in Alexandria; Cairo's free clinics, or Medical Consultation Centers, are referred to in government publications as Dar al-Istashara al-Tibbiya, Mahallat al-Istashara al-Tibbiya, or Bayt al-Istashara al-Tibbiya.

30. Ibid., no. 116, 10 June 1848, 1.

31. Ibid., no. 29, 7 September 1846, 1; no. 50, 3 February 1847, 1; no. 74, 20 July 1847, 1; no. 105, 21 February 1848, 1.

32. It should be noted again that diagnosis was imprecise at this time. First aid (is'āf) appears self-evident. Infectious diseases (amrad 'adiya) may refer to skin eruptions like measles, which were recognized as being communicable. Shock (turbah) has been explained as any physical disturbance considered to have resulted from a sudden fright or shock. Smallpox appeared only in the first semiannual report, covering the period 5 December 1845 through 24 June 1846; apparently, an epidemic occurred in Abdin/Ezbekiyah where 565 cases were reported, and the remaining 42 cases occurred in Darb al-Jamamiz, Khalifiya, and Old Cairo. Venereal disease, al-ifranji or al-ifranki, did not distinguish between gonorrhea and syphilis. With regard to internal illnesses (amrād batiniyah), the prevalence of gastrointestinal disorders makes it seem likely that they constituted a large proportion of the ailments. Injuries or wounds (jurūb) may refer to broken bones

for which patients presumably were referred to the hospital, in contrast to "first aid," denoting minor injuries. Eye ailments are listed either as "awjaᶜ alᶜayin" or as "ramad," the all-purpose term for ophthalmia.

33. Max Meyerhoff, "A Short History of Ophthalmology in Egypt during the 19th Century," *Bulletin of the Ophthalmological Society of Egypt* XX (April 1927): 34; Dr. N. Kahil, "Une ophthalmologie Arabe par un praticien du Caire du 13ᵉ siècle, 7ᵉ de l'Hégire," *Comptes rendus du Congrès* Internationale de Médicine Tropicale et d'Hygiène, II, 241.

34. Muhammad Ali al-Baqli, "De l'ophthalmie externe et de ses principales variétés," thèse presentée et soutenue à la Faculté de Médecine de Paris le 27 Novembre 1837 (Paris: Rignoux et Cie, 1837), 16–21, 30–39.

35. *Egyptian Gazette,* no. 17, 16 June 1846, 2; ENA, *Ministry of Education,* register no. 2112, 103, 29 December 1846.

36. *Egyptian Gazette* no. 46, 4 January 1847, 1; no. 52, 17 February 1847, 1; no. 53, 26 February 1847, 1; no. 70, 17 June 1847, 1. The frequency of treatment of eye disorders by surgery and medication is indicated in the following tables of returns from two clinics for the months of April and May 1848.

Ophthalmological Treatment by Survery, April–May 1848

	al-Salibiya Clinic	al-Jamaliya Clinic
Trichiasis	85	85
Ptergium	5	4
Entropion	3	6
Ectropion		3
Sebaceous cyst	1	
Cataracts		4
Styes	4	1
Symblepharon		3
Cystic swellings	—	1
	98	107

Ophthalmological Treatment by Medication, April–May 1848[a]

	al-Salibiya Clinic	al-Jamaliya Clinic
Corneal opacities	156	41
Acute Catarrhal conjunctivitis	58	140

	al-Salibiya Clinic	al-Jamaliya Clinic
Nebulae	56	
Fibrolic conjunctivitis	4	3
Chronic blepheritis	3	18
Chronic catarrhal conjunctivitis	46	
Trachoma	57	40
Purulent conjunctivitis ("Egyptian ophthalmia")	37	26
Phlyctenular		1
Keratitis		4
Congestive glaucoma	—	1
	417	274
Total	515	381

ªIbid., no. 120, 26 June, 1848, 1; no. 121, 4 July, 1848, 1. For the layman, the most common eye disorders listed may be defined very simply as follows: trichiasis—inward turning of the eyelashes; entropion—inversion or turning in of the eyelid; pterygium—a fleshy mass of thickened conjunctiva covering part of the cornea and disturbing vision; staphyloma—protrusion of the cornea or sclera of the eye; symblepharon—adhesion between the eyelid and eyeball; keratitis—inflammation of the cornea; phlyctenular—small vesicles or pustules on the cornea or conjunctiva.

37. Meyerhof, 49, 50–51. Muhammad Awf Pasha and Muhammad Alwi Pasha were the last two Egyptian directors of the ophthalmic section at the medical school in the 1890s.

38. Ali Mubarak, VII, 21–22; XIII, 45–46.

39. Neuroutsos, 41–42.

40. Egyptian Gazette, no. 81, 7 September 1847; Clot-Bey, Compte rendu de l'état de l'enseignement médical et du service de santé civil et militaire de l'Egypte au commencement de Mars 1849 (Paris: Victor Masson et Fils, 1849), 21–32; "Organization du service médico-hygiènique des provinces en 1840," in coll. no. 8, Faculté de Médecine, Paris, 27–32; Neuroutsos, op. cit., 44, 54, 59. The two decrees were dated 19 June 1842 and 22 August 1847.

41. See Grassi's "Observations" following the Table of Organization for the Provincial Health Service, Appendix 3.

42. Clot-Bey, Compte rendu . . . 1849, 22–23, 28–32.

43. ENA, Ministry of Education, portfolio 50, register no. 2094, 22 January 1844; Dr. Perron refers to the "sanitary or public health service" in a

letter to the editor of the *Gazette des Hôpitaux,* 3 December 1844, 565–566; Schoelcher, 40–41, praises the "Sanitary Service."

44. Joseph Hekekyan-Bey, journal entry dated 24 June 1850, 346b, 347a, Vol. III; *Journals, correspondence, and other papers of Joseph Hekekyan-Bey,* British Library, additional mss. no. 37450. Joseph Hekekyan was an Armenian in Muhammad Ali's service who received training in England in engineering under the pasha's sponsorship.

45. Rafalowitch, op. cit., passim. Rafalowitch spent two weeks in Alexandria but did not mention visiting Cairo. He seems to have been briefed by the Quarantine Board, for he stated (p. 504) there were 72 district physicians in Lower Egypt, but during his tour he referred to only 41, which would make the missing number of Egyptian medical officers for the governorate of Gharbiyah an unlikely 31.

46. Rafalowitch, 260, 264, 496, 507–508, 520.

47. Ibid., 512. When Rafalowitch questioned the Egyptian physician in Damanhur about the obvious nonenforcement of sanitary regulations in the city, the medical officer sighed and said, "They never listen to what I say" (ma 'isma'shi kalam abadan'!).

48. Schoelcher, 40.

49. Ibid., 41; Klunzinger, 81–83.

50. Rafalowitch, 496.

51. Duff-Gordon, 157.

52. Godard, 17, 37–38. Dr. Godard identified Fantah, the site of the provincial clinic, a village of 4,000 people which at that time was the capital of Radat al-Bahrain province in Lower Egypt.

9: The Continuing Evolution of Concepts of Disease and Medicine

1. Two articles that discuss present views on the relative weight of factors contributing to the disappearance of plague—nutrition, housing, vectors, quarantines—are Andrew Appleby, "The Disappearance of Plague: A Continuing Puzzle," *The Economic History Review* 33 (1980): 161–173; and John D. Post, "Famine, Mortality, and Epidemic Disease in the Process of Modernization," *The Economic History Review* 29 (1976): 14–37.

2. Wakil, in Pollitzer, 33, 509, 513, proposed that the brown rat established itself in Upper Egypt after perennial irrigation was introduced.

3. In *Egypt in Revolution: An Economic Analysis* (London: Oxford University Press, 1963), Charles Issawi notes a rise in real per capita income and in the level of living during the latter half of the nineteenth century (p. 18), but neither increased earnings nor a higher living standard extended to the lower classes. Those who claim a more adequate food supply as a

contributing factor in population increase have not suggested that housing and environmental conditions for the urban and rural poor improved during the nineteenth century.

4. Grain is a preferred food for rats, and the husks provide ideal nesting places for fleas; therefore, even empty cereal sacks have been implicated in carrying plague. Cotton in its unspun state is an ideal medium for transporting fleas, and they breed freely in the debris of cotton seed dust. Rats also can subsist on a diet of raw cotton seed and use the fiber as a nesting material. Hirst, 312, 315, 316–319.

5. Kemal, 17. Safeguarding London's drinking water supply from contamination therefore reduced the incidence of waterborne disease, in spite of public health authorities' skepticism toward Snow's evidence. Winslow, 271–278.

6. Hirst, 413. The antiplague costumes worn by contagionist physicians and derided in Alexandria in 1835 also reappeared in the twentieth century in the protective antiflea uniform worn by sanitary squads fighting plague in China. The outfits consisted of a one-piece suit open only at the neck and wrists, top boots, rubber gloves, and a white skull cap, supplemented, if pneumonic plague was feared, by goggles and a respirator covering nose and mouth. Hirst, 440.

A Russian plague commission conducted a series of experiments in Cairo in 1843 to study the effect of heat as a disinfectant; FO 78/541, Barnett, 15 May, 19 July, 18 December 1843; Cattaui, III, 685, 686, 712, 728, 738.

7. Pollitzer, *Cholera,* 7; Albert Colnat, ed., "L'âge du Cholera," in *Les Epidémies et L'Histoire* (Paris: Editions Hippocrates, 1937), 180.

8. Cited in Norman Longmate, *King Cholera: The Biography of a Disease* (London: Hamish Hamilton, 1966), 188.

9. Richard H. Shryock, *The Development of Modern Medicine: An Interpretation of the Social and Scientific Factors Involved* (London: Victor Gollancz, 1948), 309.

10. Benjamin D. Paul, ed., *Health, Culture and Community: Case Studies of Public Reactions to Health Problems* (New York: Russell Sage Foundation, 1955), 2.

11. The information in the following pages is drawn from Charles Issawi, "Asymmetrical Development and Transport in Egypt, 1800–1914," in William R. Polk and Richard L. Chambers, eds., *Beginnings of Modernization in the Middle East* (Chicago: University of Chicago Press, 1969), 383–400; "Egypt Since 1800: A Study of Lopsided Development," *The Journal of Economic History* 21 (1961): 1–25; "Middle East Economic Development, 1815–1914: The General and the Specific," in M. A. Cook, ed., *Studies in the Economic History of the Middle East: From the Rise of Islam to the Present Day* (London and New York: Oxford University Press, 1970),

408–411. See also references to the works of Gabriel Baer in Chap. I, "Muhhamad Ali and the Egyptians."

12. Stanley Lane-Poole, *Cairo: Sketches of Its History, Monuments and Social Life* (London: J. S. Virtue and Co., Ltd., 1898), 256.

13. Lady Lucie Duff-Gordon, *Letters from Egypt* (London: Routledge & Kegan Paul, 1969), 118. In the 1890s, an Egyptian doctor complained bitterly that the mass of people still shunned their own trained physicians in favor of old wives' remedies, while the wealthy snobbishly patronized only Europeans who, he claimed, in some cases had training inferior to Egyptians. 'Abd al-Rahman Effendi Ismail, *Tibb al-Rukka (Old Wives Medicine)*, John Walker, trans. and ed. (London: Luzac and Co., 1934), 15–18, 87–94.

14. Amira El Azhary Sonbol, "The Creation of a Medical Profession in Egypt during the Nineteenth Century: A Study in Modernization," (Ph.D. dissertation, Georgetown University, 1981), 180ff., describes the maldistribution of medical personnel during and following the British occupation. Most Egyptian doctors were employed by the government, but as railway health supervisors, port inspectors, and so forth, and very few served the rural areas of Upper or Lower Egypt.

15. "Egypt," in *Encyclopedia of the Third World*, George Thomas Kurian, ed. (New York: Facts on File, 1978), 444.

16. Victor W. Sidel and Ruth Sidel, *A Healthy State: An International Perspective on the Crisis in United States Medical Care* (New York: Pantheon Books, 1983), 201.

17. Margaret Pelling, *Cholera, Fever, and English Medicine, 1825–1865* (Oxford: Oxford University Press, 1978), 146–202, rightly points out that members of the medical profession held a broad span of views on the etiology of infectious diseases—the telluric, electric, and ozonic theories; the animalicular and fungoid; the zymotic or humoral—and the professional consensus, as distinguished from the official (Board of Health/governmental) view, was a modified or contingent contagionism, which assumed specificity in epidemic disease but posited a greater role for the environment in disease causation than strict contagionism.

This study has emphasized the official status of the miasmatic hypothesis as a scientific justification for domestic and international policies adopted by the government to control epidemic disease.

18. Antoine Barthèlme Clot-Bey, *De la Peste observée en Egypte: Recherches et considérations sur cette maladie* (Paris: Fortin, Masson et Cie., 1840).

19. An enlightening study examines the expansion and contraction of definitions of "medicine" and "disease" among practitioners of three medical specializations: Stephen J. Kunitz, "The Historical Roots and Ideological

Functions of Disease Concepts in Three Primary Care Specialties," *Bulletin of the History of Medicine* 57, no. 3 (1983): 412–432.

20. Donald Seldin, "The Intimate Coupling of Biomedical Science and Physician Education," *Clinical Research* 23 (1975): 282, quoted in Kunitz, 418.

Index

Abbas Pasha, 45; postgraduate medical study abroad under, 46

Abu Zabel: Hospital, 136, 140; Medical School, 34, 140

Agricultural development, 18; capitalism, impact on medical care, 19

Al-Attar, Shayk Hasan ibn Muhammad, 27; description of 1801 plague in Upper Egypt, 76

Al-Azhar, 44; curriculum, 34

Al-Baqli, Muhammad Ali, director of Medical School, 47; surgeon, 141

Al-Jabarti, Abd al-Rahman, 27; views on anti-plague measures, 75–78

Anglo-Ottoman trade convention (1838), 18, 159

Bilharz, Theodor, discovery of schistosoma haematobium, 45

Black Death, 1, 2; medieval Muslim experience, 72. *See also* Plague

Bowring, John, opposition to quarantine, 74

British Native Passengers Act (1858), 102, 103

Broussaisism, 36–37

Brownism, 36, 37

Chadwick, Edwin, and sanitary reform, 8

Cholera, 3, 49–68; epidemic of 1831, 51–57; epidemic of 1848, 57–64; epidemic of 1865, 65–67; epidemic of 1881, 104, 107–108; in Hijaz, 52, 65; 101–102, 108

"Cholera Conference," 1855, 101–102

Clinics, in Cairo, 142–145

Clot, Dr. Antoine Barthelme, 6, 26, 83, 89, 121; anti-contagionist stand on cholera, 64; anti-contagionist stand on plague, 87–88; awarded title "Bey," 42; biography, 33; ideological dogmatism, 165; observations on diseases in Egypt, 30; promotion of Egypt's Medical School, 32, 34–48; smallpox vaccination program, 114–115, 119; on women health officers, 122–125, 127–129

Constantinople, 97; 1866 agreements on cholera control, 102

Contagion, 2. *See also* Disease

Contagionism and anticontagionism, 5

Curry, Charles, health officer, vaccination campaign, 116–119

De Lesseps, Ferdinand, 108

Desgenettes, General René, 26

Disease: causation theories, 1–3, 97–98, 105–106; concepts, ontological and physiological, 1–2; continuing evolution of disease concepts, 165–166; dissemination accelerated by Suez Canal opening, 103; specificity, 2

Dispensaries. *See* Clinics

Drug usage in Egypt, 28–29

Duff-Gordon, Lady Lucie, 151, 161

Dysentery, 30, 31, 152

"Eastern Question," 3

Egypt, nineteenth century: civil adminis-

231